Social Welfare: Institution and Process

Social Welfare: Institution and Process

HELEN M. CRAMPTON

KENNETH K. KEISER

UNIVERSITY OF UTAH

Random House, Inc. NEW YORK

To
Bert Keiser and Pete Mickelsen,
whose enthusiasm for life
provided us the blueprint for living.

This book owes much to a workshop sponsored by the Council on Social Work Education in June 1967 at Estes Park, Colorado. During the course of the meetings it became evident that there was a need for a textbook on social-welfare institutions, a need that the authors had felt for some time. In considering plans and developing outlines for the book, Mereb E. Mossman, Dean of Faculty at the University of North Carolina and director of the Estes Park workshop, was the first person to offer encouragement. Alex Zapharis, Associate Professor of the School of Social Work, University of Denver, and coordinator of the workshop, was most helpful in his suggestions and advice; he later reviewed the completed manuscript and offered many specific recommendations that have been adopted.

This textbook was written for a particular course, Social Welfare as an Institution, offered in many undergraduate social-welfare programs. After teaching the course and finding that no one book fulfilled the needs of the course at the undergraduate level, we developed this textbook to introduce students to the complex matter of social-welfare agencies and the processes by which they function in American society.

We are indebted to a number of professional colleagues and associates who offered advice, help, and good will along the way, and we gratefully acknowledge their assistance. At the University of Utah there were Rex Skidmore, Dean of the Graduate School of Social Work; Ted C. Smith, Chairman, Department of Sociology. To Sherman Merle, Professor of Social Work, Catholic University, Washington, D.C.; Raymond H. Clark, Associate Professor of Sociology, Weber State College, Ogden, Utah; Martin W. Scheffer, Assistant Professor of Sociology, Boise State College, Boise, Idaho; John H. Compton, Assistant Professor of Sociology, University of Iowa; and Robert L. Deaton, Associate Professor of Sociology, University of Montana, we also wish to express our thanks.

The following persons representing the Federal, state, and county welfare agencies in Utah and elsewhere have been most helpful: Kay A. Desserich, Director, and other members of the Division of Staff Development, Department of Public Welfare; James A. Anderson, David R. Franchina, William G. Geurts, David C. McShane, John R. McCall, Patrick B. McNamara, Larry L. Peterson, Reverend Roger K. Prescott, and Stephen L. Petty.

Theodore Caris, Dorothy Grosvenor, and Arthur Strimling of Random House, Inc., have offered constant assistance and encouragement. For help of several kinds we are grateful to James H. Johnson, Raleigh E. Riggs, Eva Bowersox and Pat Butterfield.

In writing this book we have drawn on the combined experience that has come from some years of university teaching and professional work with the aged, federal prisons, courts, welfare departments, child-welfare and adoption agencies, and minority groups. This experience has also demonstrated the compelling need for an integrated approach to social-welfare agencies.

This book, then, is an answer to an apparent need, and, thanks to the assistance of friends, associates, and our long-suffering families, we offer it to undergraduate classes in social welfare, whose members will be called upon to face awesome responsibilities in this modern world.

November 1969   H. M. C.
                                                            K. K. K.

CONTENTS

PART ONE: **Historical Perspectives on Social-welfare Institutions and Processes**

**PART TWO: Society's Struggle to Solve Social Problems
The Greene Family**

Chapter

PART THREE: Contemporary Social Forces

Part One

HISTORICAL PERSPECTIVES

ON SOCIAL-WELFARE

INSTITUTIONS AND PROCESSES

INTRODUCTION

Social Welfare: Institution and Process explores the history and philosophy of social-welfare institutions and their relationship to other social institutions in the United States. Emphasis is on the role of social work in various interrelated social-welfare institutions.

No attempt is made to discuss all such institutions, but enough of them are described to provide a clear picture of their interrelations and importance on the current scene. Change through both planned and spontaneous movements is also examined.

The book is divided into three parts. The first examines both historical and sociological implications of social-welfare institutions. The second describes various national attempts to solve problems in the past. An example of a multiproblem family is given to assist the reader in understanding the practical functioning of interrelated social-welfare institutions. The final part treats existing social forces, with an emphasis on what the future holds for social-welfare institutions and processes.

This book includes a collection of facts drawn from the past, an interpretation of these facts in the present, and a prognosis for the future of social welfare. It focuses on the gradual modification of social policy in the United States, in order to provide students with a basic understanding of the evolution of programs and services to meet the changing needs of people. This approach will help students to understand, evaluate, and analyze the relations between the development of social-welfare institutions and the values underlying them.

This text was written primarily for use by teachers and students in the course "Social Welfare as an Institution." The material is presented in such a way that it can also be used in the undergraduate introductory course in social welfare. An overview of contributions to social change and the pressures and means that bring about innovations is included. It is hoped that the book will also help to enhance the student's respect for the dignity of the individual, increase his sensitivity to human needs, and stimulate his awareness of contemporary society and the dynamics of social change.

The development of social-welfare study is apparent in the historical progression of changes in social-welfare ideology and practice in American society. Institutions as "blueprints for behavior" are constantly undergoing change, and we believe that this process of change is highly significant for modifications of social-welfare policy. Contemporary correctional philosophy and services to veterans, for example, have resulted from a combination of economic, political, and social factors acting to produce ideological change.

Chapter I

HISTORICAL PERSPECTIVES
ON SOCIAL WELFARE

A description of the historical development
of social welfare, with emphasis on events
whose significance remains strong today,
is provided.

Any definition of social welfare must, of necessity, reflect a combination of theory, ideas, and processes that have emerged over the last hundred years. Social-welfare institutions have developed in a response to human needs in society. It is therefore apparent that such institutions must be multifaceted, drawing upon the expertise of such interrelated disciplines as economics, social work, politics, medicine, religion, and psychology. The goals of such institutions reflect the values of the society in which they function.

The authors agree with Edmund A. Smith,[1] who argues that social welfare is the collective concern of society for its individual members, and with Nathan E. Cohen's emphasis on the positive role that government must assume in meeting social and economic problems.[2] We define social welfare operationally as a system that embodies a multifaceted approach to social and economic problems, reflecting social values and using the expertise of interrelated disciplines for the collective good.

Social welfare has been known by a variety of names over the centuries. Although precepts and ideology about the poor and needy have changed, the basic premise that human beings should help one another has not altered in respect to the indigent. From the beginnings of recorded history some people have not been able to meet the minimum requirements of society either economically or emotionally. Several ethical codes and systems have been based on what has been considered desirable treatment of the poor and helpless. Humanitarianism was perhaps the basic impetus for the evolution of American social work. Interwoven in the fabric of such values as individualism and democracy has also been concern for the welfare of fellow human beings. Agreement on ways and means to help the unfortunate has not always been present; such lack of consensus has resulted partly from historical developments and ethical systems that have impeded full awareness and agreement.

All patterns of culture known to anthropologists have emerged from a need to protect the group, a need that has also manifested itself in the cohesion and solidarity of people undertaking the care of the less fortunate. Many of our social values reflect such patterns: compassion and mercy, good will and loyalty are qualities evolved from the need to provide for those who cannot provide for themselves. Along with attitudes inculcated to protect the group have come the institutionalized means through which societies have provided for the poor. These means which have become increasingly complex throughout history, reflect society's intention of caring for those of its members who cannot care for themselves.

In medieval Europe the Church, following the Judeo-Christian tradition of incorporating biblical guidelines on charity into its practice and teaching, fed and took care of the poor, largely through monasteries. Later, trade guilds and cities experiencing the first by-products of industrialization helped with relief programs and allocated public funds to relieve destitution. With the breakdown of the feudal structure in western Europe, traditional forms of poverty were replaced by new ones, and new ways had to be devised to deal with them.

English Beginnings

Before the passage of the Elizabethan Poor Law of 1601, which for the first time established legal and secular responsibilities toward the poor, a series of economic and social changes had taken place in European society. Enclosure laws and dependence on foreign markets and New World treasure led to new production techniques, from cottage industry to factories. Also, traditional employment in small villages was losing ground to the enticement of urban areas, with the result that many more people were vagrant or at least much more mobile than formerly. To discourage vagrancy, which was viewed with alarm by the British government, a statute of 1531 licensed the aged and destitute to beg, thus restricting their movements throughout the country. In 1536 another statute prohibited begging and tried to classify the poor into groups according to age and need. Subsequent statutes attempted to clarify both the groups needing help and the amount of responsibility to be assigned to citizens and government. By 1601 England was thus ready for social reform.

Enactment of the Poor Law in 1601 established public policy on the state's responsibility for care of dependent persons. This law codified existing practices and statutes on the handling of destitute cases. Its dominant features were acknowledgment of the parish as the proper unit of administration and establishment of a system of separate charges for each parish. The law's basic intent was to repress begging, to use employment as the chief means of assistance, to establish almshouses for the handicapped, to apprentice children for work, and to allow a broader use of houses of correction for both the idle poor and petty offenders.

The major provisions of the law reflected the new spirit of wanting to do something more than inflict "cruel and unusual" punishment on vagrants and mendicants:

1. Overseers of the poor were to be appointed annually by the justices in each parish. In addition to church wardens, the overseers were to include two to four "substantial householders."
2. Able-bodied persons who had no means of support were to be set to work.
3. The funds necessary for implementing the act were to be raised by taxing every householder.
4. Power was given to the justices to raise funds from other parishes in the vicinity or even within the same county if insufficient funds were available locally.
5. Overseers were authorized to bind out poor children as apprentices, subject to the consent of two justices. A "woman childe" could be bound to the age of twenty-one or marriage and a "man childe" to the age of twenty-four.
6. Local authorities, with the consent of the lords of manors, were

empowered to erect workhouses on waste lands. Building costs were to be borne by parishes or counties.

7. The mutual responsibilities of parents and children to support one another were extended to include grandparents.

8. Justices were authorized "to commit to the House of Correction or common gaol, such poor persons as shall not employ themselves to work, being appointed thereto by the overseers."

The Law of Settlement and Removal of 1662, or the Settlement Act was undoubtedly a logical consequence of the system of poor relief established in 1601. As the parishes were responsible for the relief of destitution, they wanted to be certain that they were supporting their own poor. According to the settlement act, the necessity, number, and continual increase of the poor, not only within the cities of London and Westminster, but also through the whole kingdom is very great and exceedingly burdensome. By reason of some defects in the law, poor people are not restrained from going from one parish to another and, therefore, do endeavor to settle themselves in those parishes where there is the best stock, the largest commons, or wastes to build cottages, and the most woods for them to burn and destroy; and when they have consumed it, then to another parish and at least become rogues and vagabonds . . .[3] The Settlement Act provided a system for dealing with these migrants. Upon a complaint made by church wardens or overseers of the poor, an undesirable person who entered a community could be removed within forty days of his arrival and conveyed to where he had last been legally settled. An individual did not have to request assistance to merit removal. He merely had to appear "likely to be chargeable to the parish." Fortunately, the punitive and harsh settlement act did not set the pattern for subsequent poor-law legislation. In fact, soon after its passage Parliament became interested in a project to employ the poor that was positive in approach and optimistic in tone. Numerous private and public efforts were made to relieve the unemployed by finding them useful work.

This interest in setting the able-bodied poor to work coincided with the rapid industrial development of England. Belief in work for the poor as morally therapeutic, as well as beneficial to the economy, manifested itself in the passage in 1772 of a law that resulted in the immediate construction of workhouses. These houses provided stocks of goods and skilled supervisors necessary to train the poor in domestic and semi-skilled tasks for eventual employment. Rigid discipline was exacted: Attendance was required at numerous religious services and daily prayers, and the day's activities were severely organized. Penalties were typical of the time: confinement in the stocks and whipping, for example.

The law gave to the overseers the right to refuse relief to anyone who was not willing to enter the workhouse. All members of a family had to accompany the father. Poor people were quite naturally willing to undergo almost any hardship rather than submit to the regime of the workhouse. Conditions in most workhouses were deplorable. The sick and the poor, the young and the old were mingled regardless of sex. So bad were the conditions that such reformers as Jonas Hanway and Thomas Gilbert undertook a crusade to bring them to the attention of the public. As a result of their efforts, the Gilbert Act was passed in 1782 repealing, in effect, the act of 1722. Thenceforth, instead of forcing the able-bodied poor to go into workhouses, the parishes would provide them with assistance in their own homes until suitable employment could be secured for them. Once again the doctrine of public responsibility for the relief of human destitution took a constructive form.

The Industrial and French Revolutions

The Industrial Revolution of Europe can be studied more effectively in both its dimension and impact on the social order by first examining the old order of European society. Wealth and power rested mainly on concepts of land and kinship, social class, and religion. The uncontested power of the monarchy was an integral part of the system.

Social research on the Industrial Revolution in England, has centered mainly on the conditions of the working class—perhaps because labor became degraded under industrialism—and on the dissolution of the craft guilds. Added to the loss of pride in one's work was the wrenching of many workers from their families, parishes, and villages to urban areas that were crowded, lacking in kinship ties, and distinguished by lower standards of living. The feudal and patriarchal relations characterizing England's preindustrial society gave way to commercialism and urban values.

Along with the change in status of the common laborer there was another far-reaching change in the economic system. As Robert A. Nisbet points out, conservatives of that time objected to the transfer of political power from land ownership to more abstract wealth represented by shares bought and sold on the market.[4] This change was especially irritating in a country like England, which for centuries had preserved the continuity of land ownership through laws of primogeniture and a value system that made such ownership virtually sacred.

The trend toward urbanism intensified the loss of community identity, and social disorganization and alienation began with the mushrooming of huge cities. With changes in locale came changes in the traditional roles of men and women, and with each technological advance came greater dependence on machines and further subjugation of the individual.

In other parts of Europe the processes of change were also in operation. The French Revolution did much to change family, Church, employment, and property institutions. New laws reflected the shift from rural and feudal values to contractual relationships. Property rights changed considerably, particularly as primogeniture was replaced by equal division of land among the owners' children.

Perhaps the most far-reaching change affecting both the family and the Church was the transfer of education from home and Church to the state. In effect, the French Revolution terminated feudalism and all it implied and initiated a new social system in France, one that embodied new directions for the people of the nineteenth century and their descendants.

Nisbet views the results of the Industrial Revolution in England and the French Revolution in terms of three concepts that have also had much to do with the formulation of later social-welfare measures: individualization, abstraction, and generalization.[5] Individualization is a kind of separation of people from their communities, religions, traditional occupations, and family structures, resulting in individual rather than group orientation. Abstraction results from the evolution of values experienced in concrete terms—such as protection—to reliance on impersonal institutions such as police forces. The generalization process categorizes people from a personal, face-to-face relationship to that of a more general quality, going beyond the community-state context to international implications.

History of American Poor Laws

Concepts of public responsibility for dependent persons in the American Colonies were similar to those in England. Most of the colonists came from England, attracted by the prospect of religious freedom, the lure of adventure, or the opportunity for economic independence. They brought with them their English manners and customs, social and legal institutions, and philosophical approaches to human existence. They also imported the poor-law system.

Under the Colonial system of poor relief, the administrative unit corresponding to the English parish was the town. Some poor people became the responsibility of the province, a broader unit of government. Poorhouses were erected for the care of the indigent sick. Little distinction was made between dependence caused by physical and mental disabilities and that caused by economic failure. Anyone in need of financial help was considered a pauper, and to be a pauper was to be a failure in an increasingly individualistic society.

Voluntary agencies and charities also developed; by the beginning of the nineteenth century they had become a sprawling array of overlapping and poorly administered organizations. Following trends that had begun in England, Germany, and France, a movement to make private philanthropy more systematic, ensuring complete coverage of donors and avoiding duplication of both services and requests for contributions emerged.

In the midst of the Industrial Revolution in the nineteenth century in the United States, thousands of people lived in degradation and squalor. Basic reform in the working conditions of these people was needed and from this need grew the beginnings of factory legislation. At the same time the "settlement" movement, an attempt to assist people from Europe with their relocation problems, began; its proponents viewed the problems of the new arrivals to this country as related to their ethnic and racial differences. The first charity organizations, now called "family-welfare services," date from this era. Most of these efforts were imbued with the philosophy of helpful service and neighborliness to help people in distress.

After 1880 there was a trend to consolidate the charities then in operation. Better care of neglected and orphaned children was developed, and interest in proper care of the feeble-minded and criminals began to be expressed. The end of the nineteenth century and the beginning of the twentieth brought reforms in housing and slum clearance, including the Federal housing program. The public health movement, health education, and the first juvenile courts also appeared during this period. There was an awakening to social needs and ways of ameliorating social problems, and social-welfare theory was beginning to make itself heard.

The underlying objective of "scientific charity" was rehabilitation of the individual, rather than an attack on social problems in general. The organizing of charity had little to do with social reform. In the early stages volunteer friendly visitors actually performed the "services." The paid workers were investigators and administrators of the programs. The "friendly visitor's" most important qualification was "moral insight" and not any special knowledge or skill.

Viewed in retrospect, the assumption that "friendly visitors" from higher economic and social levels, equipped only with good will, could modify the attitudes, behavior, or life styles of the poor seems naïve. When applied to non-English-speaking immigrants, who came in waves in the latter part of the nineteenth century, the paternalistic effort to "uplift," though benevolently intended, was a failure.

Around the turn of the century voluntary agencies became increasingly preoccupied with training social workers. The theme was no longer "not alms, but a friend" but "professional service." [6] Although the scientific development of social diagnosis and treatment was fostered, the broad theme of public responsibility for conditions beyond the control of individuals was neglected.

The Great Depression

The stock-market crash of October 1929 brought an entirely new look at poverty and provisions for poor relief. Even though some funds had previously been provided by tax money and private charitable organizations, they had been extremely limited and unevenly distributed. Part of the difficulty was that the poor laws had not had much revision since 1600. The world's economic, social, and political institutions had changed considerably since then, yet the poor were still viewed by the populace much as they had been for 300 years. The upheaval of the Great Depression revealed many disparities in the laws. Nineteenth-century values had stressed individual responsibility. It was considered each individual's moral duty to accomplish as much as he could. Harold L. Wilensky and Charles N. Lebeaux take this analysis one step farther. [7] In summing up the competitive struggle, they assert that the notion that failure is cause for guilt and shame is incorporated in the value system. They also point out that economic individualism goes beyond employment and material successes, that American education is based on individual achievement and competition. Adding to the complexities at the end of the nineteenth century was the huge demand for cheap labor, which was supplied largely by European immigrants. Many of the new arrivals did not grasp that responsibility for one's own fate and a high degree of independence were fundamental to American culture. For many it was bewildering to do work that must have seemed incomprehensible at times, as well as highly impersonal in nature.

The Great Depression made it obvious that one could not always be master of one's fate, that causes and effects completely beyond individual control could cause deprivation, misery, and poverty. An estimated 15 million people from the middle class and upper middle class were unemployed, and the rationale that a man failed only because he did not work hard enough was refuted. Many of the new destitute had been self-supporting until the Depression. Because the need surpassed the capacity of existing agencies, in 1932 the Federal government devised several temporary programs to provide employment for the needy, some of which are still in existence today. It took widespread deprivation among groups that had formerly prospered under industrialization to convince many people that they could accept public assistance without feeling that their integrity was in doubt.

Some of the better-known programs were the Works Progress Administration (W.P.A.), the Federal Emergency Relief Administration (F.E.R.A.), the Civilian Conservation Corps (C.C.C.), the National Youth Administration (N.Y.A.), the Public Works Administration (P.W.A.), and the Civilian Works Administration (C.W.A.). Although works programs helped those who were only temporarily unemployed, many of the aged and handicapped could not be assisted under them. It was for these groups that a more permanent system of help was established under the Social Security Act of 1935. This act provided for Federal grants to states, to be used along with state funds to make assistance payments through three main programs—Old Age Assistance, Aid to the Blind, and Aid to Dependent Children respectively. The Social Security Act also provided for a system of social insurance (Old Age Insurance) to be financed by contributions from employees, employers, and the Federal government. Other provisions of this law included a program of vocational rehabilitation; Federal aid to states for public-health activities, including maternal- and child-health programs and crippled children's services; Federal grants to states for child-welfare services in rural areas and areas of special need; and unemployment insurance. Many of these programs will be discussed in greater detail in later chapters.

In 1950 the Social Security Act was amended to provide for joint Federal-state participation in making grants to persons who are totally and permanently disabled. Titles I, IX, X, and XIV are the parts of the Social Security Act that provide for public-assistance payments for Old Age Assistance, Aid to Dependent Children, Aid to the Blind, and Aid to the Disabled. Responsibility for aiding needy persons not included in these four categories is still upon the states and local communities. One of the main criticisms of the act is that the programs and amounts of available assistance vary according to the states' ability—and willingness—to match funds.

The public-assistance titles of the Social Security Act do reflect growing recognition of human dignity. For example:

1. Money is paid to individuals to spend as they see fit (instead of to almshouses or in the form of grocery orders).
2. State restrictions on clients' use of assistance payments are prohibited.
3. Each client has the right to a fair hearing to challenge decisions he may feel are unfair or not in his best interest.
4. The recipient is protected against disclosure of confidential information (in contrast to such past indignities as published pauper lists).
5. Lengthy residence requirements are prohibited for assistance eligibility.
6. Assistance payments are made in cash to permit recipients to continue living at home without interruption of family life because of economic need.

As far as implementation of the act is concerned, there are certain requirements that help to ensure efficient and responsible service to clients, as well as sound administration:

1. A single agency in each state administers or supervises the assistance program.
2. States participate in financing public-assistance programs.
3. Such programs must be in effect in each subdivision of the state.
4. The same eligibility regulations apply throughout each state.
5. Each state has a merit system for selection of personnel to administer the public-assistance programs.

The Federal government has constantly encouraged the states to provide such additional services to public-assistance clients as rehabilitation programs (to facilitate self-support), improved medical care, help in strengthening family life, and help in attaining social independence. The latest revisions of the Social Security Act provide for Federal aid to states in making these services available.

Social-welfare agencies began moving toward a form of social insurance in the 1930s. The Federal Security Administration initiated a two-part program: public economic assistance and Old Age and Survivors Insurance, with certain restrictions on budget allocations and eligibility. Some critics of the system, ~~notably Philip Klein~~, deplore the means test prescribed for applicants, claiming that it tends to exclude the truly destitute person.[9] There has long been a question of how to establish the degree of deprivation that should entitle a client to help. In the past, payments were determined by the available funds rather than by need. Financial assistance may have been less than that required by the client, but had to be based on departmental appropriations.

American social-welfare agencies reflect compounds of ideologies, values, and traditions that must be understood in the light of their development and legislative bases. One interesting side effect of the Judeo-Christian tradition is the connotations of moral superiority attached to charity. To those with superior social status and wealth it was but a short step to assuming moral superiority over those less fortunate. Class consciousness thus came into being.

In the United States, with its equalitarian emphasis and great demand for laborers, both of which favored the dignity of the worker, class consciousness was not quite as entrenched as in Europe. Nevertheless, there was evidence of the elite's fear and distrust of the lower classes, notably its reluctance to support the poor and particularly the idle poor. The prevailing ethic of the American people, based on individual efforts, resourcefulness, and an expanding society, labeled anyone unable to be completely self-sufficient a "failure." The majority of people felt only contempt for those less fortunate than themselves.

NOTES

1. Edmund A. Smith, *Social Welfare—Principles and Concepts* (New York Press: Association, 1965), p. 17. Stresses the collective requirements, responsibilities, and dynamics of social welfare.
2. Nathan E. Cohen, *Social Work in the American Tradition* (New York:

Dryden Press, 1958), pp. 6–8. Evaluates the evolution and present direction of social work as a profession.

3. Nicholls, Sir George, *A History of the English Poor Law,* Vol. I (London: P. S. King and Son, Westminster S. W., 1898), pp. 279–284.

4. Robert A. Nisbet, *The Sociological Tradition* (New York: Basic Books, 1966), pp. 21–42. Examines the developmental framework of both empirical sociology and theoretical sociology.

5. *Ibid.* pp. 42–44.

6. Herman B. Stein, "Observations on Determinants of Social Work Education in the United States," in *An Intercultural Exploration: Universals and Differences in Social Work Values, Functions and Practice. Report of the Intercultural Seminar, The East-West Center, Hawaii, February 21 March 4, 1966* (New York: Council on Social Work Education, 1966), pp. 163–164.

7. Harold L. Wilensky and Charles N. Lebeaux, *Industrial Society and Social Welfare* (New York: Free Press, 1965), pp. 191–192. Explores the impact of industrialization on the availability and organization of social-welfare services in the United States.

8. Philip Klein, *From Philanthropy to Social Welfare* (San Francisco: Jossey-Bass, 1968), pp. 260–261. Describes social-welfare activities connected with livelihood, medical care, child welfare, and psychotherapy.

9. *Ibid.* pp. 51–53.

SUGGESTED READINGS

Feldman, Frances L., and Frances Scherz. *Family Social Welfare.* New York: Atherton, 1967.

  Comprehensive treatment of family therapy in social work.

Pumphrey, Muriel W. *The Teaching of Values and Ethics in Social Work Education.* New York: Council on Social Work Education, 1959.

  Report of a three-year study of curriculum in the education of social workers.

Smalley, Ruth E. *Theory for Social Work Practice.* New York: Columbia University Press, 1967.

  A theory for social-work practice developed in an introductory text on social-work methods.

Chapter II

DYNAMICS AND EFFECTS

OF SOCIAL CHANGE

*This chapter offers an analysis of how change
results from recognition of needs and
from various attempts to cope with
existing problems.*

The American "way of life" is both elusive and vaguely defined. It is
elusive in that it has been undergoing change since the original
colonies were settled. It is vague in that different people define it in
different ways. The fifteen-year-old son of a white U.S. Senator would
not experience his day-to-day living as would the fifteen-year-old son
of an urban Negro welfare recipient. These two examples represent
opposite ends of a continuum, and neither boy's attitudes, values, and
beliefs would correspond precisely to those of a person occupying a
mean position on the same continuum. Their views on many issues
would be different because they would have been exposed to different
circumstances. The present and future orientations of each boy would
also be quite disparate. Vocational preparation, for example, would
probably represent one of the widest gulfs separating the two boys. An
observer would likely consider their respective educational choices as
"natural" to the American way of life. The Negro boy's overcrowded
school, inadequate diet, substandard housing, and ill-fitting second-
hand clothes would necessarily have shaped an outlook different from
that of the middle-class white boy.

The differences in this example exist now, have in the past caused problems, and will continue to do so in the future. Society is taking a more active interest in such disparities in the quality of life and is attempting to guarantee a minimum standard of living to all people. This effort is relatively new, although the problem was recognized in the past. It has taken efforts to assess the values involved in the social process and to establish goals that would alter that process. A definite value conflict arises whenever any change is introduced. Change is never desired by everybody, but the assumption of the democratic process is that the preferences of the majority of people will prevail.

Many efforts to initiate change have failed to recognize the necessity of benefiting the largest number of people possible. Others have been relatively successful, revealing that in a democratic society the dynamics of change can operate independently of total involvement; but the results affect all. Example programs that have been successful in bringing about change despite opposition will be given in this chapter.

Change-oriented groups invariably encounter opposition and resistance. The experience of American society with Prohibition is an example, one in which the opposing forces eventually triumphed. Sometimes a person or a group advocating change that challenges prevalent values overreacts as does the opposition, by both violent and nonviolent means. Three general alternatives are open to a change-oriented group that is overwhelmed by opposition: to continue the attack, to retreat, or to do nothing. An attack could include fund raising to continue the fight, fact-finding studies to combat misrepresentation by the opposition, or a "summit" meeting to negotiate differences. Retreating might include policy changes for the sake of appeasement, exclusion of particular persons or groups from participation because the organizational image would suffer, or a decision to disband.

It would not be possible to predict the outcome of any of the three alternatives without considering all the variables in the specific instances. One can, however, evaluate the past success or failure of these methods. It is possible to find a group that is doing nothing about a problem and to discover that change is nevertheless taking place in the direction of the group's stated goals. Similarly, retreat sometimes permits a gathering of strength with which to attack anew. The reader is cautioned against assuming that frontal attack by change-oriented organizations is the only route to success.

Four examples of change-oriented groups will be discussed in terms of value conflicts, efforts at initiating change, resistance encountered, and ultimate achievements.

The Ku Klux Klan

Neither the original Ku Klux Klan of the Reconstruction period, with its racism, atrocities, and secrecy, nor its modern image will be treated here. The organization, also known as the "invisible empire," did, however, reflect interrelation of the concepts with which we are dealing in the period from 1915 to 1930, when American society was undergoing pervasive change, which influenced its attitudes toward minority groups and civil disobedience.

The revival of the Klan in 1915 was influenced by three particular factors. One was David W. Griffith's motion picture *The Birth of a Nation,* in which the South was pictured as being "saved" and restored to white supremacy through fear, violence and hatred during the Reconstruction period. Another was the writings of a newspaperman and senatorial candidate from Georgia, Tom Watson, who strongly urged the rebirth of the Klan. The final impetus came from an opportunistic white supremacist, "Colonel" William Simmons. From Simmons' emergence to prominence in 1915 until 1920, when two professional organizers were employed, the Klan membership stood at approximately 5,000. Within a year and a half the two "agents" had increased it to 95,000, simultaneously realizing a profit of 80 percent to themselves on each $10 membership fee.

The charter granted to the Ku Klux Klan by the State of Georgia in 1915 listed patriotic, benevolent, military, ritual, social, and fraternal aims, but were soon belied by the waves of Klan persecution and violence that followed. The Klan promoted the idea of "100 percent Americanism," which did not include being Negro, Roman Catholic, Jewish or born outside the United States.

The phenomenal rise in membership did not result from recognition of unjust oppression on the part of unjustly treated victims. Before 1920 members of the Klan were not deliberately recruited; only after indicating interest would a man be invited to participate in Klan rites. The organization's goals were much too nebulous for analysis and too unstable even for adequate definition. For example, anyone not a member of the Klan was considered an "alien," a term that could be applied in whatever context was convenient.

The Klan set itself up as the moral protector of America. In Louisiana, people were tarred and feathered, a woman was flogged, a Roman Catholic priest was shot dead in public, and others were ridden out of town on a rail—all in the name of "Americanism." Twelve people were horsewhipped in one month by local Klansmen in the Southwest; the victims had no recourse to authorities, who feared that inquiries "would bring criticism to the investigators." [1]

Robed Klansmen paraded in Montgomery, Alabama during the last days of World War I carrying banners warning spies and pacifists to leave town. Similarly, throughout the Southwest they publicly threatened bootleggers, seducers of young girls, prostitutes and gamblers. They also engaged in many attacks on Roman Catholics and were responsible for a national anti-Catholic crusade. A Klan official spoke in behalf of the Klan *and* the Anti-Saloon League against Governor Alfred C. Smith's Presidential candidacy. Governor Smith was a Roman Catholic. [2]

As far north as Illinois, the Klan battled its way into control of an entire town, Herrin, Illinois, attacking private homes and the "un-American" element. This "un-American" element consisted of citizens of Herrin whose national origins were predominantly Italian and whose faith was Roman Catholic. Both attributes removed these people from the category of "100 percent American," the Ku Klux Klan slogan invented by the professional "agents." In 1923 Klan membership was reportedly 3 million, the states of Ohio and Indiana had the highest membership of any states in the northern United States.

Perhaps one of the most significant points is that the general membership believed that Klan activities were justified, that they were not only upholding the law but also doing so in obedience to Holy Scripture. Their rationalizations seem bizarre and pathetic now, but less than twenty years later the people of Germany were being exhorted on similar grounds by Adolf Hitler, German nationalist and proponent of Aryan supremacy.

Although it is not our intention to analyze the personality of the typical Klan member, it is noteworthy that the symbolism of the organization speaks rather loudly for itself. The costume, a hooded robe, set members as part from other citizens; they were able to identify themselves a part of an "in" group while retaining their anonymity behind the hooded mask. These features, in addition to the jargon and secret passwords are suggestive of feelings of insecurity and inferiority. The Klan's activities in the name of "Americanism" and "justice" were conducted without much fear of exposure or reprisal. People were whipped, tarred and feathered, and otherwise tormented for "suspected" crimes and violations of the "Protestant" value system.

Not only did the Klan play on the ignorance of the general public, it also took substantial advantage of prejudices grounded in fear and mistrust. For instance, the Negroes, according to the Klan, threatened to take jobs from white men and were rapists of white women. Roman Catholics were suspected of participating in plots to move the Vatican to America and of storing guns and ammunition in the cellars of their churches. Jews were believed to be manipulators of the economy and therefore responsible for such social ills as inflation and unemployment.

The human impulse to seek solidarity with others was played on by Klan propaganda, particularly its "brotherhood" image, but the majority of members probably did not totally believe in the Klan "line." It seems implausible that the Klan could muster 100 percent support and enthusiasm for the many "causes" it adopted.

The Klan aligned itself not only against Negroes, Roman Catholics, Jews, foreigners, and "sympathizers" with the enemy but also against other citizens. The hooded reformers were concerned with preserving the chastity of white women, combating adultery, enforcing parental homage, fighting against bootlegging, and closely observing "shady" business dealings. Almost no pursuit was immune from their inspection.

The involvement of the Klan in politics is a story in itself. Klan support accounted for some candidates' election almost unopposed. The Klan was less violent in the North than in the South and the Southwest. In Oklahoma, where Klan violence was greatest, a white candidate for the legislature who was not endorsed by the Klan was tarred and feathered by them, even though he lost the election.

The Klan supported Bible reading and opposed the teaching of evolution in public schools. It adopted the hymn "Onward Christian Soldiers" as its anthem and opposed anything other than "old-time religion" with revivalist overtones. Quite often the Klan would participate in charity drives, usually of its own devising. Widows received gifts, children were remembered at Christmas, and the show of force at local churches often insured attention of members of the community. The reported total of charitable donations by the Klan in 1921 was $1 million. This figure is believed to be fairly accurate because the Klan always exhibited its philanthropy.

Many Protestant ministers were Klan members and fiercely echoed the "hellfire and brimstone" tone of the Klan in their preaching. So strong was this connection that some clergymen became preachers for the Klan exclusively.

The political power of the invisible empire began to wane in the late 1920s. Much success had been enjoyed by various candidates who had received Klan support, but growing public disapproval of the hooded raiders had begun to make such endorsements a political liability. By 1930 the Klan was more important spiritually than physically, or as a political force.[3]

In reviewing the activities of the Ku Klux Klan for the fifteen-year period ending in 1930, we can see the value conflicts that eventually brought about repudiation and censure. Aside from its desire to be the moral protector of American society, the Klan met opposition to its "100 percent American" anti-Semitic, and anti-Catholic doctrines. Its efforts at initiating change were brutal and often indiscriminate. Resistance was encountered from both its victims and an aroused general public. Its ultimate achievement was to inspire disrespect for the power it so unjudiciously exercised.

The Temperance Movement

Several organizations were formed in the United States during the first half of the nineteenth century with temperance as their goal. The Moreau, New York, Temperance Society (1808); the Massachusetts Society for the Suppression of Intemperance (1813); and the America Temperance Society (1826) all preceded the more active and renowned Women's Christian Temperance Union (W.C.T.U.), founded in 1874. The leadership of these earlier groups was initially drawn from Congregational and Presbyterian ministers, who recruited reformed drunkards and held meetings that paralleled religious revivals in emotional appeal and vigor.

As Americans became first concerned and then alarmed about urban conditions arising from industrialism, a rigid set of values reminiscent of New England Puritanism began to emerge. Such qualities as industry, fidelity, courtesy, frugality, consideration for others, cleanliness, and sobriety were lauded as cultural imperatives. It was a simple step for members of the W.C.T.U. to conclude that those who had succumbed to "demon rum" had fallen from glory because they had disregarded these imperatives.

The pleas for abstinence and prohibition were closely tied to a rising middle class in which the Protestant Ethic was ingrained. The middle class of the nineteenth century had frowned on "emotional outbursts." Also, it was a time when it was unthinkable for a teenage son to flagrantly defy and disobey his father. Consumption of alcohol could cause people to violate these rules of propriety.

Skid row, habitat of the hopeless alcoholic, was not as prevalent or as well populated as it is in American cities today, but it was nevertheless considered a disgrace, rather than "retreatist subculture," a term used by contemporary sociologists.[4]

Female suffrage was emerging as a cause at about the time that the Prohibitionist Party, whose main plank was opposition to the sale of liquor, was formed. An attempt by one W.C.T.U. leader to throw the organization's support behind both female suffrage and the labor movement failed, however. Partially as a result of this failure, the W.C.T.U. became less active after that and eventually lost control of the temperance movement to the Anti-Saloon League.

The Anti-Saloon League had its headquarters in Westerville, Ohio, one of the strongholds of the Ku Klux Klan, which strongly supported prohibition. It is possible that mutual interests motivated the alliance between the two organizations, for the combined claimed membership of the two groups included much of the adult population of Ohio in 1920 and therefore represented political and social strength sufficient to control almost any proposed legislation. With the enormous support they could offer each other, it is little wonder that both movements were successful in their efforts.

The Anti-Saloon League not only encouraged nondrinkers to protest liquor traffic but also advocated that imbibers "sign the pledge," a written promise to abstain from alcohol. Its techniques and slogans were unsophisticated by current standards. The Young People's Co-operative Temperance Bureau, an adjunct of the Anti-Saloon League, attempted to involve youth in the crusade for a "saloonless nation."[5] The League carried on postcard campaigns and issued posters and leaflets. The *Anti-Saloon League Year Book 1916*, showed the relations of pauperism, crime, insanity, and other social ills to alcoholism. One argument was that in Maine, which had had prohibition before 1915, 127.3 people per 100,000 were listed as paupers, whereas in Connecticut, only 25 percent of whose people enjoyed prohibition, 201.3 people per 100,000 were defined as paupers. The League did not, however, publicize the fact that in New Jersey, with the same prohibition ratio as Connecticut, only 84.1 people per 100,000 were paupers. This type of information was offered to the public during the struggle to bring about the "great experiment," as Prohibition was to become known.

The Committee of Fifty, a group of scholarly men assembled in 1893, made one of the most thorough and impartial studies of the liquor problem to that date. Their conclusion was that the saloon, as any other public-supported business, would supply what its clientele demanded, and therefore presented no imminent threat to the moral fiber of America.

Many people of the latter part of the nineteenth century were involved directly or indirectly in the temperance question. They took sides or issue with the Bible, medicine, statistics, prophecy, and one another. Some saw liquor as the root of all evil. Everybody saw the symptoms—economic, moral, legal, medical—of excessive alcoholic consumption, but none saw it as a disease.

The argument was taken up in popular songs. "Behind Those Swinging Doors" spelled out the ills of drinking, whereas "Saloon" glorified fellowship, escape from the wife, and haunting memories of close harmony with "the boys." The concluding line of "The Drunkard's Lone Child" spells out the sentiments of the Anti-Saloon League. On a dark and ominous night, in a raging storm, a child waits outside a saloon in the cold for her father. The song ends with a prayer aimed at all children subjected to a similar fate: "God pity poor Bessie, the drunkard's lone child." [6]

The temperance movement had sufficient strength to bring about real change—the Eighteenth Amendment to the Constitution, the Volstead Act of 1917. The Twenty-First Amendment subsequently repealed it, demonstrating that change can occur before the entire population is ready for it. Evidently many of the apathetic voters that did not exercise their franchise were upset with the results and only came forth when the consequences became disturbing to them.

Social drinking has now become solidly entrenched in middle-class American culture; the cocktail party has become an institution. Liquor is available even in so-called "dry" states today. The primary long-term effect of the temperance movement was to promote keen awareness of the problems of manufacturing, transporting, selling, and taxing of alcoholic beverages.

The Humane Movement

A summary description of two social movements like the Ku Klux Klan and the temperance movement reveals not only the conflict of values inherent in social change but also the effect of these movements on society. Although the third example is perhaps less well known to the public, the same principles apply. When religious and moral significance is attached to social change, as it was in the Ku Klux Klan it usually accompanies an economic factor; for example wholesale killing of Negroes by the Klan would have been economically disastrous, for the most menial and undesirable jobs were filled by Negroes at very small wages.

Initiation of another movement, the American Society for the Prevention of Cruelty to Animals (A.S.P.C.A.), was also influenced by economic factors. Not that the people seeking change were not sincere —public acceptance *was* tied to safeguarding an investment. If a race horse was mistreated it could become an economic loss. The same was true of other livestock. Smaller animals like cats and dogs were not the original objects of concern, but interest in their welfare grew to great proportions in the last third of the nineteenth century.

An act authorizing the A.S.P.C.A. was passed by the New York state legislature in 1866. The bylaws of the society spelled out its objectives, including not only prevention of cruelty to animals but also promotion of such enforcement measures as arrests, convictions, and fines. The power of arrest was placed in the hands of "agents" who were to take arrested people before a magistrate immediately.[7] This police function now has been assumed by law enforcement officials.

As had many other movements, the A.S.P.C.A. had originated in England. A similar organization was formed in Germany in 1839. The movement soon spread from Europe to South America and the United States. Within three decades it had thus become international in scope.

The American impetus for treating animals humanely came from the founder and first president of the American society, Henry Bergh. After delivering an emotional lecture in 1866, Bergh was assisted by the news media in arousing public sentiment for his cause. Action on the issue was rapid. The Bergh lecture was given in February 1866, and the New York legislature acted in April of the same year.[8]

Movements geared to the prevention of cruelty to animals inspired similar efforts in behalf of children. The aims of the West Virginia

Humane Society, included protection of animals, the aged, and children. Colorado organized in 1901 a state bureau for the "prevention of wrongs to children and dumb animals." By 1903 the American Humane Association had been incorporated for the purpose of coordinating policies of state chapters.

Although the fines collected from violators were a source of income for humane societies, the largest sources of funds were private donations, membership dues, and bequests. Various chapters would regularly advertise, "Remember the [humane] society in your will."

The Humane society, as it is generally called, has secured legislation controlling driving, working, beating, mutilating, maiming, and killing of animals and the amounts of food, water, rest, and shelter to be given.

The suffering of animals used in sporting events was brought to the attention of the American public. Horse racing was a popular spectator sport, and the grueling contests occasionally killed the horses. Cock fights and dog fights were also popular, and the deaths of the combatants were common.

The humane societies scored another success in the fight against mistreatment of animals: New York passed a law making it illegal to shoot pigeons—which the sportsmen of the day looked upon as an infringement of their rights. Animal fights have now been outlawed in virtually all states, over the protests of many "sportsmen." Not only the past impact of the humane movements can be assessed, its future achievements can also be predicted with some confidence. It is extremely unlikely that a bull fight will ever be held in the United States.

The issue that has received most attention in this century is vivisection, the use of animals for scientific research. The influence of the humane movement has been sufficient to obtain laws requiring painful experiments and treatment procedures on animals to be carried out under anesthetic to avoid unnecessary suffering.

Concern has also been registered for the comfort of animals en route to the slaughterhouse; they must be segregated according to kind when being transported any distance.

The humane movement has been successful not only in achieving state and Federal legislation but also in gaining support from schools and churches. Curricula and books for children are reviewed to see that humane principles are promoted. Sermons from the pulpit support humane principles. Citizens are thus reminded continually of the philosophy of preventing cruelty and humane treatment of animals and people. Whereas a man in the United States of 1860 could beat his horse to death on the street before a crowd of interested spectators, the same act would soon be halted today. This shift in attitudes has resulted from the perseverance of a group dedicated to bringing about changes in values.

Society offered little resistance to restrictions on the treatment of children sought by humane societies. The societies did not challenge the right of a parent to discipline his child unless his methods were extreme, yet states began to take more active interest in the welfare of children as a result of the humane societies' concern.

Children did not become objects of concern for the humane movement until the case of a young New York girl who had been brutally beaten by her stepmother in 1874.[9] The police in their search for someone who might assist the battered child, approached the A.S.P.C.A. No laws existed that could be used either to protect the child or to prosecute the person beating and tormenting her. And so a movement originally founded to protect dumb animals eventually took up interest in protection of children and thus affected the lives of many people.

Mechanization has eliminated the need for animals in most industry and transportation, but there is still concern for livestock and game animals. Mistreated children can be placed under the jurisdiction of child-welfare agencies and juvenile courts. The humane movement met with relatively little resistance, other than that inherent in any widespread change of attitude of the general public.

The War on Poverty

The final example of social movements in this chapter, the War on Poverty, reveals processes similar to those of the other movements discussed, but that came about through government initiative, rather than through organized effort among individual citizens. In his message to Congress on March 16, 1964, President Lyndon B. Johnson submitted the Economic Opportunity Act of 1964, pleading that the United States "declare war on a domestic enemy which threatens the strength of our Nation and the welfare of our people." [10] The act established the Office of Economic Opportunity (O.E.O.) to administer the program; the act consisted of seven titles aimed at creating opportunities for the disadvantaged. This represented the first major nationwide effort to combat this internal problem of such consequence since the legislation pertaining to the problems of the Great Depression. R. Sargent Shriver, first director of the OEO, summarized the titles of the act:

Title I. *Youth Programs*

Part A—Establishes a Job Corps to provide education, work experience, and vocational training in conservation camps and residential training centers. Administered by OEO.

Part B—Establishes a work-training program under which the Director, OEO would enter into agreements with State and local governments or nonprofit organizations to pay part of the cost of full- or part-time employment to enable young men and women, 16 to 21, to continue or resume their education or to increase their employability. Administered by Labor Department.

Title II. *Community Action Programs*

Part A—Authorizes the Director of OEO to pay up to 90 percent of the total costs of financing antipoverty programs planned and carried out at the community level. Programs will be administered by the communities and will mobilize all available resources and facilities in a coordinated attack on poverty.

Part B—Authorizes the OEO Director to make grants to States to provide basic education and literacy training to adults. Administered by the Department of Health, Education, and Welfare.

Title III. *Programs to Combat Poverty in Rural Areas*

Part A—Authorizes grants and loans to very low-income rural families where such grants or loans are likely to produce a permanent increase in the income of such families. The OEO Director may provide assistance to nonprofit corporations to acquire lands to be reconstituted into family farms. Administered by Department of Agriculture.

Part B—Sets up a program of assistance to establish and operate housing, sanitation, education, and child day-care programs for migrant farmworkers and their families.

Title IV. *Employment and Investment Incentives*

The OEO would be authorized to make, participate in, or guarantee loans to small business on more liberal terms than possible under regular loan provisions. Administered by the Small Business Administration.

Title V. *Work-Experience Program*

Authorizes the Director of OEO to transfer funds to HEW to pay costs of experimental, pilot, or demonstration projects designed to stimulate the adoption by the States of programs providing constructive work experience or training for unemployed fathers and needy persons.

Title VI. *Treatment of Unemployment Compensation and Income for Public Assistance Purposes*

A policy declaration that an individual's opportunity to participate in certain programs under this act should neither jeopardize, nor be jeopardized by, his receipt of unemployment compensation or public assistance.

Title VII. *Administration and Coordination*

Authorizes the Director of OEO to recruit and train VISTA volunteers to serve in specified mental health, migrant, Indian, and other federally related programs including the Job Corps, as well as in State and community anti-poverty programs.[11]

The implementation of the Economic Opportunity Act of 1964 signals the first time in the history of the United States that a concerted attack has been made on a national problem. Not that other movements have not been important, but the O.E.O.'s target is poverty, and no social problem has had more far-reaching effects. Poverty affects approximately one-fifth of the people in the United States.[12] Beside efforts to provide for sufficient income the attack extends to such symptoms as inadequate education, housing, and employment and to other home-management difficulties.

The fact that the ultimate impetus for the War on Poverty came from the President, rather than from a special-interest group, does not affect the questions of social dynamics to be examined. Since World War II the United States has had several occasions on which to examine its policies and practices connected with poverty. Recognition that basic civil rights have been denied to certain groups and individuals and the discovery of a corresponding high incidence of poverty among these groups led to a more penetrating analysis of the problem. A serious conflict in values involving public accommodations was revealed. The existence of separate public facilities for the races was one example, and the continuing nationally condoned custom of denying housing on the basis of race is another. But even when not deliberately excluded, many members of ethnic or minority groups cannot afford more convenient and comfortable facilities.

Ultimately many causes of poverty were brought to light, and the Economic Opportunity Act of 1964 was offered as a means to attack them. The program met resistance, essentially that expressed by Senators Barry Goldwater and John Tower.[13] Their main objections were that O.E.O. might affect virtually every person and community in the country—also, the costs of the program to the taxpayer. This cost of additional services would have to be paid from budgets that had already been pared; moreover, additional sources of revenue, according to their position, would have to be developed. The Senators also contended that the further costs of such a program had the potential of creating financial burdens for all levels of labor and management.

NOTES

1. Charles C. Alexander, *The Ku Klux Klan in the Southwest* (Lexington: University of Kentucky Press, 1965), pp. 22–35. Alexander examines the moral authoritarianism of the Klan in Texas, Louisiana, Oklahoma, and Arkansas from 1915 to 1944.
2. *Ibid*. p. 238.
3. *Ibid*. pp. 208–232.
4. David J. Pittman and Charles R. Snyder, eds., *Society, Culture and Drinking Patterns* (New York: Wiley, 1962), p. 100. This book is an analysis of the factors inherent in the consumption of alcohol.
5. Ernest H. Cherrington, ed., *The Anti-Saloon League Year Book, 1916* (Westerville, O.: Anti-Saloon League, 1916), p. 311 *Anti-Saloon Year Book*. This book offers a strong defense of the temperance movement.
6. George Ade, Ray Long, and Richard Smith, *The Old-Time Saloon* (New York: Smith, 1931), p. 132. The authors have compiled nostalgic tales of the taverns of yesteryear.
7. Roswell C. McCrea, *The Humane Movement* (New York: Columbia University Press, 1910), pp. 20–21. McCrea describes the growth of the humane movement in the United States and its lasting effects on society.
8. *Ibid*. p. 11.
9. *Ibid*. p. 135.
10. President Lyndon B. Johnson, *Message to the Congress of the United States on the Economic Opportunity Act of 1964* (Washington, D.C.: Government Printing Office, March 16, 1964). U.S. Department of Health, Education and Welfare, *Health Education and Welfare Indicators* September, 1964, p. vi, Government Printing Office, Washington, D.C.
11. U.S. Senate Committee on Labor and Public Welfare, *The War on Poverty* Report 1218, 88th Congress, 2nd Session Senate Document 86

(Washington, D.C.: Government Printing Office, July 23, 1964). p. 132.

12. Johnson, *op. cit.* p. vi.

13. See U.S. Senate Committee, *op. cit.*, minority (Republican Party) views. p. 138.

SUGGESTED READINGS

Arthur, T. S. *Ten Nights in a Bar Room.* Chicago: Donahue, c. 1913.
    A dramatic portrayal (fictional) of the evils of drinking.
Ashbury, Herbert. *The Great Illusion.* New York: Doubleday, 1950.
    An informal history of Prohibition.
Hapgood, Norman. *Up From City Streets.* New York: Harcourt, 1927.
    A biographical study of Alfred E. Smith and the politics of the 1920s.

Chapter III

*Society's shifting values, attitudes, and
expectations about woman's role, the child's
place, and the rise of the middle
class are described.*

Woman's Changing Role in Society

If women's realization that they were treated as inferiors existed before 1800, there is little evidence that they did anything about it. The first Woman's Rights Convention was held in 1848 and published a list of conditions that many women wanted changed; the convention was the beginning of the feminist movement, an outgrowth of women's participation in antislavery agitation. Women wanted a degree of equality that would raise them from the status of "things." This feeling was more prevalent among married women, probably because a woman's status was determined by her husband, and it was they more often than single women who were active feminists. They complained that a husband could force his wife to obey laws that she had had no voice in enacting. They involved her property, wages, and, if so decreed by the husband, her liberty. A woman was denied formal education beyond high school. She was expected to "submit" to sexual intercourse but forbidden to enjoy it or to express herself through active participation. In effect, she was denied her own identity.

Reaction to the movement to secure women's rights was varied, but the preponderance was negative. Misunderstanding and misinterpretation of the feminists' motives were common. Although today some would feel early feminists suffered from penis envy and nymphomania others feel that women were misunderstood largely because they were breaking away from the role in which they had been cast for so long. The word "man" is now often used in a generic sense to include both men and women, but its use in the Bible and in legislation was interpreted then to mean only the male sex. Feminists were thus regarded as revolutionary. Potent support for the male argument was lent by the Bible. Women's desire to "speak in church," "be the head of the family," or not "be in subjection to husbands" was contrary to Scripture, they were told. From this entrenched position men began to attack personalities in the movement, thus obscuring the real issues.

Men had grown complacent in their secure belief that women should stay in their kitchens and be happy about it. Discontent seeped through the country, causing previously dutiful wives and mothers to wonder about expressing their true potentials. As the feminist movement gained momentum, females became less willing to accept the subservient roles assigned them. Even most colleges were under male dominations, and the first females to gain admission were prepared mainly for "intelligent motherhood" and "properly subservient wifehood." [1]

Not only did women receive unequal consideration in education, but they were also subordinate in marriage, religion, citizenship, and employment. Divorce courts created and managed by males did not look favorably upon allowing children to remain with a woman who complained about her lot or who was unfaithful or disobedient to her husband. A proposed Constitutional amendment granting female suffrage was defeated in 1869 and again in following years. The individual states reacted differently; Wyoming, Colorado, Utah, and Idaho granted women state franchise in the early 1890s. Nationwide suffrage for women, however, did not occur until the Nineteenth Amendment to the Constitution was passed in 1919.

More and more women came to believe that they had potential contributions to make to society that were more challenging than baking, cooking, washing, bearing and raising children, and other homemaking duties. The feminists compared their position to that of slaves. But many other women not only resigned themselves to the unlikelihood of change but also accepted their situation. But, as women began to work outside the home, their financial contributions gave them a new voice in the home. Once removed from the circumscribed home duties and allowed to meet people in similar circumstances, women became more difficult for men to control.

The efforts of women to obtain rights were not directed at assuming male roles nor at achieving domination over men. Those men who made such charges belied their own security. Not only was the rise of feminism a challenge to their own sense of adequacy; it was also considered a shocking affront to the mores. Contrary to the expectation of opponents to feminism, however, women became less rather than more bitter as they won what many termed "concessions." They were eventually able to compete in business, education, politics, and industry, although never yet on equal terms. The legal, medical, and engineering professions, for example, still have few female members.

The gains made by the feminists did not come without sacrifice. Women were assaulted by police and put in jail for picketing (sometimes in freezing weather); they caused national hysteria by going on hunger strikes and chaining themselves to the White House fence. As difficult as the struggle for rights was, many women were dedicated to the cause with a near fanatical zeal. Description of the hardships encountered by the feminists reveal their fortitude, dedication, and perseverance.[2] They fasted, slept on floors, and engaged in fisticuffs with men, all of which evidently produced an esprit de corps among the lady combatants that was virtually impossible to counter. Although some participants probably believed themselves to be martyrs, writers claim that most feminists did not.[3]

When the United States entered World War II, its women had already won the legal right to vote. Not only were they aware of the gains that American women had won, but they were also learning how women in other countries had progressed. Simone de Beauvoir discusses the history of female subservience and international involvement in women's efforts at "liberation" before 1942.[4] The Depression years, according to Ruth Cavan, had a sobering effect on youth in general.[5] During the 1920s many young girls had taken up smoking, drinking, and extramarital sexual intercourse in protest of the double standard of conduct for men and women. Early feminists had considered sexual freedom and equality their rights as persons; they refused to accept sex simply as a function that they were expected to perform.

As more men were mobilized for the war effort in the early 1940s, it became necessary for industry to seek other sources of labor. Two important resource pools were tapped: the elderly and women. It was recognized for the first time that women were capable of engaging in a wide range of industrial occupations. During the Industrial Revolution, when women were already exploited to a greater degree than those in other labor categories, industry had tapped two other sources of cheap labor: immigrants and Negroes. Because of an absolute labor shortage women were paid equal pay for equal work, and they performed competently in positions formerly occupied by men. Their work proved satisfactory; however, there are positions in the factory system today that have been known predominantly as women's trades since the war. Women employed during World War II started far above the highest level achieved by women several decades earlier. They donned overalls, welding caps, work gloves, and other practical clothing to work in defense plants, drive buses and taxicabs, and work in other crafts and trades. Nurses were vital to the armed forces; all levels of training in medicine were offered both in and out of the military services.

The freedom of women in the 1920s had declined somewhat in the 1930s but expanded again during World War II. In 1945, at the end of the war, a new era had arrived for women on an international scale. The U.N. Commission on the Status of Women pressed for equal rights for the sexes in all its member nations. This ideal may never become a reality, but it is a goal for millions of women in the present and countless numbers in the future.

The Child's Place in Society

Traditionally, the child has been a subordinate person in our society, and adulthood has been postponed a little longer in each succeeding generation. The transition from childhood to adulthood took place at an early age during the expansion of the Western frontier, usually of necessity and often abruptly. The child of earlier times could do very little to fight the existing system, and by the time of his emancipation from home he had become identified with the established culture. He not only had little desire to rebel, but he was encouraged by society to marry, rear children, and earn a livelihood for himself and family. This was in accord with the dictates of a society that stressed individual endeavor, ambition and independence for the adult. The child was expected to adhere to a rigid and well-defined behavioral pattern.

Society's expectations of its children have changed since pioneer days. Then, women were expected to remain in the home and virtually assume total responsibility for the daily care of children. If a mother of that time was discontented over her role and bitter about her lack of freedom of expression and individuality, her child very likely absorbed some of her hostility. The father often took no active interest in his children until they had reached their teens—and then only in his sons. The mother's dissatisfaction and the father's distance created an atmosphere for children that was not conducive to positive emotional health.

Such conditions existed well into the twentieth century. Children were given more freedom in 1900 than in previous years but were expected to behave as small adults. Whereas children of six or seven had been working for wages less than fifty years previously, in 1900 children the same age had to attend school. They were frequently told that they were to be seen and not heard. They were expected to run errands for adults without receiving much money or other rewards. The school experience was often a combination of regimentation and strict discipline. A teacher could administer corporal punishment unhampered by the interference of parents. Often the teacher was the only professional staff member, serving as instructor, administrator, custodian, and substitute parent.

Most children were not encouraged to remain in school much beyond the sixth or seventh grade, by which time they were regarded as a young adult and therefore economic assets on farms or in industry. The expectations of society at that time, transmitted by the process of socialization, reflected the demands of an industrial complex for inexpensive labor. The average child was socialized by example and sanctions into acceptable behavioral patterns. Serving as a model for the youth of that era was the dominant, "self-made" man. Although this model lacked much of the sophistication of today's ideal, it was popular then, for American history abounds in success stories of men who had been "on their own" since they were fourteen or fifteen. Today, there is some confusion existing over a single hero-model inasmuch as the "organization" man is as highly regarded by some, as the rebel leader is by others.

Socialization of the child, which is the transmission of values from one generation to another, involves orientation of the person toward his role and function. Children in past generations had been conditioned to "face reality" about their places in adult-determined society.

Like most other forms of behavior, the ability to "face reality" had to be learned. The child was taught that the best way to ensure his comfort in the future was to expose himself to present hardships and to overcome them through his own resources. Adults advised young people of the middle and lower classes to postpone gratification for the moment and to work toward nobler values in the future.

It was already difficult for teenagers of 1920 to pass up fun and immediate rewards for remote and uncertain gratification, and the young people of today do not look upon conformity to these values as the ultimate in aspirations as did their counterparts several decades ago. Instead they now ask to "hear it like it is," without moralizing or embellishment. They do not accept the axioms of adults as unadulterated truth, for they have been instilled with a spirit of inquiry bordering at times on revolution against the established system. They exclaim their distaste for world conditions and loudly blame adults for creating those conditions. Some protest against military service that they are obliged by law to perform. Although considered irresponsible and too immature to know what they are talking about by some adults, these young people have raised questions that cannot go unanswered. They want to know, for example, why they should be bound by laws in whose enactment they have had no voice; laws that commit them to potential hazards like war, laws that restrict their freedom, impinge on their rights, or generally restrain them from self-expression.

The child's place in society has changed and will continue to do so. There will be changes in systems, practices, approaches, and attitudes connected with children. Those with the responsibility for rearing children will initiate some of those changes themselves and will transmit others.

Oscar W. Ritchie and Marvin R. Koller describe three systems of raising children: child-centered, child-oriented, and child-dominated.[6] In the child-centered system adults maintain control but focus attention on children. A child-oriented system is one in which children are the main participants but their efforts are directed to goals defined by adults. The child-dominated system is one in which older children define their own goals. None of these systems, however, adequately explains the changes in child-rearing practices from 1900 to World War II. As events like Prohibition, the Depression, and World Wars I and II changed the living patterns, attitudes, and values of the nation, the role of the child was also redefined. The family lost many of its traditional functions to other institutions, primarily the school and the

TABLE 1

*Child-Rearing Patterns Reported as Characteristic
of Families of Emotionally Healthy Children Compared
with Relevant Patterns Reported as Characteristic
of Very Poor Families*

Emotionally Healthy	Low-Income
1. Respect for child as individual whose behavior is caused by multiple factors; acceptance of parental role in child development.	1. Misbehavior defined in terms of concrete outcomes; reasons for behavior not considered; parental projection of blame on others.
2. Commitment to slow development of child from infancy to maturity; parental acceptance of stresses and pressures at each stage because of ultimate goal of raising "happy," successful child.	2. Lack of goal commitment and belief in long-range success; parental emphasis on child's "keeping out of trouble"; orientation toward fatalism, impulse gratification, and alienation.
3. Relative sense of competence in handling child's behavior.	3. Sense of impotence in handling children's behavior, as well as in other areas.
4. Discipline chiefly verbal, mild, reasonable, consistent, based on needs of child, family, and society; more emphasis on rewarding good behavior than on punishing bad behavior.	4. Discipline harsh, inconsistent, physical, involving ridicule; depends on whether child's behavior annoys parent or not.
5. Open, free, verbal communication between parent and child; control largely verbal.	5. Limited verbal communication; control largely physical.
6. Democratic rather than autocratic or laissez-faire methods of rearing, with both parents in equalitarian but not necessarily interchangeable roles; companionship between parents and children.	6. Authoritarian rearing methods; mother chief child-care agent; father, when home, mainly a punitive figure; little support and acceptance of child as an individual.
7. Parents' general confidence in own competence and satisfaction with themselves and their situation.	7. Low parental self-esteem, sense of defeat.

TABLE 1 (Continued)

Emotionally Healthy	Low-Income
8. Intimate, expressive, warm relationship between parent and child, allowing for gradually increasing independence; sense of continuing parental responsibility.	8. Large families; more impulsive, narcissistic parental behavior; orientation to "excitement"; abrupt, early yielding of independence.
9. Presence of father in home and absence of severe marital conflict.	9. Father not at home (under certain circumstances). Marital conflict.
10. Free verbal communication about sex, acceptance of child's sexual needs, channeling of sex drive through "healthy" psychological defenses, acceptance of slow growth toward impulse control and sexual satisfaction in marriage; sex education by both father and mother.	10. Repressive, punitive attitude about sex, sexual questions and experimentation; sex viewed as exploitative relationship.
11. Acceptance of child's aggressive drives and channeling into socially approved outlets.	11. Alternating encouragement and restriction of aggression, primarily related to consequences of aggression for parents.
12. Open to new experiences; flexible.	12. Distrust of new experiences; constricted life, rigidity.
13. Happiness of parental marriage.	13. High rates of marital conflict and family breakdown.

church. Training in cooking, home maintenance, farming, automobile driving, and religion is conducted outside the home. Playthings include models of cars, stoves, guns, and other items used by adults, fostering children's identification with the adult world of which they will soon become a part.

Another route to identification with adult roles and attitudes is exposure to television. Left to themselves children are usually honest and direct in their dealings with people, exhibiting an absence of guile that also makes them vulnerable to the suggestions of others and places them in potentially exploitable positions. Children are conditioned through their interaction with others, and it is sometimes difficult for them to separate reality from fantasy. As a result, television advertising and programming may have both calculated and accidental impacts on children.

Children are now evaluated more on the basis of individual merit than were the children of frontier days by adults. A parent's responsibility is to rear the child in an atmosphere of acceptance and warmth. Concern for the welfare of the child through his developmental stages has become paramount. Based on the assumption that some children will eventually hold positions of leadership, society seeks to avert problems inherent in its definition of the child's role.

A government publication, *Growing Up Poor*, provides several interesting comparisons between patterns of parental behavior associated with emotionally healthy children and those of low-income parents.[7] Table 1 summarizes such parental patterns.

That the child of today is treated quite differently from his counterpart of an earlier time is clear from the characteristics in the first column of Table 1, which reflects the idealistic child-rearing patterns of today. It is also observable in prevailing efforts to forestall children's coming of age. Most middle-class parents not only frown upon marriage for their children immediately after graduation from high school but also prefer that they wait until after college. It is not uncommon for young men and women to remain financially dependent on their parents during their college years. A redefinition of the child's role has evolved, and the parent generation looks upon this extended dependence without alarm. This change is directly related to attitudes of the middle class, which has enjoyed an elevation in status and possession of material goods unequaled in history.

The Rise of the Middle Class

The middle class in the United States, comprising the majority of the population, can now possess many comforts of life, in addition to such necessities as food, clothing, and shelter. What may once have been considered a luxury, like automobiles, is now regarded as a necessity. The labor force almost tripled between 1890 and 1964, and that during the same period of seventy-four years the number of females in the work force rose 505 percent, compared to an increase of 330 percent of all females in the population.[8] In 1864 the work week was approximately sixty-five hours.[9] Now more people work shorter hours for higher wages. The total monetary value of all goods and services produced in a country during a given year is defined as its Gross National Product (G.N.P.). The G.N.P. of the United States has had an overall increase of 2.9 percent since 1900.[10] This figure is an accurate index of the rise of the middle class, which encompasses both the main producers and consumers of products.

One element in middle-class purchasing power, applied to both necessities and luxuries is the contract or installment plan. Instead of saving earned cash toward the price of a desired purchase, one can make a down payment, or deposit, at the time the buyer takes possession and then pay the balance in regular installments until the price plus interest or "carrying charges" or "service charges" has been paid. These additional sums are similar to the interest on a loan, which is, in effect, what has been negotiated between buyer and seller.

Installment buying has increased both relative and absolute purchasing power. Generally, a person's credit is calculated at about ten times his gross monthly pay. By increasing its purchasing power by at least ten times, the middle class has been able to raise its standard of living.

From this rising potential consumption of goods and services comes the obvious need for greater production, which, in turn, creates employment for more people and thus increases potential consumption. This system is not without fault. People sometimes overextend themselves financially and risk losing the products that they have contracted to buy. Loss of work may result in the consumer's inability to keep up the installment payments. Such other problems as forgery, misrepresentation, and fraud exist, but the system appears able to continue functioning and bettering the middle-class standard of living.

The middle-class person has not only been able to raise his material standards but he has also been able to impose his values relating to education, religion, free speech, morality, and various Constitutionally guaranteed rights upon society. A person expects his child to receive free public education and will complain if it is not forthcoming. He insists on his right to free speech and free assembly and will speak out for causes that he favors. Religious persecution is now mostly a matter of the past, and outcries against religion are heard only when a Constitutional violation is suspected. Violations could center around such issues as military deferments, taxation or praying in public schools. The issue itself, as opposed to the stated religion of a person would most likely be questioned. People can claim nudism as their religion without fear of persecution, as long as they practice it privately.

The middle-class American is concerned more about himself, his family, and his immediate environment than about larger events that appear to affect him less. Although he generally avoids "getting involved," he is determined in his efforts to overcome any deterrent to his ascending power. It is when the problem becomes personal to him that he attempts to muster forces to solve it. He joins the fight the fastest and expends the most energy when the problem becomes internalized and a solution is visible.

NOTES

1. Eleanor Flexner, *Century of Struggle: The Woman's Rights Movement in the United States* (Cambridge, Mass.: Harvard University Press, 1959). p. 30.
2. For example, see Ida Wylie, "The Little Woman," *Harpers*, November 1945, pp. 402–409. This article depicts the trials and tribulations of activists in the feminist movement.
3. Alma Lutz, *Created Equal* (New York: Day, 1940), pp. 295–307. The personality of the typical suffragette is discussed.
4. Simone de Beauvoir, *The Second Sex* (New York: Knopf, 1953), pp. 679–715. Offers an international historical perspective on the feminist movement.
5. Ruth Cavan, *The American Family* (New York: Crowell, 1953), pp. 537–543. Presents the thesis that the family has developed its ideals and forms in interaction with other parts of the social order.
6. Oscar W. Ritchie and Marvin R. Koller, *Sociology of Childhood* (New York: Appleton, 1964), pp. 26–28. Offers an analysis of the various factors that produce children's attitudes and behavior in society today.
7. Catherine S. Shilman, *Growing Up Poor* (Washington, D.C.: Government Printing Office, 1968), pp. 28–29.
8. Murray Gendell and Hans L. Zetterberg, eds., *A Sociological Almanac for the United States* (New York: Scribner's, 1964), Almanac, p. 65.
9. *Ibid.* p. 15.
10. *Ibid.* p. 11.

SUGGESTED READINGS

Bottomore, T. B. *Critics of Society: Radical Thought in North America.* New York: Pantheon, 1968.

Suggests the role of fundamental social criticism in our society.
Davis, Allison. *Social Class Influences Upon Learning*. Cambridge, Mass.: Harvard University Press, 1950.

The process of learning viewed with emphasis on the status of the child.

Part Two

SOCIETY'S STRUGGLE TO

SOLVE SOCIAL PROBLEMS

THE GREENE FAMILY

We have constructed a multiproblem family for the purpose of illustrating social problems and assisting the student to decide on the appropriate use of community resources. The Greene family is fictional, but its problems are genuine and represent a composite of the difficulties that commonly come to the attention of social-welfare agencies.

The problems of the Greene family are initially outlined on what most agencies call a "face sheet," which is usually placed at the beginning of the case record of a client. The face sheet in this text has been constructed by the authors so that the student can observe the steps involved in a case. Before meeting the client a worker often has no more information on a case than that in the face sheet. But an experienced social worker often can formulate tentative decisions and possible courses of action from such identifying information.

Following the face sheet we have provided factual descriptions of individual members of the family, from which we have intentionally omitted mention of family members' feelings. The three basic steps in processing a case are study, diagnosis, and treatment. Study is the collection of factual material on the case, diagnosis is interpretation of the facts, and treatment is mobilization of resources to solve the problems identified in the diagnosis.

Subjective material, or individual points of view, is used in the diagnostic phase of the process. We shall illustrate it in the form of comments from each person in the family, couched in what the authors believe is typical language. The reader will thus become aware of the various ways in which the same problems can be viewed. In arriving at a diagnosis, a "helping" professional must guard against interpreting facts until the attitudes, values, and beliefs of the clients about those facts are taken into consideration. This is in keeping with our definition of the helping services, which includes those professional disciplines directly concerned with the prevention, alleviation and relief of social problems and with assistance to people in order to aid them in realizing their potentialities.

Following the family members' views is an evaluation of the individual strengths of each. The purpose of this evaluation is to pose questions that must receive attention before a treatment plan can be formulated. Neither the facts collected by the worker nor the subjective views of the family members will provide answers to all the questions that must be answered before proceeding with treatment. A hasty conclusion is to be avoided, for the "obvious" solution often depends on over-simplification of the total problem.

A summary of the various social-welfare resources available to help solve problems like those of the Greene family concludes this chapter. No attempt is made here to solve each problem listed. Instead, the reader is shown how to approach interrelated difficulties through existing resources. Relatively few people are aware of all available community resources, but those in the helping professions are expected to be. Although the Greene family might come to the attention of one social-welfare institution for a particular problem, it would eventually also receive help through other agencies to which it was referred.

The Face Sheet

A person who needs help is often confused, bewildered, and on the brink of panic. His problem is the most important thing in his life at the moment. When a solution is not immediately forthcoming or the solution that he has adopted is unavailing, his problem becomes worse. Seldom does his initial description of the problem encompass all the difficulties he is experiencing. The problem of one family member has effects on others in the family. Most problem families are thus multiproblem families.

To understand and evaluate the problems of the Greene family, we must first study the facts recorded on the face sheet. The face sheet is usually a one-page form used by social-welfare agencies to identify a particular case. Virtually thousands of different kinds are in existence, but all contain one essential ingredient: identifying information. In order to keep the face sheet one page in length, various coding procedures are used. For example, the number assigned the family members in item 10 of our sample face sheet is seen in relation to former marriages (item 8). This makes it possible to identify the person about whom the initial notation pertains.

Case Histories

The information on any face sheet is limited. A better understanding of the family can be obtained from the narrative portion of the case record. In the following example, certain standard items such as relatives on assistance, former residences, family physicians and military assignments have been omitted, and the emphasis is given to the family members only. Some of the standard headings one would find in the narrative portion are reason for requesting help, living arrangements, health, home and household practices, economic practices, family unity and emotional atmosphere, education, individual behavior and adjustment, social adjustment, diagnosis, and treatment plan. Additional headings would be entered by the caseworker for circumstances peculiar to the case, and progress notes would be added to help other readers to understand the case.

The following case study is a typical report of a multiproblem family that is designed to show the many facets of a situation in which a worker becomes involved. It should be understood that the average

FACE SHEET

1. Surname	Maiden Name			Case Number-Suffix		Date Applied
GREENE				3647613 - 7		5-16-68

		Man	Woman	6. Military Record		7. Soc. Sec. No.
2.	Color or Nationality	Cauc (Mex)	Cauc	Dates of	30 Dec 42 21 Jan 46	1. 172-20-4501
						2. 528 31-2695
3.	Religion	Catholic	Lutheran	Numbers 933065		3.
						4.
4.	Guardian			Service	Army PFC	5.
5.	Present Marriage	15 Sep 46	—	Type of Discharge		

Former Marriages:

8. Name	Date	Place	Status & Degree	Date & Place	Soc. Sec. No
(2) Dale Peters	9 Sep 42	Thorny Ariz	Deceased	— 1944	unk -?

9. Addresses	Telephone	Living Arrangements
218 Belmont, Ill Metropolis USA	none	Renting - 95.00 + utilities Ted C and william Realtors

10. Family Members	Birth date	Verification of Birthdate	Education
1. Harold	22 Dec 25	Luce, Texas	
2. Olive	25 Jul 27	Karlan Texas	
3. (Barbara)	27 Nov 46	Metropolis	
4. Marvin	26 Feb 49	"	
5. Robert	15 Apr 52	"	
6.			
7.			
8.			

11. Others in Household	Relation	Relatives	Relation-ship	Address
Angela White	Mo. # 2	David Green	Bro # 1	1115 Island Ave. Reid, Georgia
Barbara Compton	Dtr 1 & 2	Richard White	Bro # 2	PO BOX 750, DRAWER Y, Mont.
Raymond Compton	Son # 3			
John Johnson	Son # 3			

12. Other Agency Conferences	Problems from Agency Point of View	Dates
Alcoholics Anonymous -	Ref wants to see Harold & Olive	
Red Cross (Mr. McNamara)	- Can't locate for release	
Childrens Aid Society		
Veterans Admin -	Dr Carruth wants claim withdrawn	
Vocational Rehab -	Inquire about WIN for Barbara	
Juvenile Court -		
Employment Services		

13. Remarks

Raymond Compton, son # 3, placed for adoption with Aid - Mrs. Stryen will report - See Arkava's report on court hearing.

case worker is under pressure of time and caseload; as a result, his reports do not always reflect the highest standards in composition. The report, of necessity, must be brief and cannot be redone, due to these very real pressures.

Harold Greene

Harold Greene was born on December 22, 1925, in a small rural farm area in Texas. He was the fourth oldest in a family of nine children. His mother was Mexican-American and his father Caucasian-American born and raised in Texas. Harold Greene continually denied his Mexican ancestry from the time he was a small boy, and later in life this attitude caused him numerous difficulties because his physical characteristics made his denials extremely unconvincing.

When Harold was nine years old his mother died in childbirth. His father, who was left with the sole responsibility of raising nine children, yielded to the pressure and deserted the family three months later. All nine children became wards of the state and were placed in separate foster homes.

During the next two years Harold lived with five different foster families. When he was twelve years old his paternal grandparents took him into their home, where he remained until he enlisted in the army in 1942. During his years with his grandparents, Harold was never allowed to forget that he was an "orphan" and should "thank God" that his grandparents were considerate enough to take care of him and that they had sacrificed a great deal to take him into their home.

Harold's three years in the army passed without incident, and he was given an honorable discharge in 1945. A year later he was convicted of armed robbery and sentenced to one to twenty years in the state penitentiary. After serving three years in prison he was paroled, having been promised a job in a printing firm as a result of the training that he had received while incarcerated. Harold remained in this job until 1965, at which time he suffered a back injury in an automobile accident, necessitating a spinal fusion. He drew his last paycheck in May 1965. Since his injury Harold has been content to draw his monthly social-security disability check and has shown no interest in returning to the labor market.

Harold married Olive on September 15, 1946. The marriage, although apparently stable, has many underlying problems, resulting in the present unhealthy marital relationship. Verbal communication between Harold and Olive is virtually nonexistent, and the same situation exists among all family members. At present Harold has withdrawn almost completely from the world around him and spends much of his time recalling happier days.

Olive Greene

Olive Greene was born on July 25, 1927. Like her husband, she was born in a rural area of Texas. She was the oldest of twelve children. The family lived under poverty conditions; its only income came from the sale of produce raised on its small farm. Olive describes her childhood as happy but difficult. Although Olive can describe her childhood as happy, she can also vividly recall several incidents when her father molested her, beginning when she was nine or ten years old.

Olive married when she was fifteen years old and four months pregnant. This marriage lasted two years and was dissolved when her husband, in a fit of rage, killed both his child and himself. Olive is very reluctant to talk about this marriage, and whenever the subject is brought up her eyes fill with tears and she makes every attempt to avoid discussing it.

Shortly after the death of her first husband Olive began to drink heavily. Her drinking has continued to the present time; the amount she consumes, however, varies according to the pressures that she feels. She by no means thinks that she has a drinking problem and insists that she takes only an occasional social drink.

Olive married Harold Greene approximately one year after the tragedy. She was again pregnant at the time of her marriage, and she states emphatically that she doesn't know "why in the hell" she ever let herself get into "such a mess."

Olive has held fairly regular employment during her second marriage, working primarily as a motel maid. She has stated many times that her work has interfered with her performance as a mother, but she feels that she must work because her husband won't.

For the past several months Olive has been suffering from dizzy spells, and she recently had to terminate her employment because of them. A brain tumor has been diagnosed, and she is presently under a doctor's care. The family applied for welfare assistance, and it receives AFDC (Aid to Families of Dependent Children).

Olive has been unable to assume any responsibility for what she describes as "the mess that I'm in." She feels that she has been a victim of circumstances beyond her control.

Angela White

Angela White was born February 14, 1902. She is Olive Greene's mother. According to Mrs. White, she came through the "school of hard knocks," working hard for everything that she has received. She had one "successful marriage" lasting twenty years and resulting in twelve children. Her husband died of a heart attack at forty-five, and Mrs. White had two subsequent marriages, both ending in divorce.

Mrs. White is an aggressive, domineering person. She still looks upon Olive as her little girl and imposes upon her a great deal. Mrs. White is unwilling to allow Olive to make independent decisions, and Olive seems quite content in this relationship. Mrs. White never hesitates to express her negative feelings about Harold to the entire family. She has insisted many times that Harold is the sole cause of any family difficulty.

Mrs. White spends a great deal of time reminiscing about old times and uses her past as an example of how Olive and Harold should raise their children. She seems to be quite oblivious to changes in the world during the past fifty years. She is a definite advocate of "What was good enough for me is good enough for anybody."

Mrs. White is receiving welfare assistance under Old Age Assistance (OAA). She is very dissatisfied with her status on public assistance, claiming that she would much rather be working and earning her own way. At present Mrs. White is the dominant member of the Greene household. All decisions are made with her approval. It appears that she has taken up permanent residence with the Greenes and has no intention of moving out.

Barbara Greene Compton

Barbara Greene Compton was born on November 27, 1946, when her parents had been married approximately three months, and Mr. Greene has continually denied being Barbara's father. These denials and ensuing fights with Mrs. Greene often took place in front of Barbara. Shortly after Barbara was born Mr. Greene was convicted of armed robbery and was sentenced to the state penitentiary. During his imprisonment Mrs. Greene worked as a motel maid to support the family, and Barbara was left in the care of numerous babysitters.

Barbara was always a shy, withdrawn child and had practically no friends. Her favorite pastime was to play with paper dolls by herself in her bedroom. Barbara disliked school intensely, and her scholastic record was poor. She quit school midway through the tenth grade because of pregnancy and ran away from home to live with her Negro boyfriend, Bob Johnson. Both her parents and Bob's parents disapproved of this relationship, but neither took any direct action to dissolve it. Barbara remained with Bob for approximately six months, until he left to seek employment in another state. Barbara never heard from Bob again, and she is certain that the only reason he left was because her parents frightened him away. One child, John Greene Johnson, was born as a result of this relationship, and Barbara refused under any circumstances to consider placing this child for adoption.

Immediately after Bob's departure Barbara began to frequent local bars looking for warmth and affection, however temporary in nature. It was in one of these bars that she met Ted Compton, who was an army private home on leave. She married Ted after knowing him for only two days. Shortly after Ted returned to his unit he went AWOL and defected to Russia. Barbara was pregnant with Ted's baby, and when the child was born she relinquished custody to the Children's Aid Society so that he could be placed in an adoptive home.

At the present time Barbara is very confused. She has not been successful in anything that she has tried, even though she appears to be the brightest member of the Greene family. She has no plans for the immediate future although she is extremely dissatisfied with her present situation.

Marvin Greene

Marvin Greene is a nineteen-year-old mentally defective boy. The origin of Marvin's retardation is unknown. Mrs. Greene attempted a self-induced abortion when she was four months pregnant with Marvin because the child was unwanted. Marvin also had scarlet fever when he was thirteen months old.

The severity of Marvin's retardation is apparent in his behavior. (It should be noted that Marvin has never undergone any psychological testing.) He can neither read nor write and is unable to maintain a train of thought long enough to explain a complete idea. He attempts to speak rapidly but is not coherent when he does. Most of Marvin's time is spent watching television, primarily cartoons.

When Marvin was a young boy, the family doctor encouraged Mr. and Mrs. Greene to place him in a training school for mental defectives. Although they agreed that it was a good idea, they failed to follow through with the application. Marvin is also epileptic, subject to frequent grand mal seizures. Medication has been prescribed for this condition, but the family is often negligent in seeing that Marvin takes his medicine.

It is understood by the entire family that Marvin is not "normal," but no mention is ever made of his being mentally retarded.

At present Marvin appears to be basically happy and does not appear to be dangerous to himself or others. For the most part he is ignored by his family; he often embarrasses the others with his unusual behavior, however.

Robert Greene

Robert Greene was born on April 15, 1952, and is the youngest member of the Greene family. He is regarded as the problem child in the family, and neither of his parents has been able to control his behavior. He quit school after completing the tenth grade. Before leaving he was placed on probation by the juvenile court for possession and use of marijuana. Robert looks upon this record as a status symbol, for a great many of his friends are also on probation. Harold and Olive show no reaction to the fact that Robert has quit school or has been placed on probation by the juvenile court. They refuse to accept any responsibility for either event and merely shrug it off, saying, "That's Robert, and we can't do a thing with him."

Robert is presently trying to grow a beard. His efforts are being thwarted by nature itself, and only a few lonely and sparsely placed whiskers adorn his chin. His attempt to grow a beard has gone unnoticed by his family. Robert is planning to marry his girl friend Maria, who is three months pregnant. He is presently unemployed and has no idea how he will support a wife and baby, but he is certain that everything will work out okay.

At the present time Robert's only confidant is his probation officer, who has managed to establish a close relationship with him. Robert appears to be at a crossroads in his life, with one road leading to further delinquency and eventual commitment to the state industrial school and the other to responsible behavior and a productive life.

Family Statements

The narrative portion of the case record would be essentially the same, regardless of what agency collected the material. Following are examples of the way the authors believe that individual family members would verbalize their views on family problems. The statements are couched in the language common among people in circumstances similar to those of the Greene family. In preparing this material the authors have had the benefit of their own experience and the consultation with interviewers from many social-welfare agencies, representing more than 30,000 client contacts.

Harold Greene

Here I am minding my own business when that damned mother-in-law of mine comes barging in on us. She feeds my wife so full of bull that naturally she invites her to live with us. Olive always was tied to her mother. She could never do a damned thing without checking with her first, and now here's the old biddy living with us. I don't have a chance with those two ganging up on me. Oh, what the hell, maybe if I ignore them they'll leave me alone.

If that isn't enough, Barbara and those two bastard children of hers show up. Now there's a good example of how screwed up my wife and her mother are—look at how Barbara turned out, and it's all their fault. If they'd have just listened to me, Barbara would have been a good girl. But no, they have to continually nag at her, just like they do with me, until Barbara runs away and gets herself pregnant by some nigger. She really showed them. She never would have married that punk who ran away from the army if Olive hadn't of nagged her into it. Oh, what the hell, maybe if I ignore her and the kids, they'll leave me alone.

Then there's Starvin' Marvin, what a dumbbell! He really takes after his mother's side of the family. That kid is so dumb he thinks I've said something nice when I call him Starvin' Marvin. I'll never forget when Robert tried to teach that idiot how to swim. He was so dumb, he couldn't tell his hands from his feet. And what a sight he made in a swimming suit, he looked just like a big fat blob. Oh, what the hell, maybe if I ignore him, he'll leave me alone.

I wonder how Robert is getting along on probation? I'll have to talk to the kid someday. I could teach him a lot of tricks on how to snow the probation officer and keep him off your back. But Robert's too big for his britches. He thinks he knows more than his old man, but I got news for him. I'm a lot smarter than him. I never got no sixteen-year-old girl pregnant when I was out chasing around. Oh, what the hell, maybe if I ignore him, he'll leave me alone.

I'd give anything if I could leave this dump and go back into the army. Those were the days—what great times I had! I can see myself now—I'm a first sergeant in an infantry company, barking out orders. The men are jumping at my command. Oh, what the hell, I know I can never go back to the army. My back won't let me.

You know, if it wasn't for my bad back, I could be just about anything I wanted to be. I'm certainly smart enough, and I'm strong as an ox, but my back just keeps getting worse. The Social Security doesn't seem to care enough to do anything. They just keep sending that measly check every month. A guy just doesn't have a chance when the cards are stacked against him like they're stacked against me. Oh, what the hell . . .

Olive Greene

What a mess, what a mess. My husband just doesn't care. If he would just go out and get a job and support the family, everything would be all right. Lord knows I've done everything I can, working my fingers to the bone cleaning those rooms at the motel. By the time I get home at night I'm just too tired to do anything, and Harold refuses to help me. Thank heavens my mother's living with us now. She's been such a great help in the past, and now she can help me with taking care of the kids and cleaning the house.

I'm so nervous with all my responsibilities. The only way I have to relax is to take an occasional drink, and then Harold jumps all over me, which makes me even more nervous. He says I'm an alcoholic, but I know I'm not—I can quit drinking anytime I want to.

No one seems to understand me. I wonder how they'd feel if someone they loved killed their child and themselves too. Why, oh why, did he do that? Everything would have been all right if he'd have just grown up and assumed some responsibility.

You know men are just not to be trusted. My father raped me when I was small, my first husband was nothing but a little boy, and he killed my baby, and Harold is a lazy good-for-nothing bum. I wonder why men are like that. Everything would be all right if men would be as responsible as women.

I wish Barbara would find a place of her own. She and her children are such a burden, and she does nothing to help around the house. I don't understand why Barbara went bad; I did everything I could. I guess if Harold had of just taken more of an interest in her everything would have been all right.

Robert is such a problem. I just can't control him anymore, and besides I can't work at that motel all day long and then come home and spend time with Robert. I'm just too tired, and Harold should realize that Robert takes after him—getting into trouble with the law and raising hell around the house. Everything would be all right with Robert if his dad would just spend more time with him.

Marvin is such a dear boy, but he takes so much of my time. He just doesn't seem to understand what I tell him, and I'm always losing my temper and yelling at him. I just don't know what to do about him. I feel so helpless. I guess everything would be all right if Marvin were just smarter.

Things have really gotten bad lately. With me the only one working in the family we've had to apply for welfare. The welfare people seem nice enough but they don't seem to understand, and they ask all those personal questions. What are they going to do with all that information? Besides having to apply for welfare the doctors have told me I have a brain tumor. What a mess, what a mess.

Mrs. White

There's that lazy no-good Harold sitting with his nose glued to the television. I tried to tell Olive that he wasn't good enough for her, but she went and married the bum anyway. If she'd of just listened to me she wouldn't be in this mess now. If I was married to Harold I'd make sure he toed the mark, and I wouldn't take any back talk from him either. Why, when my third husband was around, he always did what I told him.

I wonder why Olive did this to me? Why, she could have had her choice of any number of men. I remember little Roger Smith—if Olive had of listened to me, she would have married him, and she'd have been happy today. It's probably still not too late for her to find a good man if she'll just get rid of Harold.

Things just aren't the same as they were in my day. Why, I wouldn't sit still for all this nonsense with Barbara, and I'd have made sure that Robert was a good boy. Parents these days are too easy, and it seems like the kids are taking over. Things are just too easy for everybody. Why, in my day I had to walk ten miles through rain, snow, and sleet to get to school. Nowadays kids just jump into their brand-new cars and away they go—and nobody knows where. Let me tell you, the whole world is turning soft.

I worked hard all my life to give my kids everything, and look what it's got me. No one gives a damn about me except Olive, and look at the mess she's in. It's all that she can do to handle her own problems without bothering about me.

I wish there was something I could do with my time. I'm used to hard work, and now that I *can't* work anymore I don't know what to do with myself. It's a shame that someone can't use a retired healthy woman who's willing to work—if I could just return to the good old days!

Barbara Greene Compton

What a zoo! I hate living here with Mom and Dad always fighting and Grandma just laying around, expecting everyone to wait on her. No one seems to care about anything or anyone, it's just as though they'd all given up living.

Poor Dad, if Mom would just quit nagging him and leave him alone, maybe he'd feel like doing something. It's been that way for as long as I can remember, with Dad just sitting back and letting Mom, and even Grandma, beat him to death with words. That's the very reason I ran away from home. I couldn't stand the constant fighting and no one seemed to care whether I lived or died. It wasn't until I met Bob that anyone really loved me. It didn't matter to me that he was a Negro, we had so much in common. Neither one of our parents approved of the relationship so we never married, but the happiest time in my life is when I had his baby. Mom and Dad managed to finally scare Bob away, but they'll never be able to take John away from me.

Then came Ted. I'm sure I just married him on the rebound from Bob—I never did love him. I thought he could provide me and my child with security, inasmuch as he was in the army and drawing a regular paycheck. When he went AWOL and defected to Russia, I felt a sense of relief to be rid of him. Even the ridicule I've suffered since his going to Russia has been worth it. The only big regret I have is that I was pregnant when he left and had that damned kid. I'm sure that I've done the right thing in allowing Children's Aid Society to place Raymond in a home where he will be wanted and cared for.

I'm so confused—I don't know what I want anymore. At one time I thought I wanted to be a model, but then again I just don't know. Maybe the best thing for me is to find a nice guy, get married, and settle down. But who would want me? Mother of a Negro child, married at one time to a man who defected to Russia. I guess I'm just a born loser and will just have to be content with what I have.

Oh, I would give anything to get out of this zoo. Look, there's

Marvin drinking a glass of milk with half of it slobbering down his chin. Why didn't Mom and Dad put him away when he was younger? He's always embarrassing the whole family, and he'll never get any better. It's unfair to expect anyone to baby someone all of their lives.

The one bright spot in this family is Robert. If Mom and Dad would just take an interest in him and spend some time with him, he could be a good boy. It's a shame to see a boy as smart as Robert waste all his talents. Oh well, it's just like wishing that hell would freeze over to expect Mom and Dad to change at all. It looks like the only way Robert will ever get out of this zoo is to be committed to the state industrial school or get married. What a choice!

I hope I can stay here without going completely out of my mind until something good breaks for me. Wow! What a zoo!

Marvin Greene

What a wonderful day—everything's just great. I'm Batman, and I'm the toughest good guy in the world, and I can beat up any crook. Look, here comes a crook now. I'm going to—oh, my shoe's untied. Think I'll tie it.

I think I'll go outside and play catch with my friends. I'm probably the best catcher in the whole neighborhood. Better ask Mommy and Daddy first 'cause they'll wonder where I am. They might even think I'm lost. But they shouldn't worry 'cause even if I did get lost, I could find my way back. I was an explorer once, and I was lost in Africa. There I was surrounded by lions and tigers, and I didn't have a gun. All of a sudden they charged me and . . . Gee, I wish I had a dime so I could buy an ice-cream cone.

I wonder if any of the kids would like to play house or doctor. That's lots of fun. Last time we played house I got to be the daddy. That was the most fun of all. I got to go to work and make lots of money and . . . Think I'll go get a glass of milk.

I'm going to be a doctor when I grow up. I'll be able to fix people up when they get hurt and give them pills when they get sick and. Gee, it's a wonderful day.

Robert Greene

My family is nothing but a bunch of zeros. They don't give a damn about anyone or anything. When I quit school I went home and made the big announcement, "Hey folks, I've quit school." The only thing those numbskulls could say is "That's nice. When are you going to get a job?" I might just as well have come home and told them, "I just got a haircut." They couldn't have cared less.

And when I got picked up for smoking pot Dad said, "Well, when I was a kid I never did such terrible things." I don't give a damn what he did or didn't do when he was a kid. Mom said that I'm just like the old man and she can't do a thing with me. Well, maybe one of the reasons she can't do a thing with me is that she's never tried. I'll bet if I really got into trouble, they'd pay attention to me.

I wonder what's with the older generation? They're just not with it. They haven't got the slightest idea what's happening in the world today. Look at the old man sitting on his fat fanny in that chair with his eyes glued to the television and drinking his beer. He hasn't left that chair long enough to even know whether it's winter or summer outside. And poor Mom, she's so busy feeling sorry for herself and all her responsibilities that she hasn't got time for anything else—except to hit the bottle every night.

And look at Grandma just sitting there doing absolutely nothing. There's no way of knowing what's going on in that old lady's head, and that's scary. She can look holes right through you, just like she can see inside you.

Why don't those people get off their dimes and get out into the world and find out what's going on? I mean, it's just plain stupid to sit around the house all day long like a bunch of vegetables when so much is happening.

I guess the best thing for me to do is to marry Maria and get away from the place. I don't really want to marry her, but I know I should. The baby's got to have a name, doesn't it? And who's going to take care of Maria if I don't? I'll just have to go out and get a job and support Maria and the baby. But what can I do?

Evaluations

After studying the material on the Greene family one can see many of the complex individual and family problems. For the purposes of this text, a complete discussion of the dynamics involved in the problems, their subtle interrelations, and the pathology implied in family attitudes is not possible. Consideration will, however, be given to strengths that are not immediately apparent and to areas that could be explored to arrive at a workable treatment plan.

Perhaps the first question is what factors have operated to keep this family intact for twenty-six years? Also we would want to take a look at the work history of Mr. Greene before his back injury, which might indicate his capacity to benefit from retraining for employment.

Mrs. Greene has assumed the responsibility of supporting the family. Such a decision reflects strength, which may also have lent emotional support to other family members.

There is also a question about Mrs. White's future contributions to the family. It would be well to consider the positive effects of both her leaving and her staying with the family unit.

There is not sufficient information here to establish whether or not Barbara is satisfactorily fulfilling her role as a mother to John. It is possible that she could benefit from some type of vocational training, but her aptitudes and interest in such training have not yet been ascertained.

Marvin Greene, although limited intellectually, may have potential for increased learning. Whether or not he could ever relieve the family of his support is conjectural. Another unanswered question is whether or not a nonresident training program for people like Marvin is available in the area.

As we begin to assess Robert's strengths, the question of his ability to rechannel his delinquent behavior arises. It is also important to consider the positive relationship that he has been able to form with his probation officer. There is insufficient information at present to determine Robert's ability to make concrete plans for his future.

Community Resources

Answers to the questions posed here would help to provide a basis for planning treatment. In our concluding discussion we shall show how community resources can be used both to answer these questions and to help the Greene family alleviate some of its problems and make future plans.

Harold Greene

Because of his honorable discharge from the army, Harold may be entitled to benefits from the Veterans Administration. A consultation with his parole officer may be helpful in better understanding Harold. The local Office of Vocational Rehabilitation may be able to offer him training that would once again make him employable. The United States Employment Service (U.S.E.S.) can assist in the evaluation of his work potential and offer assistance in locating employment.

Olive Greene

An appointment with the community mental-health clinic or Alcoholics Anonymous (A.A.) might help Mrs. Greene to recognize her drinking problem and motivate her to solve it. A medical specialist on the staff at the welfare department could help to obtain treatment for her brain tumor, including hospitalization, surgery, and after care. The Family Service Society of America (F.S.S.A.) could provide counseling services aimed at solving the problems of disorganization that threaten to disrupt the family even further. Mrs. Greene may qualify for unemployment insurance which would help the family with some of its financial problems.

Angela White

Mrs. White's age, capacity for work, health, and desire for change must be considered. The social worker from the welfare department could assure her of medical and financial attention. Alternatives to her present living arrangements could be explored. Various volunteer programs in the community might possibly have useful work for her, with or without pay.

Barbara Greene Compton

The American Red Cross would be the agency best equipped to find the father of Raymond Compton and to secure a release for his adoption. The child-welfare division of the department of public welfare can assist her in obtaining adequate day care for her other son, John Johnson. Either through the welfare department, U.S.E.S., or the Office of Vocational Rehabilitation she could begin a training program to prepare her for employment. The public health nurse could instruct her in child care.

Marvin Greene

In some areas service clubs such as Kiwanis International, Rotary International, and the Lions provide centers for mentally retarded children that offer day-care programs. These centers offer not only custodial care but also supervised activities that help to socialize the child. An evaluation of Marvin's mental capacity could be obtained through the welfare department, the community mental-health center, or an affiliate of the National Association for Retarded Children.

Robert Greene

The probation officer of the juvenile court should be asked what latitude Robert has in his activities. Ordinarily juvenile courts are committed to the principle of encouraging whatever plan is in the best interest of the child. Any interest shown by Robert in the Neighborhood Youth Corps (N.Y.C.), the Job Corps, U.S.E.S., or adult-education classes would thus probably be applauded by the court.

SUGGESTED READINGS

Ruben Hill. *Families Under Stress*. New York: Harper, 1949.
Adjustment to the crises of war separation and reunion.
John Levy and Ruth Monroe. *The Happy Family*. New York: Knopf, 1938.
Marriage, family, children and home management are discussed with emphasis on participation by all members.
Albert Frederic Philip. *Family Failure*. London: Faber and Faber, 1963.
A study of 129 families with multiple problems.
Benjamin Schlesinger. *The Multi-Problem Family*. Toronto: University of Toronto Press, 1963.
The multiproblem family, a review and annotated bibliography.

Chapter IV

THE IMPACT OF INDUSTRIALISM

ON THE OCCUPATIONAL LADDER

Problems relating to employment, immigration,
mobility, aging, and trade unions are reviewed,
in order to familiarize the student
with the impact of industrialism
on the American social system.

The Industrial Revolution, by which Western societies moved from agricultural to technological bases, had its origin in England's technical development from 1760 to 1840. During that period new materials, methods, and machines were devised, and new production concepts took hold. People who had formerly been self-employed in rural settings were encouraged to relocate to urban areas where resources, facilities, and expertise were centered.

This shift in population brought many problems, like those connected with health, to be discussed in Chapter 7. Problems of employment and unemployment are the main topic of this chapter. The Industrial Revolution affected interpersonal relations as well. The worker accustomed to face-to-face contact with his employer and coworkers was compelled to adjust to a subordinate position in a highly impersonal system embodying greater social distance from authority and mechanical accounting for his activities.

Although the Industrial Revolution originated in England, other countries soon began the process of industrialization. In the United

States the invention of the cotton gin in 1793 by Eli Whitney, a firearms manufacturer added impetus to the process. This invention did more to promote industrialization of the textile industry than did any other single factor. It brought with it many problems, however. One such problem was the more rapid development of the factory system, under which workers were subjected to the supervision and discipline of foremen. The various jobs required little training and no understanding of the total system. The people pouring into the cities supplied ready replacements for those who dared to show distaste for the system. As machinery and processes became more complicated, the need arose for people trained in technology and engineering. Such people were more difficult to find and as a result were treated with greater deference.

The common factory laborer, on the other hand, was subjected to many inconveniences like long hours, low wages, and harsh supervision, from which he had no recourse. If he rose to skilled worker, he was often, through a management "blacklist" denied the opportunity to change jobs locally because of his value to his employer. He could not migrate to another country because he was never able to accumulate the cash reserve to pay for such a move. He was used to having some agricultural pursuit during lean times, perhaps raising crops for barter, but without these advantages in the urban centers, his existence depended entirely on some kind of industrial work. He was expected to, and often did, work as many as thirteen hours a day. Children five years old were routed out of bed before daybreak, put to work at things like picking lint from the floor and putting it into bags, and not allowed to return to their beds until after dark. Furthermore, in 1802 some of these children had been declared paupers and placed under apprenticeship to cotton-mill owners. In 1832 approximately half the New England factory labor force was composed of children. (Women fared no better; they were not even given time for maternal duties.) Not until 1938 did passage of the Fair Labor Standards Act begin to put an end to child labor. This act made it unlawful for a person under eighteen to engage in hazardous occupations. It set a minimum age of fourteen for most "after school" jobs and sixteen for occupations during school hours. (Compulsory education over the previous 100 years, had had much to do with developing the attitudes of those who supported the Fair Labor Standards Act.)

To gain a more accurate impression of the general attitude toward work hours, it is necessary to look at relevant legislative efforts between 1884 and 1901. During that time Congress defeated bills that would have set the minimum age for factory workers at ten.[1] A bill that would have limited the hours of children under twelve years of age to ten was shelved. In 1890 a bill to limit the hours of women cotton-mill workers to sixty-six a week was defeated. In 1900 a measure that would have prohibited the employment of children under twelve in factories was voted down. In 1902 a bill fixing the minimum employment age at ten and prohibiting children under twelve from working night shifts was passed.

The increasingly specialized technology of the nation increased the need for trained individuals. It was necessary to educate members of the work force not only for their immediate jobs but also for replacement at all levels. For replacement at the lowest echelon, training was minimal, but for semiskilled and skilled jobs higher up the occupational ladder greater inconvenience was thrust upon the employer. One obvious solution was on-the-job training, sometimes provided according to the ladder concept, preparing for the next step up at each phase of training. The fact that the employee found avenues of advancement open to him under this system appears to have been incidental to management goals, however. Workers were not always allowed to train for the next highest job; however, race, religion, illiteracy, or some other factor unrelated to performance might block their advancement. These injustices, as well as other kinds of oppression such as starvation wages and blacklists at the hands of the "capitalists," stimulated organized efforts to find a solution—labor unions, to be discussed later in this chapter.

U.S. Employment Service

The problems confronting people seeking work were not of a kind to be alleviated by unions or on-the-job training schemes. Although an employer might have a need and although there were people trained to meet that need, they did not always find each other. This problem came to prominence in 1922, when New York State began an inquiry that ultimately resulted in the organization of employment offices throughout the country.[2]

The U.S. Employment Service (U.S.E.S.) was first organized as a result of the drain on manpower caused by World War I and became a permanent legal reality through the Wagner-Peyser (Social Security) Act of 1935. The U.S.E.S. helped meet the manpower needs of industry and labor until after World War I, when its activity began to decline. It is now part of the Bureau of Employment Security, Manpower Administration, U.S. Department of Labor. The need to match men and jobs was recognized during the Wilson and Harding administrations, and the law establishing Federal obligation to provide such an employment service also established an interstate clearance system, a more uniform set of procedures to follow, an inspection system, and Federal subsidies. The U.S.E.S. met the needs of industry and labor until after World War II, when its activity declined.

Registration with the U.S.E.S. is available free of charge to all citizens of the United States. An employer notifies the local U.S.E.S. office of job vacancies. Then, and only then, may the office refer qualified prospects for positions. The U.S.E.S. is itself an Equal Opportunity Employer, as well as subject to Title VI of the Civil Rights Act of 1964, which makes it mandatory to refer a person for employment regardless of race, creed, or national origin. If an employer does not avail himself of the service, however, there is no way in which the U.S.E.S. can properly influence him.

The services offered by U.S.E.S. do not infringe in any way on the freedom of private agencies, which often charge fees on a percentage-of-income basis. A private agency charging 10 percent of the wages of a client for a three-month period has an incentive to find work for the client rapidly and at the highest rate of remuneration possible. Private agencies are often criticized, however, for charging fees without rendering services in return, for sending applicants to firms in which vacancies do not exist. The client of such an employment agency has been told to see a particular company and file an application for work. Most firms show people the courtesy of accepting applications even though recruiting efforts may be temporarily halted.

It is the task of both private and public employment agencies to reach potential workers. U.S.E.S. has staffs devoted to publicity, liaison with other government agencies, and public relations. The agency strives for standardization and uniformity of job classification. Its *Dictionary of Occupational Titles* (*DOT*) [3] includes descriptions of more than 22,000 jobs, broken down into seven classifications:

1. 0—professional and managerial
2. 1—clerical and sales occupations
3. 2—service occupations
4. 3—agricultural, fishery, forestry, and kindred occupations

5. 4, 5—skilled occupations
6. 6, 7—semiskilled occupations
7. 8, 9—unskilled occupations

These main categories are further subdivided until it is possible to define even the most unusual jobs according to the system. For example, 0–45.31 indicates strip-tease artist. Each job description includes the industry in which it is performed, other names by which it is known, and the specific duties involved:

Strip-Tease Artist (*amusement and recreation*) *0–45.31*—peeler; teaser. Walks about stage in accompaniment to music, and gradually divests herself of clothing. May also dance and sing.
Top Screw (*agric.*) *3–37.20—top waddy.* A *Foreman.* Has charge of a group of cowpunchers (colloquially called screws or waddies) riding after cattle on the open range.

The DOT was first published in 1939; its latest edition, in two volumes, appeared in 1965, with job descriptions compiled by trained analysts. It is available to the public and used extensively by schools, libraries, vocational counselors, the armed forces, the selective service, and even foreign countries. It classifies, describes, and codes practically every legal occupation in the United States.

The skills required for a position may be classified according to the DOT description. An interviewer simply checks employers' requests for this particular work. As more offices adopt computerization the digit system will lend itself readily to such use.

The U.S.E.S. assists thousands of people in testing, interviewing, recording qualifications, referral, placement, and training. Those with special problems like age, inexperience, illiteracy, and physical handicaps receive individual counseling and testing especially suited to their needs.

In 1962 the Human Resources Development program, dedicated to achieving total employment of the disadvantaged, was initiated by the U.S.E.S. Its activities include seeking out and helping those who could become employable. Of the many publications available from the Superintendent of Documents, Washington, D.C. and containing employment information on a wide variety of occupations, two are of particular value: *The Occupational Outlook Handbook* and *The Occupational Outlook Quarterly.*

The Occupational Outlook Handbook provides information on the nature of the work, location of employment opportunities, training and qualifications necessary, advancement possibilities, earnings and working conditions, and sources of additional information for 700 occupations.

The Occupational Outlook Quarterly contains information about the most promising jobs today and in the future, how to qualify for them, where to obtain education and training assistance, and the growth and change of the labor force.

These publications and others available from the same source are useful to vocational counselors, students, teachers, and industrial and professional organizations that need reliable occupational information.

State departments of education can purchase these publications under Title II of the Elementary and Secondary Education Act or under Title V(a) of the National Defense Education Act.

Unionism: Another Step Up the Ladder

Labor unions, also known as "labor federations" or "trade unions," had a stop-and-go existence in the United States until the American Federation of Labor (A.F.L.) was formed in 1886. Earlier organizations like the Knights of Labor were forced to operate largely in secrecy because of fear of retaliation by the industrialists. But as the voice of workers began to be heard, secrecy became less necessary, and membership in the labor movement increased. The National Labor Union, formed in 1866, advocated such advanced concepts as the eight-hour day and foresaw the potential political power of labor.

The A.F.L. abandoned its original efforts to bring all workers from all occupations under one central authority but did profoundly influence the thinking of the working class. For one thing, people became aware of the "union-made" label, and the support in promoting the goods of one union in exchange for similar commitments from other unions. A remnant of this early camaraderie is the "sympathy" strike, in which workers in allied fields strike to assist the cause of another "brotherhood" or "local."

Union membership, and concomitant voting privileges have been an issue in the United States for many years. (The closed shop has since been outlawed.) Two extreme forms of factory organization have caused much turmoil and unrest: the "open shop," where an employee is free to join or not join a union, and the "closed shop" (now outlawed), where only one union is represented and membership is mandatory. In closed shops, the bargaining power of the employees is always a potent force with which management must reckon. The open shop is a potent force for management, especially if several unions cannot agree on terms among themselves. Both systems have advantages, as well as disadvantages, for both labor and management.

The open shop permits workers greater latitude in finding employment but may force management to negotiate with representatives of several groups instead of only one. The disadvantage to labor is the necessity for each union to negotiate for benefits that may then be enjoyed by members of other unions or nonunion members who may or may not have supported its efforts. Furthermore, if one union is successful in obtaining benefits already granted to another union, an endless cycle of negotiations, in which each union tries to "best" the others, can follow.

The closed shop offered advantages to both labor and management by obviating this cycle. It did, however, bar nonmembers from employment, thus granting greater bargaining strength to the union.

Union membership has fluctuated recently because of automation, but the number of union-affiliated workers has continued to rise since the Depression years 1929–1933.

As union membership has increased over the years, wages have risen, and working conditions have been improved. But with increased numbers have come internal problems that raise questions about the purposes and activities of unionism, and competition for members has also developed.[4]

A strike is a voluntary work stoppage either to protest an employers' terms or to force management into negotiations favorable to workers. There are several types of strikes, ranging from the sit-down strike, in which employees stop work but remain at their stations, to the general strike, which may encompass all trades within an industry.

If a self-employed individual either hires nonunion help or contracts for services using nonunion labor, his operation can be slowed down or halted by refusal of union suppliers to deliver essential goods or services. Used on a large scale, this tactic can have a significant impact on the nation's economy.

In a lockout, once used by management in its bitter struggle against unionism, employers closed shops rather than negotiate with the unions. Other methods employed by management to combat unionism included private armies, espionage, strikebreakers, and written and oral propaganda.

Unions, originally formed to serve only as a bargaining force, have taken on a different complexion. Today men work under contracts, and negotiations precede the termination dates of the contracts. The United States regulates unions more closely than does any other nation. One explanation is the vast number of citizens involved. Union membership rose from 2.9 million in 1932 to 17.8 million in 1956.[5]

There is still much speculation about workers' willingness to remain on strike despite financial hardship. On April 2, 1968, 18,000 employees of the Kennecott Copper Corporation in Nevada, New Mexico, Utah, and Arizona returned to work after 260 days on strike. The wages lost during this period averaged $5,091 per employee. The final settlement included an increase of 54 cents an hour, to be given in three stages. Corporation accountants, as reported in the local newspapers, calculated that at the new wage rate it would take slightly more than eight years for the lost wages to be regained.[6] The present contract expires in 1971, five years before the lost wages can be recouped. Contract negotiations in 1971 without a strike would be the only way in which lost wages could be recovered. The same source [7] estimates the cost of the strike to the economies of the four states at more than $96 million. Several factors were not taken into consideration in preparing this figure. Departments of public welfare in these states were unable to collect child-support payments from striking fathers and thus had to assume this burden. Because "unemployment" was voluntary, men were not eligible for unemployment-compensation insurance. The unions had temporary relief funds, and when they were exhausted used their credit to stock large supplies of food for distribution. Two further financial burdens were imposed in the states during this time. First, special dispensations made the strikers eligible for public assistance, and the strikers began to take jobs that would otherwise have been filled by others. By the time the strike ended, many Kennecott employees were drawing unemployment compensation from second jobs.

The citizens in general, and strikers' wives in particular, complained bitterly about hunger, lost wages and depleted savings, as well as disruption of family life for many. Yet it was considered a hollow victory; contract negotiations will have commenced and another strike possibly started before the wage losses have been regained. The company offered an increase of 25 cents an hour in early negotiations before the strike, which would have represented an average gain of $500 instead of a loss of $5,000 incurred by striking. By remaining firm in their positions, labor and management failed to achieve a mutually beneficial solution. Because of severe effects on the livelihood of the strikers, future negotiations will probably be conducted differently. One proposal that will be favorably considered is that negotiations proceed without a work stoppage.

Union membership carries with it a definite loss of autonomy for the worker. His union, bargaining collectively for the entire membership, can fix his hours of work, his wages, and his channels for seeking relief from grievances. He loses the chance to bargain with the employer independently. This loss of autonomy also has political implications; for example, a worker can risk losing his membership (and thus his job in certain instances) if he voices support for the "wrong" candidate. An expelled union member has little recourse to lawful remedy for nobody has a legally guaranteed right to membership in a voluntary organization. As a result, membership may be denied on any grounds that the organization imposes. Under the Taft-Hartley Act of 1947, however, union membership cannot be a condition of employment. Since 1920 penalties have been invoked for discrimination in employment because of membership or nonmembership in any union organization.[8]

Melvin W. Reder points out that wages have to a great extent become institutionalized and that as a result many other factors are considered in assessing job satisfaction.[9] Contract negotiations today involve retirement and other benefits as much as they involve wage rates.

A penetrating account of the rise of unionism is given by Lester Velie, who touches on such subjects as gangsterism, corruption, politics, and certain colorful personalities in the trade unions.[10]

Membership in a union involves an "initiation" fee and regular dues. Some initiation fees are so high that they are prohibitive unless there is a sponsor, an established member of the union, to lend the money. Most unions require members to meet certain minimum standards, thus ensuring a level of competence for a person in a given job. As a result, an unscrupulous sponsor can capitalize on such a debt by charging the contractor for master craftsman's work to be done by his protégé at the wages that he earned before membership. Every trained craftsman sometimes must work to repay their sponsors in excess of an even exchange of work for the money.

Unionism is but one of many steps that American workers have taken to secure and protect their jobs. Next we shall turn to a discussion of a problem that may arise after a job has been secured: that of injury or accident and its partial remedy, workmen's compensation insurance.

Workmen's Compensation Insurance

In the course of doing his job a person runs a certain risk of being injured or killed. Something may drop on his foot, or he may slip and fall on a slick surface or trip down steps. Such accidents are costly both to employee and employer.

Workmen's compensation insurance eases the financial burden for all parties concerned. This program, which has an involved and interesting history,[11] became law after a series of lawsuits by injured employees against employers—the only recourse employees had. The survivors of an employee killed on the job could not sue in their own behalf. Then individual states began to pass workmen's compensation laws modeled after the Federal Employees Compensation Act (F.E.C.A.), signed by Theodore Roosevelt in 1908. By 1920 all but six southern states had such laws on the books. Not until 1948 did all existing states, Washington, D.C., Alaska, Hawaii, and Puerto Rico have adequate coverage. The aim of the law is to provide sources of both income and assistance in meeting medical expenses in the case of an injury on the job, with certain exceptions.

As with all laws pertaining to social welfare, enforcement is a problem. To help cope with the complications that arise, most states appoint industrial commissions to hear cases involving employer-employee disputes.

The benefits available to an injured employee fall into three basic categories: cash, medical, and rehabilitation. Cash benefits are paid for total or temporary disability or death. Medical benefits cover hospital and doctors' fees. Rehabilitation benefits provide the after care and retraining of disabled employees in order to make them once again employable.

As employers must bear the cost of workmen's compensation insurance, they now take an interest in safety precautions that they formerly ignored. Previously employers did not feel obligated to take safety measures, nor were they held legally responsible for them. John L. Lewis, head of the United Mine Workers of America, led the struggle to force mine owners to make their mines safer. He was successful in general mine safety reforms being implemented on a national scale. His name will be remembered as champion of the laborer, especially the coal miner.

Even though much concern exists over wages, working conditions, and safety features, there are people willing and able to work who simply cannot find employment. Automation and an agricultural surplus, thanks to mechanization, are significant factors in unemployment today. In 1966 more than 11 million people were jobless and looking for work.[12] This figure included 1.3 million men between the ages of twenty-five and forty-four, the most employable group and the group with the heaviest family responsibilities—unemployment affects all age groups within society.

Unemployment alone is not sufficient to account for the overall loss of income to society. Other considerations include underemployment, temporary work stoppages (periodic unemployment) and underpayment (less than minimum wage) for work. Those persons considered underemployed work less than forty hours a week or in positions far below their educational and skill levels. Either underemployment or a temporary work stoppage can plunge a family below the established poverty level of $3,335 for a four-member family. Earnings over fifty-two weeks at the most recently established minimum wage would be $3,328. (The minimum wage was fixed at $1.60 an hour on February 1, 1968, by an amendment to the Fair Labor Standards Act of 1938.)

In 1966 3.4 million workers suffered from five to fourteen weeks of unemployment.[13] Computed at the minimum wage of $1.60, this loss of work resulted in a loss of from $320 to $896 apiece, which would reduce minimum annual earning to $3,008 and $2,432 respectively. Both these figures are below the poverty level and would necessitate social action to raise the standard of living for these families to a minimum level. Such programs may one day take the form of a guaranteed minimum-income plan like that discussed in Chapter 11.

The impact of underemployment and temporary work stoppages helps to explain the problems connected with poverty and unemployment. Approximately 10 million workers, mostly in agriculture, retail trade, and domestic service, were receiving less than $1.60 an hour in February 1968.[14] Yet the upgrading of 10 million positions to a point at which the workers could earn $1.60 an hour would have inflationary effects on the national economy. Another problem is lack of interest in upgrading workers through training for better-paying positions because such programs would eventually drain off manpower from lower-status (and low-paying) jobs, which would then have to be eliminated or filled by the young and the incompetent.

Most workers qualify for unemployment insurance, which pays income-maintenance benefits until such time as they can locate other jobs. The aim of this program is to provide one-half the worker's weekly wages, subject to the qualifying requirements of the specific state. The average maximum period for receiving benefits is from twenty-six to thirty-six weeks. More than 16 million workers are not protected by unemployment insurance, but the majority of the work force is covered.[14]

Unemployment Insurance

The Federal Unemployment Tax Act provides income for workers who are involuntarily unemployed. The amount a person receives is determined by the length of time he has been on the job, the wages he has been receiving and the laws of the state in which his claim is filed. This program is jointly administered by Federal and state governments and financed entirely by employer contributions except in Alaska, Alabama, and New Jersey, where employees also contribute. We recognize that various restrictions and exceptions exist, but feel a comprehensive survey is not suitable in the present context.

The Social Security Act offers unemployment insurance to employees of the Federal government. This program is funded by Federal appropriations but administered in the same manner as the other, through Federal-state employment service offices.

The mechanics involved in receiving an unemployment check have been refined by U.S.E.S. in an attempt to avoid unnecessary delays and to safeguard workers' rights. A worker must go to the U.S.E.S. office with his "blue slip" and register. The blue slip is a form filled out by the employer giving identifying information and the reason for termination. The interviewer will explain to the worker his rights under the system. He is told that, to retain his eligibility for benefits, he must seek employment on his own and be available for interviews arranged by the insurance office.

Immediately following registration, the process of determining eligibility is started. At this point the amount and duration of benefits are determined. If all is in order, the recipient should receive his first check within seven days. In the event that the worker has left voluntarily, a penalty may be imposed, resulting in delay of benefits.

Receipt of benefits under this program does not prevent a person applying for public assistance as well. If his unemployment benefits are $150 a month and he would otherwise have been eligible for a public-assistance grant of $200 a month the department of public welfare can authorize a differential payment of $50 a month. Because he is seeking employment, the welfare department is likely to assign him to a work project, which is an agency-sponsored employment program under which credit toward the amount of the grant is earned instead of cash. The work assignment is always less than 40 hours per week thereby permitting men time to look for other jobs.

This program of unemployment insurance is a temporary measure. Many people exhaust their benefits before locating other jobs. Some discover that their skills and talents are no longer marketable and that they are in need of retraining. Three groups suffer most from unemployment and lack of training: Negroes, teenagers, and unskilled laborers. The solutions to their problems lie in the creation of jobs, equal employment opportunities and the availability of training programs, all of which would be corrective measures. In the next section we shall discuss measures to prevent these problems.

Preparation for Employment

Vocational guidance, according to George E. Myers, was in use in this country as early as 1908.[15] Essentially it involves matching the right person with the right job, which entails acquainting the individual with various jobs and then assessing his qualifications to see which would be most suitable. If the assessment reveals lack of training for a specific occupation, the feasibility of securing such training must be weighed.

Secondary schools throughout the nation offer students vocational guidance through a variety of means. They may hold "career days," when people from various fields describe their jobs: airline stewardesses, social workers, lawyers, and accountants, for example. Various aptitude tests, as well as individual counseling, are also available to many high-school students. They are encouraged to think about their future occupations early, so that not only will they qualify for their desired occupations sooner but also advancement in their chosen fields will be more rapid. Almost everybody has at some time held a job in which he was not interested, that held no challenge for him, or for which he had insufficient training. At best it is difficult to perform satisfactorily under such conditions. Given the optimum conditions, however, it is realistic to expect performance of consistently high quality.

The public school of today is still geared to middle-class, nondelinquent white children. It is therefore not surprising to find vocational guidance geared to the same group. As the nation addresses itself to the problems of occupational selection for all citizens, it will no longer be possible to refuse help to someone who has failed to adjust to a meaningless system he does not comprehend.

Although the school can help students with counseling for future jobs, the same opportunities should also be made available to school dropouts and adults. A source of such counseling, aside from private businesses specializing in it, is the U.S. Employment Service offices, which will assess the applicant's qualifications and counsel him on job training, vacancies, and local job availability. Where demand justifies it, U.S.E.S. offices have special units dealing with youth, professional, clerical, and blue-collar employment.

Vocational guidance can also assist the person who is already employed to improve his occupational status through training and study. Not all people are content with their jobs and seek avenues of advancement either through promotion or in other fields of endeavor. Once a son was expected to work in the same trade as his father, regardless of whether or not his talents lay in that direction. Occupational mobility is a reality today, for people can take advantage of adult-education courses at local high schools, on-the-job training programs, and college evening or correspondence courses.

Many opportunities are available to people with technical training. More employers are following equal-opportunity principles and hiring strictly on the basis of merit, which acts as an incentive to many people who previously could see little advantage in putting forth effort that would go unrewarded.

In order to understand the difficulties surrounding employment in the United States more clearly, we shall also examine the gradual assimilation of aliens into the labor force.

Immigration and Employment

For a number of years after the Civil War the individual states regulated immigration. States in the Midwest and the West offered attractive incentives, whereas some eastern states imposed very mild restrictions. The power of the states to tax immigrants simply for being immigrants was held unconstitutional in 1876. Immigrants had been recruited from abroad during the Civil War for the army. The period of national control began in 1882, when the first immigration law was enacted. This act excluded only such undesirables as lunatics, convicts, idiots, and those likely to become dependent upon the state for support.

Oriental immigration was a problem on the West Coast and met with serious opposition during the 1860s and 1870s. Originally the Chinese and later the Japanese were objects of this opposition. Many laws, unconstitutional in nature, were passed to prevent Orientals from owning land and discriminatory in other ways. Although they were later struck down by the courts, they were temporarily successful.

In 1880 China agreed to prevent all its citizens except teachers, vacationing travelers, students, and merchants from coming to the United States. Japan, on the other hand, insisted on the same rights as other nations but was denied them. Californians remained adamant in their anti-Oriental attitudes, and diplomatic relations between the United States and Japan deteriorated to a new low.

A literacy test was imposed on all immigrants in 1897, at the end of Grover Cleveland's second term. There were exemptions for the physically handicapped, for children under sixteen, and for wives, parents, and grandparents of admissible immigrants. For everyone else a demonstration of the ability to read and write—not necessarily English—was required. Cleveland vetoed legislation requiring these tests, as did William Howard Taft and Woodrow Wilson after him, but it finally passed on a two-thirds majority over Wilson's veto in 1917.

Because of swelling immigration and rumors of even more immigration, Americans became upset and demanded that the numbers of people entering the country be curtailed. As a result, the "national origins" system was initiated, under which the admissible quota from any nation was limited to 3 percent of the number of immigrants from that country living in the United States, according to the 1910 census. This figure was changed in 1924 to 2 percent of the 1890 census. The national-origins system caused a drop in European immigration to 150,000 a year. Unused quotas could not be carried over to the following year. More aliens left the country during 1931–1936 than were admitted. For Europeans the Great Depression of the 1930s was the motivating factor in returning to their homelands. Chinese males, on the other hand, had been unable to bring their families or intended spouses to this country, and many returned for that reason.

After 1890 the main current of migration shifted from moves by farmers from land-poor countries to the United States, and became a rural-to-urban movement within the United States, as a result of industrialization and urbanization.

The McCarran-Walter Act, after a hard and bitter fight, including veto by President Truman, became the Immigration and Nationality Act of 1952. It had a number of important provisions. It allowed, for the first time, racial bars to immigration to be dropped; it gave some 85,000 Orientals the opportunity for naturalization for the first time; it permitted quota-free entry of alien spouses and children of citizens; it helped keep families united in migration; it allowed the United States an opportunity to admit people with certain skills, professional knowledge, and abilities faster; it permitted an alien to make arrangements for jobs before arriving here.

An attempt at dealing with the employment problems of immigrants led to the establishment of a branch office of information at Ellis Island, in New York harbor, in 1908. It was to have served as an information center and assist the immigrant in his attempts at assimilation. Two things kept this from being a successful employment resource for newly arrived immigrants. First, they were so excited about the prospects of being reunited with friends and family that they did not take the time necessary for processing. Second, the fear of deportation kept many from returning for processing. Consequently, the office was not successful and was later absorbed into the national system.

The national system, The Employment Service, attempts to meet the particular needs of people in the work force as much as possible by offering specialized services when these are justified. Certain discriminatory practices are not permitted, and thus some of the problems of employment have been lessened. One problem has not been solved because of its irregular definition; the problem of the older person who may be physically capable of working but who encounters other obstacles. We shall discuss some potential contributions and influences of the older worker in the next section.

The Aged Worker

As discussed in greater detail later in Chapter VIII, retirement poses a problem in seeking a harmonious relationship between work and idleness. Our concern here is with the older person as an employee.

If the worker of whom we speak is one who has been involuntarily retired, his desire to remain active in the labor force may cause him to seek employment past age 65. His choices may be narrowed by circumstances such as health, or other physical handicaps as eyesight and hearing. Generally speaking, the choices that cause much concern are in the area of challenges. More often we see a person accepting a less challenging position, physically as well as mentally, even though the person has a greater potential. Since it is often true that an older person does not have the stamina, energy, interest, or experience necessary to do a job, an employer is likely to bypass him solely because of his age.

One factor of substantial importance to the employer is the number of days that the employee is absent from his job because of illness. A study of 22,000 male employees in 1952 showed that the number of days off for illness rose from 4 percent for twenty-two-year-olds to 14 percent for sixty-four-year-olds.[16] The same study revealed that twice as many accidents occur to those under forty as to those over forty years of age. One can conclude that the older worker, even though his safety record is twice as good as that of the younger worker, will be off the job three times as much. During the time that an employee is off the job the employer not only loses his services but may also have to bear the additional expense of replacing him. Few employers want to assume such expense.

The older worker in industry is faced with a number of problems, the prejudices of his employer being a significant one. Typically, the older worker appears to his employer and his fellow workers as critical, resistant to change, slow, difficult to teach, and lacking initiative and interest—a stereotype difficult for the older worker to overcome. The older person, on the job or not, is too often treated as in his twilight years with night fast approaching, and people often humor him with just that thought in mind. The older worker operating under such conditions has to combat the feeling of coworkers and his employer in addition to his own. Having lived a productive life, he may find it difficult to comprehend why others not only fail to assist him in planning for his future, but seem even to look forward to his inevitable sunset.

Women have an even more difficult time than men in finding employment after sixty-five. They have to contend with long gaps in their work histories, lack of training and current skills, and the prejudice of the personnel officers—usually men, who prefer younger, more energetic better-looking female employees. Some companies also have retirement policies that make it economically unfeasible to hire people beyond a certain age.

Not only does the shocking realization come to the older worker that nobody cares about his future, but he is also often upset by lack of appreciation for his past contributions. The young bloods of an organization go about making their own niches much as their predecessors did, without reliance on older workers' experience.

Yet many people past retirement age work—and work competently. During World War II vast numbers were hired by defense plants and demonstrated that they were dependable, adapted to regular hours and routine, and accurate and attentive to detail.

People over forty-five have difficulty finding employment, and they usually are out of work longer than are younger people. After the desirable jobs have been given to the younger workers, the older person gets what is left—usually temporary or part-time work. The prospect of relocation holds much less appeal to the older worker, and as a result he may not take advantage of an opportunity that a younger person would seize upon to better his situation. The older worker lives with the fact that he is the last to be hired and the first to be fired.

The Future

As a matter of necessity, industry must enter into collective bargaining with labor unions, largely because of the impossibility of negotiating with each worker on an individual basis. The issues involved in collective bargaining, in general by trade unions will continue to receive attention, and the economic losses caused by strikes will be averted by new proposals. In an effort to combat unemployment, labor unions must take the initiative in discouraging their members from "moonlighting," that is, from holding second jobs, so as to enable a greater number of people to find employment.

Present immigration policies reflect greater leniency than in the past and may lead to a reappraisal of the quota system. The increasing industrialization of underdeveloped countries and the concomitant demand for indigenous labor should in any case reduce considerably the influx of immigrants to this country.

Following federal policy, the retirement plans of private and public institutions will give elderly workers more consideration in the future.

Rather than special consideration being offered an elderly worker, certain stipulations will be encompassed in policies that will apply to their particular needs.

NOTES

1. Marjorie A. Potwin, *Cotton Mill People of the Piedmont* (New York: Columbia University Press, 1927), pp. 31–38. Exploitation of workers by one set of industrialists is described.
2. Shelby M. Harrison, *Public Employment Offices* (New York: Russel Sage Foundation, 1924), pp. 1–2. Originally compiled as a reference work on the growing public employment field, this book also serves as a detailed account of the birth of the United States Employment Service.
3. Division of Occupational Analysis, *Dictionary of Occupational Titles*, Vols. I, II. Employment Service, Government Printing Office (Washington, D.C., 1965), p. XXIII.
4. Sumner H. Slichter "The Position of Trade Unions in the American Economy" in *Labor in a Free Society*. M. Harrington and P. Jacobs, eds. (Los Angeles: University of California Press, 1959), pp. 17–44. Describes various practices within different unions and their repercussions for the entire population.
5. *Ibid.* pp. 20–21.
6. *Salt Lake Tribune*, April 2, 1968, p. 13.
7. *Ibid.* p. 13.
8. *United States Statutes at Large, 1919–1921*, 66th Congress, 2nd Session (Washington, D.C.: Government Printing Office, June 2, 1920), Vol. 41, Ch. 219, p. 737.
9. Melvin W. Reder, *Labor in a Growing Economy* (New York: Wiley, 1957), pp. 12–21. This book is an account of the satisfactions offered by various jobs.
10. Lester Velie, *Labor U.S.A.* (New York: Harper, 1959), pp. 3–12 and pp. 31–46. Forcible approach to exposing defects in the labor movement.
11. Herman M. Somers and Anne R. Somers, *Workmen's Compensation* (New York: Wiley, 1954), pp. 17–37. Offers a rationale for this system, the largest of its kind.
12. U.S. Department of Labor, Manpower Administration, *Highlights of the 1968 Manpower Report of the President* (Washington, D.C.: Government Printing Office, 1968), pp. 13–14.
13. *Ibid.* p. 15.
14. *Ibid.* p. 19.
15. George E. Myers, *Principles and Techniques of Vocational Guidance*

(New York: McGraw-Hill, 1941), p. 1. A basic work on occupational counseling.
16. Fourth Annual Southern Conference on Gerontology, *Economic Problems of Retirement* (Gainesville: University of Florida Press, 1954), pp. 148–149.

SUGGESTED READINGS

The Ad Hoc Committee on The Triple Revolution, *The Triple Revolution* (Santa Barbara, California: 1964).

Reprint in pamphlet form of a statement about poverty, unemployment, and technological change, which was submitted to President Johnson; includes penetrating comments on cybernation, the weaponry revolution, and human rights.

Blauner, Robert. *Alienation and Freedom.* Chicago: University of Chicago Press, 1964.

An examination of feelings of domination, futility, isolation, and discontent in employment.

Bottomore, T. B. *Critics of Society: Radical Thought in North America.* New York: Pantheon, 1968.

Presents views on the connections between intellectual dissent and theories of society.

Goldstein, Bernard. *Low Income Youth in Urban Areas: A Critical Review of the Literature.* New York: Holt, 1967.

An analysis of the occupational strivings and opportunities of "blue collar" children.

Higham, John. *Strangers in the Land.* New York: Atheneum, 1963.

Deals with patterns of American "nativism" from 1860 to 1925 and is a prime source of information on patterns and trends in labor thought.

Chapter V

This chapter is an examination of the
ever-broadening responsibilities of the
public-school system, including more
and better services to children
and their families.

Education as a social institution has undergone considerable change in the United States since Colonial times. Generally speaking, educational policy reflects social changes. What a society demands and expects of its educational system, be it very simply constructed or highly complex, is the transmission of knowledge and values, customs, and ethics from one generation to another. If the economic character of society changes from agricultural to industrial, this change will be reflected in the educational process. In essence, a study of the history of education in the United States is a study of the impact of social upheaval and growth in the country.

Schools in Colonial times offered more than five or six years of education to very few children and were limited largely to boys. In an agrarian and frontier economy less formal education was needed. With the advent of industrialization, however, a need for broader education for more people was expressed by labor and community leaders. Since 1910 increasing numbers of jobs have required higher levels of education. But there is growing awareness that to educate large masses of people is not enough for the social demands of today. Society must examine what is being taught to determine whether or not it is applicable to the needs of the social system.

In a brief look at curricula in American schools, Paul B. Horton and Gerald R. Leslie note a conflict in values between schools and communities, reflected in the types of curricula offered and those favored by the majorities in the communities, which vary greatly depending on locale and on the background and level of education of the population.[1] The traditional curriculum was intended to prepare students for college. At the beginning of the twentieth century such a curriculum based on the liberal arts was justified because many of the high-school graduates of the day were going to college. Most students could not even go to high school, however; only the middle and upper classes found it possible to continue after grade school. Today, with higher standards of training required by man's vastly expanded technological knowledge, more emphasis is placed on practical goals which in turn has caused a change in high school curriculae in general. Such areas as mathematics and the social and physical sciences have been incorporated to a much larger extent than was deemed necessary at the turn of the century. Despite more stringent entrance requirements and a more demanding curriculum, increasing college enrollment has been noted from both middle and lower classes.

A second type of curriculum, considered more practical for many students, is vocational; it has aroused much criticism among people who do not plan to go to college yet who find that vocational courses do not adequately prepare them for employment. Often, too, students taking such courses are looked down upon by others; a commercial or trade course often has lower status than does a college-preparatory course.

Perhaps the "life adjustment" curriculum has come under fire more than has any other type. Although it may have traditional course titles, the content and method is anything but traditional, in that students are placed in situations that reflect actual life problems and are expected to solve them by their individual efforts. The progressive-education movement inspired by the writings of John Dewey in the 1920s has been an underlying factor in many educational policy changes in the last forty years.[2] It has been noted that everything, "good" and "bad," in today's schools has been attributed to the progressive movement.

This view is not entirely fair but is a commentary on the public response to anything radically new and different in the educational system.

All three types of curricula reflect the needs and demands of a society that has evolved from an agrarian base to a complex, industrialized one, as well as some vestiges of older views that still cause conflict today. With urbanization and centralization of industry have come awareness of poverty and slums in much of the nation. One of the biggest and still unsolved problems is that of the uneducated segment of the population, which constitutes a large proportion of the "hard core" poor. Some 21 million people live in households whose heads have no more than eighth-grade education.[3] Clearly illiteracy is a factor in the continuing cycle of poverty, passing from generation to generation. Much concern has been shown for the plight of lower-class students, particularly in the slums. It is apparent at this stage of study of the educational system that many difficulties arising in slum schools are caused by the conflict in values and attitudes between middle-class teachers and lower-class students. Robert D. Strom's analysis highlights this conflict in a discussion of the home backgrounds of middle-class and lower-class children.[4] Differences in two basic attitudes are explored—those toward authority and toward communication. By means of the Hess maternal-competence study,[5] it has been shown that where lower-class mothers are more afraid that their children will get into trouble if they do not conform to the demands of the school, middle-class mothers are more concerned about course content and learning difficulties. Often, the ability to communicate is poor in the lower-class child because he has not had assistance in sharing information and solving problems at home. Furthermore, such children have had very limited spheres of experience, seldom venturing outside their neighborhoods. This restricts the potential variety of subjects and situations about which they can talk, as well as the paucity of vocabularies to which they are exposed.

Frank Riessman bears out this observation, suggesting that the value of education, in the sense of future benefits, is not clear to either the underprivileged parent or his child.[6] Much of the anti-intellectualism of the lower class is predicated on its orientation to the present; abstract and idealistic speculation (thinking about ideas as opposed to "things") is not understood or wanted by many people in this class. The lower-class student's self-concept is affected considerably by the attitudes of his family and peer group.

There is evidence that the teacher usually assigned to a slum school is either the least competent or the least experienced.[7] Furthermore, the majority of teachers embrace the values of the middle class, which leads to conflict. The teacher's expectations have a great deal to do with the performance of students in poverty areas. Robert Rosenthal and Lenore F. Jacobson suggest that, if teachers expect a given group to be high achievers, that group will perform well, regardless of its members' IQ scores. Conversely, if a group is expected to perform poorly, it will do so.[8] The teacher's attitude is not always of his own making. G. Alexander Moore, Jr., emphasizes that the bureaucratic process of large city schools precludes much policy making by teachers. In addition, the practice of placing new teachers in the lower-ranking classes means that the "custodial" classroom demanding closer supervision is the starting point for teachers who have had no previous experience in either teaching or interacting with the underprivileged.[9]

The public has assumed that the educational process will prepare the student to meet the demands of his society. The concept of teaching the "whole" child has been extended to include attitudes, ethics, and morals that formerly were the province of the parents. As a result of this policy change, a wide range of new services has emerged in the school.

Pupil-Personnel Services

Pupil-personnel services are those aids to students (of all grade levels) and their families in the form of teaching, individualization of problems and counseling.

The history and philosophical perspectives of pupil-personnel services define three basic functions. The first is the transmission and development of the basic knowledge and skills of society to its youth. This function encompasses the traditional concept of education and is accepted as central in almost every current philosophy of education.

A second function, which has gained increasing prominence since the beginning of the twentieth century, is to encourage each student to acquire knowledge and skills appropriate to him as an individual. Acceptance of this function implies belief that every educational institution should provide the type of dynamic learning environment that will increase the child's curiosity and desire to explore and discover things for himself. In addition, challenges must be geared to the intellectual and motivational level of each child. This requirement has posed problems for educational administrators who are faced with overcrowded schools, lack of trained personnel, and rising costs without concomitant increases in funds; all of which retard individualization of education and attempts to offer appropriate learning experiences and opportunities to slow, average, and advanced students simultaneously.

The third function is to prepare the individual to apply his basic knowledge and skills in practical situations in such a way as to fulfill not only his own personal needs but also the needs of his society. This third function includes training and preparation for employment in the nation's business-industrial complex. The school must therefore prepare each individual for occupational involvement without undermining his right to determine his own life goals.

In an increasingly complex society, it is difficult to imagine the traditional classroom teacher performing all the general educational functions outlined here. The primary competence of the teacher is in the first area, the transmission and development of basic knowledge and skills. Pupil-personnel services contribute more to the second and third functions of the educational system: stressing the uniqueness of the individual and helping him to apply his knowledge in a practical way. There is some overlapping in the functions of instructional and noninstructional personnel, however.

The growth of pupil-personnel services must not be viewed as only a reflection of a comprehensive educational philosophy. It is also, and perhaps primarily, a response to need. As has been mentioned, agrarian society was relatively simple. This country's developing technology and accompanying industrialization have created problems with which the educational system must cope creatively. The speed with which man has acquired new knowledge has resulted in job specialization in almost every area. Education, especially at the elementary level, has been slow to respond to the need for specialized personnel. Many educators still seem to think that they can be "everything to everybody," but it is simply not realistic to expect a teacher to possess all the behavioral skills necessary to meet the unique needs of each child.

It is infrequent that a doctor, lawyer, or other professional person is competent to cope with the needs of every individual. Such professionals commonly resort to referral, consultation, and collaboration with other agencies or professional people.

Pupil-personnel services represent an attempt to make available to each student the qualified specialists who may be most useful in helping him to achieve his highest personal and educational potential. These services have evolved to the point at which they can now be called the "third dimension" in education. They are more than merely an adjunct to the instructional and administrative staffs of the school; they represent an integral part of the educational scene and have evolved from a philosophy of the importance of the individual. These changes have intensified the need for diverse new approaches to education, as well as for new personnel to implement them.

There is plenty of evidence of the vital need for services provided through pupil-personnel departments. The most pressing problem is the school dropout rate. More than 33 percent of the nation's young people leave high school before completing their senior year. At that rate 7.5 million youths will fail to finish high school during the next decade.[10] Furthermore, 10 percent of the total labor force is engaged in unskilled jobs, whereas it is estimated that only 5 percent will be needed in such employment in 1980. Diligent advisory efforts may be necessary to dissuade students from leaving school before they have acquired appropriate job skills.

Between 5 and 10 percent of children in public schools have emotional handicaps severe enough to prevent them from learning in school or conforming to expectations for classroom behavior.[11] Other statistics, equally hard to ignore, indicate that our total citizenry is not as secure and stable as might be desirable. Referrals to juvenile court have increased substantially in the past two decades. Alcoholism, drug use, mental illness, crime, divorce, and illegitimacy are increasing, which may indicate that the emotional needs of many people are not being met. This means that a society composed of many maladjusted persons will show evidence of unrest, upheaval and/or disorganization. It is the school's responsibility to gear the educational experience to the child's needs.

Although the problems cited dramatically emphasize the need for sound and effective pupil-personnel departments, it must not be inferred that personnel services should be geared solely to children who are physically, mentally, emotionally, or socially handicapped. Originally the pupil-services concept was "emergency"-oriented. Referral to a specialist generally occurred in a crisis, when the obvious "problem" child needed help. But a revolution has occurred in educational philosophy, and a preventive concept has emerged. Many pupil-personnel specialists have been placed in primary grades, in order to help children early in their school careers and to prevent problems before they become serious. The Federal government has provided financial incentives to further the implementation of the preventive concept and pupil-personnel services that benefit the total school population. Bills calling for at least minimum numbers of child specialists in the elementary schools have been presented to Congress. Their purposes include helping pupils to understand themselves, helping them to understand others, and helping them to develop realistic goals and self-fulfilling attitudes.

Nearly all the available literature defines general objectives for pupil-personnel services. One article in particular encapsules eleven objectives that seem to be universally acceptable:[12]

1. To support the broad objectives of the total educational program.
2. To focus upon the characteristics of pupils, their differences and similarities—physical, emotional, intellectual, and social.
3. To gather systematic information about pupils, for example, through cumulative records, standardized tests, interviews, case studies, observation and anecdotal records, conferences with parents, sociograms, and autobiographies.
4. To use such information systematically in work with groups—grouping within classes, placement in grades and in classes.
5. To use such information systematically in work with individuals through counseling—educational, vocational, social, and psychological.
6. To provide not only for all pupils but also especially for exceptional children.
7. To provide specialized assistance to classroom teachers, through counselors, school psychologists, or school social workers.
8. To assist teachers and administrators in working with parents through parent-teacher conferences, and Parent-Teacher Association (P.T.A.) meetings.
9. To assist teachers and administrators in working with community agencies.
10. To provide on-the-job training of the teaching staff in counseling skills.

11. To provide opportunities for research to determine the effectiveness of the guidance program.

These eleven goals might be grouped into three general goals of pupil-personnel services: to guide the pupil to maximum use of his abilities, relying on theoretical knowledge of child and adolescent development; to help him form a positive adjustment between his developmental capacities and his environmental conditions, and to challenge him—and the school staff—to consider whether or not his current academic program is the most effective that he can pursue.

After this brief consideration of the general purposes of the educational process and the rationale for the existence of pupil-personnel services, it is relevant to consider separately the services most frequently provided. The historical background, development, and function of each service will be described briefly.

Child Accounting

Maintaining school attendance records became necessary after the passage of compulsory attendance laws, beginning in Massachusetts in 1852. For nearly a century after that attendance was viewed as a purely legal matter, and enforcement was the task of the truant officer. The prevailing view is much different now. Although attendance records are still maintained, the rationale has changed significantly. The state is still responsible for seeing that no child is denied the opportunity for education, and school funds are often allocated on the basis of average daily attendance. It is the responsibility of the Juvenile Court in most states to see that a child remains in school in order to receive an education. Accurate records must also be kept in order to facilitate orderly transfer from school to school, withdrawal of students, and proper class placement. Chronic absence, however, is now viewed as an indicator of stresses within the child and in his family; it is dealt with professionally to alleviate the underlying problems.

Health Services

The first known program in which medical personnel worked primarily within the schools began in New York City in 1892. The first tax-supported school nursing service was established, also in New York City, in 1902; its original emphasis was on control of contagious diseases. The purposes and scope of school health services have been progressively broadened from medical inspection to comprehensive health examinations and follow-through counseling, promotion of good health attitudes and habits, and work with teachers to facilitate learning by pupils.[13]

The School Nurse

The school nurse's duties and contributions are manifold. As a member of the pupil-personnel team, she identifies the health needs of pupils and integrates school health activities into the total educational program. She offers in-service training and consultation to teachers and other professionals. Health examinations and adequate follow-up programs are essential, particularly for pupils whose families cannot obtain such care. First-aid materials are made available, along with advice on their use. Accurate and complete health records are necessary and should be kept up to date. The school nurse ideally acts as liaison between the school and community medical agencies, and her role thus involves public relations to a great extent.

Counseling and Guidance

Counseling and guidance arose at the turn of the twentieth century as the result of pressing needs both in education and in society as a whole. They originated in an era of turbulence and transition. With industrialization and the growing importance of scientific and technical skills, education, especially at the high-school level, became a necessity for all rather than a privilege for a few. This necessity, coupled with the rapid growth of the population, contributed to greater diversity of goals among students, which hastened the development of a more varied curricula. Greater diversity meant greater problems in educational and vocational planning, remedial programs, and discipline. In the light of these developments, it is hardly surprising that educators and the general public looked to counseling and guidance services for help. Also important to the development of counseling and guidance, and more generally, of the pupil-personnel movement, were changing theories of education and what it should do for students.[14]

In the 1960s counseling and guidance programs have received much support, especially from the Federal government. Numerous national studies and commissions have emphasized the importance of good guidance in sufficient quantity. The National Defense Education Act of 1958 and its 1964 amendments established inclusion of guidance, counseling, and testing in schools from elementary grades through junior college and technical training as national policy. Other recent

Federal legislation supports counseling and guidance related to vocational training and education of the socioeconomically disadvantaged.

In general terms, the major concern of the counseling-guidance specialist is the normal developmental needs of pupils. Here are some of the specific functions that form part of this larger one:

1. To lead in planning and implementing a pupil-personnel program that will meet the individual and collective needs of pupils and facilitate the total learning process within the institution.
2. To provide individual and group counseling, so that each pupil may come to understand and function less painfully in his social, economic, and psychological environment.
3. To accumulate useful information about each pupil and to assist pupils and their parents, teachers, and administrators in interpreting it for the benefit of the pupils and the improvement of the total educational program.

An adequate supply of educational and career materials should be made available to pupils, teachers, and parents, in order to broaden occupational horizons and to encourage realistic career choices. Such materials can also be quite helpful to pupils in planning educational programs consistent with their choices.

Consultation with teachers, administrators, supervisors, and curriculum specialists is advisable, in order to design institutional programs that will serve the specific and general needs of the pupils. Parents' involvement in the educational process helps them to understand the particular needs, interests, aptitudes, and problems of their children, as well as to perceive their own roles as team members in the educational program. This is brought about through contacts with teachers, social workers and administrators as well as the P.T.A.

There should also be leadership in research related to the characteristics and needs of the local student population, as well as cooperation with the local authorities in the use of all available resources in the community.

The Psychologist

The role of school psychologist can be traced back to the first decade of the twentieth century. The educational philosophy developing at that time stressed the uniqueness of each student and his ability to learn knowledge and skills if the appropriate procedures were used. When educators tried to implement this philosophy, however, they began to recognize the vast differences among students. At first they thought that segregating slow students in special classes might enhance the total educational process. Parallel with the development of special classes was that of testing. The work of Alfred Binet (on the Binet-Simon Scale) provided the impetus for development of more exact techniques of intellectual measurement and thus supplied new tools for assessing the individual abilities of pupils. In addition, the works of Sigmund Freud and others revealed new concepts in psychology.

The importance of the school psychologist became even more clearly recognized after the establishment of municipal child-study departments in the large cities. Clinical psychology flourished. Another important factor in establishing psychologists in the schools was the new emphasis on *prevention* of mental illness, which naturally involved working with children at an early age. The potential of the psychologist's diagnostic and remedial role was thus recognized by many educators.

The school psychologist has special knowledge of child development, learning disabilities, and behavioral deviations. He must be able to identify and diagnose problems in these areas and to recommend treatment. Among his basic responsibilities as the school psychologist are conducting individual psychological examinations, interpreting them and other clinical data, and evaluating the student's learning or behavioral problems.

The provision of therapeutic services for students, as individuals and in groups, is one of the school psychologist's duties, as is reporting his evaluations and relevant follow-up data to the appropriate school or other agency personnel so that they can initiate corrective procedures. His participation in the school team contributes immeasurably to the understanding of the learning and behavioral problems of individual students and to effective treatment.

In-service training programs operated by the school psychologist can help both students and their parents to interpret diagnostic information. Securing parental approval and cooperation for corrective measures is an important, and sometimes highly diplomatic, task that also falls upon the psychologist.

The school psychologist should serve as an adviser in curriculum planning and should cooperate with teachers to provide programs and facilities for exceptional children.

The Social Worker

The origin of school social work is usually traced to the early 1900s, when educational systems in large cities began to assume more responsibility for dealing with truant children and school administrators assigned visiting teachers the responsibility for constructive enforcement of attendance laws. The visiting-teacher program was initially financed by community agencies, but after it had become established the schools themselves assumed the cost. These early school social-work programs were developed within individual school districts, and consequently their organizational structures varied greatly from place to place. The need for someone to work with educational problems arising in the home environment was universally recognized. The development of school social work was also related to the first widespread and vigorous attempts at special education—adjusting school programs to individual pupils' capacities and needs. Recognition of the need to plan curricula for children with wide-ranging disabilities encouraged the adding of noninstructional personnel to the school staff.

Despite an encouraging start, school social work developed more slowly than did the other pupil-personnel services. When noninstructional personnel are few because of a limited budget, the school psychologist is frequently regarded as a more useful member of the educational team than is the social worker because of his testing skills and psychology's concrete contributions to educational programs, especially those for exceptional children. Another inhibiting factor has been the emphasis in Federal legislation on financing of school counseling and guidance programs rather than on social work. Recently, however, Federal programs to encourage economic opportunity, education of the disadvantaged, and studies of school dropouts have stressed the need for additional social-work services. Many professional people realize that the educational institution cannot operate with maximum efficiency and effectiveness in isolation from other social institutions, including the family. The useful role of the social worker in integrating the functions of school, home, community, and the many social agencies is becoming more fully understood. The child can benefit more when his intellectual and psychological characteristics are examined in the context of his social environment.

The school social worker brings to the pupil-personnel team another perspective on the needs of pupils: relating their behavior to environmental factors outside the school. The social worker's main contributions to the pupil personnel team are:

1. To provide casework services to individual students and their parents, in order to help the students to improve their social, emotional, and academic functioning.
2. To provide group work services to students and parents when evaluation indicates they could benefit from this kind of help.
3. To take advantage of community resources to obtain for students specialized help that is not available in the school.

Two essential tasks of the social worker are to evaluate the needs of individual pupils and to help children and parents accept special programs. This latter task includes forming and participating in parent discussion groups on such subjects as parental roles and personality development. Family therapy designed to create meaningful communication and healthy interaction patterns can be broached through such groups. They may also provide opportunities for home contacts, from which significant information can be obtained to aid in decisions concerning the student.

Social workers can help administrators and other school personnel gain additional understanding of personality dynamics, as well as assisting in implementation of sound mental-health principles in the educational process. Other peripheral but important duties of school social work include research and in-service training programs.

This discussion of the various functions of the pupil-personnel team does not include special-education programs or speech- and hearing-therapy classes because there is a trend toward integrating these services into the regular instructional program of the educational system. The team members listed above represent only a portion of people engaged in the helping services, which includes those professional disciplines directly concerned with the prevention, alleviation and relief of social problems and with assistance to people in order to help them realize their potentialities.

Federal Aid

A problem of increasing importance—and controversy—is that of Federal aid to education. It has long been known that inequalities exist among the states because of the inadequate financial resources in some. What has not been so widely recognized is that better-endowed states are experiencing migration from poorer states. Horton and Leslie point out that states with the lowest school expenditures often have the highest birth rates.[15] Many of the young people who migrate to large cities thus have not been trained to function in urban society, and the cities must cope with not only educating their native populations but also the migrants.

Historically, local school districts have been autonomous. Before World War II parents and other interested members of the community were usually the guiding forces in the educational system. Local problems and issues were resolved by people within each community, and outside help was not encouraged. The financial structure of education at the time, based almost exclusively on property taxes, was a reliable indicator of wealth in a community. Hollis P. Allen, however, notes a shift from a property-tax base to one more appropriate to an industrialized economy; in 1956 only 25 percent of the country's wealth was in taxable property.[16] Clearly the schools should share in other revenues, for property taxes fail to provide for all educational needs. Gradually, as the tax base in local school districts has become more inequitable, states have become more involved financially.

As density in the ghettos increases, property taxes are less able to support education for the numbers of children living there. The property tax collected on a tenement housing forty children is substantially less per capita than that collected on a suburban home with two children. As a result, the most overcrowded schools often have the smallest operating budgets. This problem is further complicated by the fact that public services, such as fire and police protection, are more concentrated in these areas, thus raising the costs within districts that are already overburdened financially. The Federal government, through its broader tax base, can draw upon more sources of wealth than can the individual states. The concept of Federal aid to education is not new; various statutes have granted funds to institutions of higher learning, notably the land-grant colleges, for more than 100 years. In 1958 $1 billion was provided over a four-year period by the National Defense Educational Act for scholarships to students; this figure has since been increased. The Vocational Education Act (1963) provides appropriate financial aid, in addition to which the Manpower Development and Training Acts of 1962 and 1963 support the vocational training of adults and dropouts more than sixteen years old through tuition and subsistence payments.

The real question about Federal aid is thus whether or not it should be extended to general education. The main issue is control. Many educators believe that Federal aid could equalize educational opportunities throughout the nation but fear Federal restrictions on the funds. The prerogatives of states and local districts to allocate the money to various purposes are considered paramount; extra money is needed and wanted but with no strings attached. Other aspects of the problem are amounts of money allocated, racial segregation and public funds for private schools. There seems to be no consensus on these issues. But we believe that they must be resolved if true equalization (rather than uniformity) of educational opportunities is to be accomplished.

A National Perspective

Although almost everyone agrees that formal education is necessary, there is much controversy over how much, when, where, and to whom it will be most valuable.

The problem of a teacher shortage is aggravated by insufficient funds. Only recently have teachers improved their status to any appreciable degree with better pay and fewer restrictions of personal freedom; many educators believe that there is still vast room for improvement in public attitudes toward the profession, since the teacher is a vital force in the lives of the children of the nation.

Changing social patterns mean changing school responsibilities. There is a conflict over what should be taught—only the traditional three "R"s or courses geared to current social needs. It is not accidental that pupil-personnel work in the last twenty years parallels the social movements of the same period. Arthur A. Hitchcock remarks that, in order to make education work in a democracy, pupil-personnel work must be recognized as an answer to national needs.[17]

The nation's educational problems are compounded by greater social mobility, a constantly shifting population. For members of the middle and upper classes moving to other parts of the country, mobility does not usually present serious problems; but for migrant workers who follow crops and harvests for employment, to name only one example, educational problems are numerous. The migrant child very often lives in deplorable conditions, has a poor diet, and lacks time to go to school. He must adjust to many different schools and changing environments without attaching himself to any community. It is small wonder that illiteracy is high among migrants. Although the Migrant

Health Act was passed in 1962, it was not until 1966 that an amendment to the Elementary and Secondary Education Act of 1965 provided special funds for meeting some of the educational needs of children of migrant workers.[18] Perhaps with greater public awareness of this particular problem and with greater citizen involvement, conditions for the migrant worker and his children may improve.

To sum up, a basic problem confronting educators and taxpayers is determining the value of education, of how much investment per person is feasible. The main tenet upon which education in our society is based is that civilization as we know it is impossible without education for everyone. And with the advance of technology and automation, this tenet is stronger than ever before.

The Future

There is little doubt that broad social changes affect educational institutions. It is through education that both the traditions and new ideas of a society are disseminated. Much of the struggle over curriculum has centered on values—what is important to the society and what is not.

The National Education Association (N.E.A.), founded in 1906, and now the largest professional association in the world, has gone on record in support of more Federal funds for school construction and teachers' salaries. Certainly, until the teaching profession is more favorably regarded by society, the scarcity of teachers will continue. Whether or not organized labor will attract many more teachers than it already has is still a question, but it is likely that there will be more organization among teachers in the future, particularly in the urban centers. Recent strikes by teachers have demonstrated the need for arbitration and recognition of employment problems in the schools.

It is quite possible that with equalized aid from Federal sources teaching in slum areas will change. Teachers will be trained specifically to deal with students in poverty areas and will be made more aware of cultural differences, value orientations, and attitudes in themselves and their students. There have been suggestions that teachers be assigned on a national, rather than a local, basis, so that in trouble spots new teachers will not have to confront failure in such areas.

Pupil-personnel services will be of even greater importance, and among their broader range will be training programs to attract capable people into the teaching profession.

Many problems of educational institutions may never be solved to everyone's satisfaction. Curriculum, teaching methods, the teacher shortage, and finances, both Federal and local, are long-term problems, needing continual reconsideration.[19] The process of accommodation to a changing social order, with its concomitant pressures, will loom as the most important factor in the schools of tomorrow.

NOTES

1. Paul B. Horton and Gerald R. Leslie, *The Sociology of Social Problems* (New York: Appleton, 1965), p. 307. The authors present data on social problems and interpretation of those data within a theoretical framework.
2. Lawrence E. Cremin, *The Transformation of the Schools* (New York: Knopf, 1961), p. 22. Offers a clear description of the progressive-education movement.
3. Horton and Leslie, *op. cit.*, p. 308.
4. Robert D. Strom, *Teaching in the Slum School* (Columbus, O.: Merrill, 1965), p. 15. Discusses the complex problems of slum schools.
5. Robert D. Hess, "Maternal Teaching Styles and Educational Retardation," in E. Paul Torrence and Robert D. Strom, eds., *Mental Health and Achievement* (New York: Wiley, 1964), 1965, Chapter II.
6. Frank Riessman, "The Culture of the Underprivileged: A New Look," in Staten W. Webster, ed., *Knowing the Disadvantaged* (San Francisco: Chandler, 1966), p. 59. This article is one of many collected for *The Disadvantaged Learner*, an excellent three-volume study of poverty.
7. Delmo Della-Dora, "The Culturally Disadvantaged: Educational Implications of Certain Social-Cultural Phenomena," in Staten W. Webster, ed., *Understanding the Educational Problems of the Disadvantaged Learner* (San Francisco: Chandler, 1966), p. 270. *Educating the Disadvantaged Learner*, the third volume in *The Disadvantaged Learner* (see note 6), offers valuable new teaching strategies.
8. Robert Rosenthal and Lenore F. Jacobson, "Teacher Expectations for the Disadvantaged," *Scientific American*, 218, No. 4 (April 1969), pp. 19–23.
9. G. Alexander Moore, Jr., *Realities of the Urban Classroom* (New York: Praeger, 1967), p. 6. The author discusses migration, low income, and the ethnic backgrounds of students in ghetto schools, as well as the "culture shock" encountered by teachers.
10. *The National Elementary Principal*, 43, No. 5 (April 1964), p. 5, "Educational Notes."

11. California State Department of Education, *The Education of Emotionally Handicapped Children* (Sacramento, Calif.: March 1961).
12. Harry Smallenburg, "Studying the Elementary Guidance Program," *The National Elementary Principal*, 43, No. 5 (April 1964), pp. 15–18.
13. Glenn A. Saltzman and Herman J. Peters, *Pupil Personnel Services: Selected Readings* (Itasca, Ill.: Peacock, 1967), pp. 78–84.
14. Ruth Barry and Beverly Wolf, *Modern Issues in Guidance Personnel Work* (New York: Columbia University Press, 1963), pp. 111–123.
15. Horton and Leslie, *op. cit.*, p. 304.
16. Hollis P. Allen, "Federal Aid and the Problem of Control," in William O. Stanley *et al.*, eds., *Social Foundations of Education* (New York: Dryden, 1956), p. 521. Allen describes the social forces that influence education, focusing on national conditions.
17. Arthur A. Hitchcock, "Milestones in the Development of Personnel Services in Education," in Nelson B. Henry, ed., *Personnel Services in Education* (Chicago: University of Chicago Press, 1959), pp. 283–298. This book is the fifty-eighth yearbook of the National Society for the Study of Education.
18. State University of New York, Bureau of Elementary Curriculum Development, *Educating Migrant Children* (Buffalo: 1968) is a valuable resource for school districts that operate or are developing migrant-education programs.
19. Horton and Leslie, *op. cit.*, p. 325.

SUGGESTED READINGS

Eddy, Elizabeth M. *Walk the White Line*. New York: Praeger, 1967.
Examines the urban educational system and its disparities.
Esman, Aaron H., ed., *New Frontiers in Child Guidance*. New York: International Universities Press, 1958.
Describes an experimental approach to casework therapy.
Goodman, Paul. *Growing Up Absurd*. New York: Vintage, 1960.
A description of the problems of youth in an organized society.

Chapter VI

MINORITY GROUPS: THE RIGHTS OF
SECOND-CLASS CITIZENS

An analysis of the problems encountered by
various minority and ethnic groups in search
of equality is given.

Human beings have always divided themselves into groups purporting
to be superior to one another. It is a phenomenon of modern history,
however, for groups to establish a specific type of domination over
other groups based on race consciousness. Charles F. Marden and
Gladys Meyer discuss four patterns of dominance that have emerged in
the last four centuries: political annexation, colonialism, slavery, and
immigration, all of which have played a role in the building of
American society.[1]

The problems of race relations arise directly from the pattern of
dominance. For instance, the annexation of much of the Southwest
after the Mexican War produced a Spanish-speaking minority within
the United States, a minority whose members were descended from the
Spanish-Indian population of 300 years before. As with most political
annexation of lands, there was discrimination toward those who had
lost the war.

The colonial pattern in the United States reflected political control
by the British over the native population. Colonizing zeal drove the
Indians from the East to the Great Plains and rose again during
frontier expansion.

Enslavement and forced migration of Negroes exemplify the third pattern, slavery. Treatment of slaves in North America differed from that in South America. In South America the slave was regarded as more of an asset and was given the chance of obtaining his freedom earlier than his counterpart in North America. Furthermore, intermarriage was allowed, thus indicating a degree of acceptance practically unheard of in the United States. Slave owners in the United States stripped the Negro of human dignity. He was considered a lower form of life, not quite human. When the Civil War brought freedom for the slaves, residual ignorance about and fear of Negroes thus impeded their progress toward full citizenship rights.

In the immigration pattern domination is based mainly on cultural differences. In the late nineteenth century there was a great influx of European peasants. The considerable differences between their cultural values and those of native Americans brought special problems of assimilation, which were especially apparent in the wave of southern European immigration from 1880 to 1910. These immigrants' language, educational, religious, and ethnic differences raised serious doubts among native Americans about their desirability as neighbors.

Minorities, then, can be viewed historically as groups that have been conquered, enslaved, or admitted into society on a subordinate basis. The form of entry into a society not only distinguishes the minority from the dominant group but also establishes a pattern of majority behavior toward the minority group.

In terms of social stratification, Tamotsu Shibutani and Kian M. Kwan state that in a system of ethnic stratification it is the underprivileged who are considered the minority.[2] "Minority" is not to be taken in its literal sense of fewer in number but is to be applied to social groups with low standing in society and treated unequally by dominant groups. This theory entails delineation of the poverty stricken of all ethnic groups as a minority rather than any one specific group. James W. Vander Zanden is more specific in his definition of a minority group.[3] Using the definitive framework developed by Wagley and Harris,[4] he examines five features of a minority group:

1. It suffers from what is generally known as the "dominant group" through prejudice, discrimination, segregation, and persecution.
2. Special characteristics of the minority group, either racial (phys-

ical) or ethnic (cultural) are used to justify such treatment and
make it easy to apply.

3. A minority has a consciousness of kind, based on a group image
and on a sense of belonging to the particular group.

4. Membership in a minority is generally not voluntary but
ascribed.

5. Endogamy, or marriage within the minority group, is the rule
either by choice or necessity.

These characteristics define minority groups as we see them in our
society. Specific minorities will be discussed here because the character of welfare agencies is directly related to these groups as well as to
the thinking of dominant groups.

American Indians

From Colonial times until 1871, when Indians became wards of the
United States government, there was steady pressure on the Indians as
settlers moved into the more productive land. Alan P. Grimes has com-
mented on the "invidious distinctions of superiority" made by early
Colonists in relation to the Indian nations.[5] Such distinctions were, of
course, socially and culturally oriented. Carey McWilliams, however,
notes that, had the Indian population been more concentrated where
colonies were founded, there might have been less misunderstanding
and cultural disparity and more willingness to cooperate.[6] The en-
croachment on land once held by Indians was justified by most whites
on the grounds that they could make better and more productive use of
it. The lot of Indians did not improve until 1934, when under the New
Deal administration of President Franklin D. Roosevelt the Federal
government changed its approach and recognized the value of retaining tribal customs and land for their own specific use.

The Wheeler-Howard Act of 1934 (the Indian Reorganization Act)
was an effort to repair the damage caused by the General Allotment
Act of 1887 (the Dawes Act), under which tribal holdings had been
cut from 138 million to approximately 48 million acres.[7] It has been
alleged that the low morale and poverty of Indians today arises from
implementation of the Dawes Act.

Although Indians were granted citizenship in 1924, it was not until
1948 that New Mexico allowed Indians to vote.[8] If Indians are to
improve their status, their literacy rate must be increased and help

must be forthcoming to guarantee them employment. A conflict arises from pressures by the larger society for acculturation and the Indians' own desire to maintain cultural identifications. They often face discrimination when they leave the reservations, particularly in housing and employment.

Negroes

Because importation of Negroes to the New World colonies began as early as 1619, the United States inherited a large and subservient minority group. Slavery as a social system was based on force; the slave had no rights, and his master had many. Marden and Meyer explain that, in order to survive under such a system, slaves had to be servile and passive.[9] Even after emancipation these traits were reinforced by the caste system of the South. Physical separation of Negroes from whites, as well as Negroes' acceptance of subordination, resulted in discrimination in housing, education, and social and economic opportunities. The effects are still manifest in attitudes of both Negroes and whites. Negroes express fear, distrust, and suspicion toward the dominant white group, and whites fear Negroes who do not conform to the expected subservient role.

These basic attitudes emanating from the American caste system have a great deal to do with widespread discrimination against Negroes. Until 1941 and the American entry into World War II, Negroes had little opportunity to raise their status or standard of living. The war effort required all the manpower that could be mustered, however, and Negroes were admitted into occupations formerly closed to them; labor unions also began to accept them, although not completely.

The establishment of the Fair Employment Practices Committee by President Roosevelt in 1941 was a measure to prevent discrimination in any firm doing business with the Federal government. Generally, economic conditions improved Negro labor at that time. Social discrimination, however, continued nationwide and was reflected in the segregation of Negro and white troops during World War II. Nevertheless, with the greater mobility afforded by wartime conditions, both North and South experienced upheavals in the traditional caste system.

After World War II social forces began to alter relations between whites and Negroes. The democratic process came under scrutiny, particularly through improved mass communications. As job opportunities increased, a large migration of Negroes from the South began. Awareness of the disparity between ideal and reality led many people to try to improve race relations, not only for domestic peace and justice but also to answer criticism from abroad. With each gain in race relations, more Negroes were encouraged to press for their rights. There were, of course, counter forces. Ingrained belief in Negro inferiority and customary discrimination against Negroes are difficult to change. Various economic interests, notably manufacturing and agriculture rely upon low paid help in which discrimination and segregation play an important part.

The 1954 Supreme Court decision outlawing school segregation, *Brown* v. *Board of Education,* reversed the *Plessy* v. *Ferguson* decision of 1896, which had legalized segregation and established the separate-but-equal doctrine.[10] School desegregation in the South has been slow, however. Progress is more rapid in areas where Negroes form smaller proportions of the population, in urban rather than in rural areas, and where there is a higher educational level among the dominant white population. White reaction to desegregation in the South has been strong resistance, including legal and economic maneuvering, and has proved effective in delaying, if not actually halting, school desegregation, as well as in limiting Negro voting. Boycotts and sit-ins by civil-rights workers have demonstrated the illegality of segregation rulings but have intensified emotions in the process.

Continuity and discipline in the civil-rights movement has been provided by the National Association for the Advancement of Colored People (N.A.A.C.P.) and the Congress of Racial Equality (CORE). Although the former has been criticized by many Negroes in recent years for its conservative policies, it has publicized the Negroes' plight and, to a great extent, provided legal protection and help for them. CORE has trained demonstrators in the nonviolent tactics promulgated by Martin Luther King, Jr., assassinated leader of the Southern Christian Leadership Conference (SCLC).

The Civil Rights Act of 1957 established the Commission on Civil Rights, empowered the U.S. Attorney General to seek a court injunction against anyone interfering with the voting rights of any citizen, and established a civil-rights division in the U.S. Department of Justice. There was strong resistance in the southern states, and because of fear of reprisals five months went by before any complaints were heard by the commission. The intimidation inherent in the segregation system and the difficulty of prosecuting violators were noted by the commission. The problem lies not in blatantly discriminatory laws but in the "discriminatory application of and administration of apparently nondiscriminatory laws."[11]

The Civil Rights Act of 1960 made it a punishable offense to obstruct a court order in voting-rights cases, made it a requirement that states retain voting records for twenty-two months, and initiated a system of Federal referees in such cases of persistent denial of voting rights.

Vander Zanden points out that many stresses in the South are not entirely caused by the race question; they also result from other major changes in southern society.[12] The South's economy has changed from cotton to cattle and from rural to an urban base, as new industries have been organized during and since World War II. Such social and economic changes have undermined the traditional paternalism of the caste system, originally useful in the plantation economy, and led to status confusion for many southerners. In this respect, the South has undergone more severe social changes than has the North.

The rest of the country has not been free of discrimination against Negroes, however. Although northern Negroes are occupationally integrated to a greater degree than in the South, they experience widespread residential segregation and, consequently, school segregation, proliferating slums, intensified racial conflict, and social isolation from whites. Both public and private housing developments have demonstrated that it is possible to achieve *somewhat* successfully integrated neighborhoods, but most suburbs have not yet responded to the challenge.

The position of Negroes today reflects a certain amount of progress after many years' effort to improve their status and economic position. The Negro worker has gained in proportion to the white worker in finding nonfarm jobs. This is partially explained by the opportunities now open that were either closed or did not exist previously. Negro men in professional and technical categories have kept up with white men in percentages. Even so, the Federal Commission on Civil Rights stated in 1961 that the mass of Negro workers cannot rise above unskilled labor.[13] This fact is reflected in their earning capacity, which has risen slightly but still shows a considerable lag behind that of white workers. As for unemployment, the high incidence of Negroes in unskilled jobs means that they are the first to be laid off in an economic recession.

In the executive order creating the President's Committee on Equal

Opportunity in 1961, provision was made for equal opportunity in government and government-contract employment. Negroes today have job opportunities in the Federal government unequaled in the past, although they were heavily concentrated. In 1964 13.2 percent of Federal employees were Negro (although they were heavily concentrated in the lowest salary grades).

Labor organizations have also been integrated. When the American Federation of Labor and the Congress of Industrial Organizations merged in 1955, one stated objective was to bestow full benefits on all workers without regard to race, creed, color, or national origin and to establish a department of civil rights to implement this objective. Many trade and craft unions, however, still limit the admission of minority-group members.

Discrimination against Negroes continues in housing practices as well. In recent years there have been Federal efforts to combat residential discrimination. Executive Order 11063, issued by President John F. Kennedy, provided that agreements for Federally-financed housing must be covered by enforceable nondiscrimination pledges. Open-housing legislation, to be effective, must be followed by action on open housing in the community. Here the difficulty is in private financing; at present government action against discrimination can be taken only if Federal funds are used.

Particularly in southern rural areas, many Negroes understandably are not willing to exercise their voting rights. Poll taxes, literacy tests, and required interpretations of the U.S. Constitution have all been used by local administrators to block Negroes from exercising the franchise. Economic reprisals and physical threats have also been effective deterrents to Negro voting. Although coercion and physical intimidation are not prevalent in the rest of the country, even there Negroes have voting problems. A large proportion of the potential Negro vote is composed of poverty-stricken and illiterate people who are apathetic about their political responsibilities and unable to see how they can benefit from voting. The Negro vote, however, especially in the eastern states, is beginning to make itself felt as a political force.

Negroes' progress toward full citizenship has been painfully slow. Although technically free from bondage, until recently they have not been able to free themselves from the old stigmas of subservience, servility, and supposed subhuman ability. Legislative action and citizen involvement have reduced discrimination in employment, and there should be continued improvement in the social welfare of Negroes as they better their occupational status and increase their literacy rate. Such improvements take time, however, because desegregation in the country as a whole involves the changing of values and attitudes and, in several regions, complete reappraisal of social roles.

Mexican-Americans

As there is considerable variation among Spanish-speaking people in the Southwest, a clarification of terms is in order. Much confusion exists over such designations as Latin-American, Hispano, Mexican, Spanish Colonial, Spanish-American and Mexican-American. For purposes of clarification we will refer largely to two terms, Hispano and Mexican-American, the origins of which will be described below. The term Hispano (Spanish Colonial) refers to those whose ancestors became citizens of the United States after the Treaty of Guadalupe Hidalgo in 1848. Following the Mexican War Mexico ceded to the United States a territory that included California, Arizona, New Mexico, Nevada, Utah, and parts of other states. The Hispanos were given the option of remaining and accepting United States citizenship or of resettling in Mexico, thus relinquishing rights to their lands north of the border. These people were descendants of the Spanish conquistadors and the native Indian population. They were generally divided into two classes: upper-class property owners and peons. Many of the former had held their lands for more than 200 years.

The Hispanos of today are predominately rural and constitute approximately half New Mexico's population, although often states in the Southwest do have large numbers of Mexican-origin people. Most are socially isolated from the dominant group and live in a seventeenth-century culture, using agricultural techniques from that period. Poor health conditions arising from inadequate diet, reliance on folk medicine, and poor sanitation predominate in their rural slums.

Mexican-Americans are more recent arrivals from Mexico, usually since about 1910. Their labor was needed for cotton production in Texas as early as 1890. Much of this population was migratory; workers returned to Mexico after each harvest. From these early beginnings a steadily increasing force of migratory labor helped to harvest crops in Texas and parts of California. With the increased demands for labor during World War II, thousands of Mexican nationals, called *braceros,* were admitted to the country temporarily. But since 1964 emergency measures have been employed to restrict their numbers. These are evident in the restrictions on immigration involving agriculture which to this date have not been resolved.

It is difficult to establish accurately the total population of Mexican-Americans, but it is estimated at 3 million, concentrated in the Southwest. This culturally complex group constitutes one of the largest ethnic populations in America.

From the beginning of their immigration the Mexicans were separated from the Anglos (a term used in the Southwest for whites). The language barrier and the low educational level of the Mexican immigrants encouraged their relegation to unskilled positions. They were welcomed as laborers (usually at below minimum wages) as long as they accepted the social restrictions and did not try to cross segregation lines. They therefore formed subcommunities in which their customs and values were perpetuated and reinforced. In this respect, the Mexican immigrants were different from European immigrants because they not only held on to old-country traditions, but also often expected eventually to return to Mexico. Buffeted by Anglo beliefs that they were inferior and dirty, their main response was to avoid assimilation into American society.

World War II changed many of the traditional attitudes held by Mexican-Americans. Greater mobility opened up new employment areas and brought outside contacts to their isolated villages, in New Mexico particularly. The war did not end discrimination, but changes since then have helped to desegregate much of the area. The League of Latin-American Citizens, the American G.I. Forum (Mexican-American veterans), and civil rights legislation have brought hope and encouragement to Mexican-Americans by providing a focus for civic and social activities that heretofore were virtually impossible for the average citizen of Mexican descent. Through the Office of the Coordinator of Inter-American Affairs, intercultural relations in the Southwest have been improved.

The extent of housing discrimination is difficult to assess because there is no overt segregation. Furthermore, Mexican-Americans tend to avoid housing areas and public facilities in which they sense hostility. Whether or not a particular Mexican-American is accepted in an Anglo neighborhood depends on his social class.

Employment and union activities have to some extent opened up for Mexican-Americans since World War II, but wide acceptance of the group has been slow, particularly in rural areas that rely heavily upon Mexican-American farm labor. The situation is complicated in that many Mexican nationals cross the border illegally to do farm work, notably in Texas. Although these migrants' difficulties in learning English and their different cultural attitudes toward education are partly responsible for the low literacy rate among Mexican-Americans, segregated schools poorly equipped to teach their children have contributed as well. As George Sanchez points out, however, "overt segregation" of the Mexican-American child is no longer tolerated by the general public in the Southwest.[14] One of the encouraging aspects of school desegregation is that it has served as a precedent for attacks on segregation in other public services. In 1953 the case of Pete Hernández, a Mexican-American who had been tried for murder and sentenced in a county where Mexican-Americans had never served on juries, was successfully appealed to the Supreme Court.[15] The decision included a paragraph stating that the Fourteenth Amendment forbids discrimination not only against Negroes but also against any other group. This decision gave Mexican-Americans a legal precedent for protection against discrimination and also encouraged their leadership.

Politically, Mexican-Americans have been passive, partly because many have not obtained United States citizenship and partly because of apathy in the face of political bosses and corrupt machines in some states. The Hernández case showed Mexican-Americans that causes can be won and that independent political power is important.

The Mexican-Americans differ from other minority groups: Many are not immigrants in the usual sense, as many of their ancestors have been here since the sixteenth century. Few are wholly Indian, however, although many are directly descended from American Indians. They have not had to deny the "old country"; in fact, many return to Mexico for extensive visits. Total acculturation has not seemed desirable to most Mexican-Americans because they have their own communities based on Mexican values and attitudes. The Spanish language has furthered ethnic identification within the group; many dialects have emerged, however. What is different about Mexican-Americans is their adherence to their own culture and people. Their values and customs vary considerably from those of the Anglos, and such differences have had much to do with their slow rate of acculturation and the history of discrimination against them resulting in low socioeconomic status.

Puerto Ricans

The Puerto Rican population in the United States was estimated in 1959 at 903,000, three-quarters of whom lived in New York City. Numerically this group is not as large as some of the others discussed in this chapter, but the special problems involved in Puerto Rican immigration make this group important within the framework of welfare institutions.

Since the Spanish-American War in 1898, there has been continuous migration from Puerto Rico to the United States, which has aroused considerable distrust and fear among other groups. Many arrivals are illiterate and come from a culture predominantly Roman Catholic, rural, and politically inactive.

Many Puerto Ricans are attracted by the economic opportunities in large American cities, as well as by the encouragement of relatives already living there. For economic reasons, many of the migrants are forced to live in slum areas, where several families often live in one apartment in a dilapidated building. The educational problems of their children are compounded by the ignorance of English at home. For those Puerto Ricans who are white entrée into the larger society is possible, but for dark Puerto Ricans the chances of upward social mobility are limited. They also encounter more discrimination in employment and housing. The fierce adherence to the Spanish language among Negro Puerto Ricans is a way of distinguishing themselves from American Negroes and the related prejudices. All Puerto Ricans consider themselves a single group and marry without great attention to color; native American citizens stress color difference in a more emotionally laden way.

In the Puerto Rican living pattern, kinship plays the most important part. Much of the Hispanic tradition of close chaperonage of young girls, clearly defined roles for men and women, and early marriages are still found among the Puerto Ricans.

As most Puerto Ricans read Spanish, they consider English-language literacy tests for voting unfair. This factor does exclude many from politics and higher levels of employment. There has been controversy in New York City over licensing of professionals trained in Puerto Rico. Licensing of teachers has been slow, although the New York Board of Education uses some as substitute teachers in Spanish-speaking classrooms. The department of welfare has also followed this policy for special personnel assigned to the counseling of Spanish-speaking clients. Nurses, who are badly needed in Spanish-speaking hospital wards, are nevertheless not licensed if they have not passed examinations in English.

The Puerto Ricans are a relatively new minority group, and they have perhaps benefited from lessons learned by Americans in the past. Certainly, there has been a more systematic appraisal of their plight than of those of earlier immigrant groups. Urban-renewal programs have somewhat helped the housing problem; clergymen, political clubs, and various social agencies have brought landlords of substandard buildings to court. School-district lines have been changed to avoid having more than a 33 percent proportion of Puerto Ricans in any school, and "culture free" IQ tests are given to determine more accurately the abilities of Puerto Rican children.

Public-welfare agencies, private nonsectarian welfare agencies, Protestants and Roman Catholics have all helped to meet the needs of this new group. Spanish-language newspapers have helped to bridge the communications gap between them and the English-speaking world. Various organizations have helped to strengthen minority identification. Although membership is not large, such organizations as the Spanish Merchants Association, the Puerto Rican Civil Service Employees Association, the Spanish Club of the New York City Police Department, and the Association of Puerto Rican Social Workers all reflect increasing awareness of professional claims. Other civic and cultural groups are bringing to the Puerto Ricans a sense of belonging that is essential if they are to become more than the newest migrant group.

Other Minority Groups

At certain periods in American history there has been a good deal of discrimination against the Chinese and Japanese, but if placed on a continuum, the Oriental would occupy the middle position between the dominant society and the more vociferous minority groups. They have not assimilated to the same degree as have many Europeans in a comparable length of time because of greater cultural differences. For a long time there were also severe restrictions on Chinese and Japanese immigration. Although the Japanese-Americans had a difficult time on the West Coast after the attack on Pearl Harbor on December 7, 1941, and many were forcibly relocated to the interior of the country, there has since been a concerted effort to compensate them for the effects of land seizure and displacement. It should be noted that such widespread relocation did have a unifying effect on Japanese community life. The younger generation, many of whom had American citizenship, was given a greater voice and more civic participation was encouraged. Today both Chinese-Americans and Japanese-Americans enjoy more favorable images than in the past. Although they are still rejected socially to some extent, barriers in employment, politics, and education have lowered considerably. Their value systems, however different from those of the mainstream of American society, stress the honor and integrity of the individual, and this emphasis has done much to speed the acculturation process.

Those immigrant groups that have succeeded in assimilating into American society after two or three generations may retain ethnic characteristics but do not form minority groups as we have defined them. We have not always approached the problem of those who experience difficulty in absorbing the customs and language of our society in useful ways. Milton M. Gordon pointed out the need to concentrate on cultural assimilation.[16] The immigrant can be helped with training in necessary skills, education in the English language, and more sophisticated explanations of American politics. Yet these programs should not be implemented at the expense of the individual's identification with his primary group; he should be encouraged to retain pride in his ethnic origin while being assimilated into American society.

As far as the government's role is concerned, Gordon makes an important distinction between desegregation and integration. His view is that desegregation involves legal equality of all citizens in all public institutions, facilities, and services, and that integration involves attitudinal changes and disappearance of fears and prejudices, a more difficult process. The government's role is to pursue desegregation to the utmost, but legislation cannot directly change attitudes and fears, particularly in times of social upheaval. Integration of all minority groups will come only with an enlightened citizenry and the cooperation of vested interests.

NOTES

1. Charles F. Marden and Gladys Meyer, *Minorities in American Society* (New York: American Book, 1962), p. 6. Offers a comprehensive

review of minority and ethnic groups in the United States, as well as an overview of relations between dominant and minority groups.

2. Tamotsu Shibutani and Kian M. Kwan, *Ethnic Stratification* (New York: Macmillan, 1965), pp. 208–209. The authors have made a comparative study of contacts among peoples throughout the world in developing a theory of interethnic relations. Ethnic identity and popular notions of ethnic differences are explored.

3. James W. Vander Zanden, *American Minority Relations* (New York: Ronald, 1966), pp. 10–12. This book focuses on sociological foundations of race and minority relations and offers an excellent historical survey with a superb chapter on the ramifications of segregation in American society.

4. Charles Wagley and Marvin Harris, *Minorities in the New World* (New York: Columbia University Press, 1964), pp. 10–12.

5. Alan P. Grimes, *Equality in America* (New York: Oxford, 1964), p. 44. This book is basically concerned with equality in religion, race and representation and is particularly valuable on history.

6. Carey McWilliams, *Brothers Under the Skin* (2nd ed., Boston: Little, Brown, 1964), p. 61. The first edition is a classic in identifying minority groups and their problems. In this edition the author has added a new introduction bringing information on legislation and movements up to date. The book gives a historical perspective on each of the main minority groups, as well as an astute look at customs and values involved in discriminatory practices.

7. William A. Brophy and Sophie D. Aberle, eds., *The Indian—America's Unfinished Business* (Norman: University of Oklahoma Press, 1966), p. 18. This report is an excellent up-to-date historical survey.

8. McWilliams, *op. cit.*, p. 84.

9. Marden and Meyer, *op. cit.*, p. 224.

10. *Ibid.*, p. 292.

11. U.S. Commission on Civil Rights, *With Liberty and Justice for All* (Washington, D.C.: Government Printing Office, 1959), Chapters 4, 5 offer an abridgment of the commission's report.

12. Vander Zanden, *op. cit.*, pp. 101–118.

13. *Ibid.*, p. 475.

14. Cited in Marden and Meyer, *op. cit.*, p. 136.

15. *Hernández v. Texas*, 347 U.S. 475, 74 S. Ct. 667, 98 L. Ed. 866 (1954).

16. Milton M. Gordon, *Assimilation in American Life* (New York: Oxford, 1964), pp. 243–245. Discusses race, religion, national origins, and accompanying assimilation patterns. The author has distinguished two types of assimilation, structural and cultural, which he applies deftly.

SUGGESTED READINGS

Barron, Milton L. *Minorities in a Changing World*. New York: Knopf, 1967.

   A compilation of readings that gives a good general overview on the problems of minorities in both foreign and American contexts.

Bettelheim, Bruno, and Morris Janowitz. *Social Change and Prejudice*. London: Collier-Macmillan, 1950.

   The authors explore psychological bases of prejudice and discrimination through a study of soldiers returning from World War II.

Rubel, Arthur J. *Across the Tracks*. Austin: University of Texas Press, 1966.

   An account of people in a Texas town and the conditions under which they live.

Samora, Julian, ed. *La Raza—Forgotten Americans*. South Bend, Ind.: University of Notre Dame Press, 1966.

   A collection of papers by experts assessing the status of Mexican-Americans in the Southwest.

Williams, Robin M., Jr. *Strangers Next Door*. Englewood Cliffs, N.J.: Prentice-Hall, 1964.

   A report of a research program designed to determine the attitudes and behavior of various racial groups in the United States.

Chapter VII

THE NATIONAL CONCERN FOR

PUBLIC AND MENTAL HEALTH

This chapter describes the gradual shift of
concern for individual health to society and
of the implications of such a shift.

Concern for public health, like many other social concerns, developed
in the United States after other countries had already gained experience in the field. England had, during the turbulent period of the
Industrial Revolution, watched its urban areas mushroom and the
resulting increase in disease, epidemics, and death rates. Attempts to
eliminate squalid conditions and privation finally brought Parliament
to pass the Public Health Act of 1848. From that time on a centralized
administration saw to the upgrading of medical standards, which
necessarily involved efforts to eliminate bad housing, inadequate clothing, and improper diet.

Meanwhile the United States was receiving swarms of European
immigrants. From 1830 to 1870 the same epidemics, resulting from
inadequate sewage disposal, poor housing, and other urban problems
beset American cities. Long before any health organization came into
being its necessity was recognized. New York City formed the Metro-
politan Board of Health in 1866, and other major cities soon followed.

U.S. Public Health Service

The Federal government took no active part in public-health programs until passage of the National Quarantine Act of 1878 and the creation of the National Board of Health. This law authorized a quarantine in ports of entry for purposes of establishing controls over such diseases as typhoid. A domestic quarantine law of 1890, requiring diseased persons to be isolated (no longer in effect), as well as assumption of reponsibility for medical examination of immigrants, put the Federal government firmly in the public-health field.

In 1912 the former Public Health and Marine Hospital Service became the Public Health Service, but it was not until 1953 that it became truly national in scope. In that year President Dwight D. Eisenhower signed a law creating the Department of Health, Education and Welfare. This department includes, in addition to the Public Health Service, the following important agencies: the Social Security Administration, the Office of Education, the Food and Drug Administration, the Vocational Rehabilitation Administration, and the Welfare Administration.

The Public Health Service is charged with the responsibility for cooperating with the states in controlling epidemics and communicable diseases and with establishing and enforcing national health standards and practices. It also administers a hospital construction program, which assists the states with Federal matching funds.

An important branch of the Public Health Service is the National Institutes of Health, devoted to research in respiratory and metabolic diseases, mental health, child development, allergies, and infectious and communicable diseases.

In order to be effective, the Public Health Service must perform several other functions as well. First, it must cooperate with health organizations at all levels, public and private; second, it must provide a clearing house for information on procedures, experiments, and research available to all interested organizations, universities, and foundations; third, it must be involved in research both directly and indirectly, making information, facilities, and funds available if possible, as well as collecting, filing, and interpreting data.

Other Public-Health Organizations

Today health is also an international concern, as is demonstrated by the existence of the World Health Organization (WHO). WHO has established two major categories of nations, each with special problems: "underdeveloped" and "advanced" nations. In underdeveloped countries technological and economic advances have been slow. Experience has taught advanced countries how to solve some problems now being faced by underdeveloped nations, but there are other problems in the advanced countries that clearly indicate how much public-health services are still needed. The best example is the United States, where, despite affluence, there is still poverty and often lack of adequate housing, sewage disposal, proper diet, and control of infectious and communicable disease. High density living, uncommon in underdeveloped countries, creates problems in areas such as industrial and space medicine, highway accident prevention and air pollution.

Public-Health Nursing

The dissemination of knowledge and practical application of some medical techniques are functions of the public-health nurse. This special branch of the nursing profession serves people at home, on the job, and in the schools. In instances where municipal budgets permit, a nurse may be employed by school districts. Otherwise, school nursing service may be rendered by the public-health nurse. Nurses were visiting the poor and the sick in the United States as early as 1885, but the National Organization for Public Health Nursing (N.O.P.H.N.), organized in 1912, was the first formal group to set standards for the nursing profession on other than a local basis. This group merged with several other professional organizations in 1952 and became known as the National League of Nursing (N.L.N.).

The American Medical Association

Doctors are also interested in public health. From the activities of the medical profession many improvements in teaching, training, surgical techniques, and health standards have emerged. Physicians concerned about the sometimes lax standards of their profession formed the American Medical Association (A.M.A.), now the largest professional medical group of its kind, in Philadelphia in 1847. Its main interests at the time were public health, research, and teaching. From its rather humble beginnings the A.M.A. has grown to include 75 to 85 percent of all medical doctors practicing in the nation today. Fierce opposition to the granting of diplomas for cash after little or no study was an early principle of the A.M.A., and as a result the Association of American Medical Colleges (A.A.M.C.) was established to see that certain standards were met. There was substantial cause for concern. In 1869 the director of the Harvard University Medical School claimed that most of his students literally could not write.[1] In 1884 only three states required more than presentation of a "diploma" for a license to practice medicine. The grimly humorous story is told of one enterprising man in Indiana who displayed a Chinese napkin as his diploma.

The A.A.M.C. now takes a keen interest in all phases of training, from admission procedures, internship, and records to the staffing of hospitals, in order to maintain high standards in all phases of medical education.

Much committee work on various aspects of medicine is done without pay by A.M.A. members. This listing is not inclusive but only representative of their wide range of concern: drugs, mental health, aging, cosmetics, medical education, alcoholism, food and nutrition, automotive safety, nuclear medicine, rural health, and nursing.

It was through the efforts of the A.M.A. that a Federal health agency was formed as early as 1872. Henry I. Bowditch, president of the A.M.A. in 1877, had helped to establish the Massachusetts board of health in 1869 and had assisted at the birth of the American Public Health Association in 1872. The yellow-fever epidemic of 1878 hastened the formation of the National Board of Health, which was discontinued by Congress in 1883.

One problem with which the A.M.A. has long been concerned is that of "quackery," the practice of medicine without skill or training. Rural America in particular, where there is often too little knowledge of medical science and too little money to pay for medical services, has been open to exploitation. At one time the traveling "medicine man," who claimed that his elixir, usually a fluid with a high alcoholic content, would remove warts, restore hair, improve eyesight, or increase sexual potency, was commonplace. His departure from town was usually a hasty one. His worthless mixture was usually harmless but was definitely misrepresented. Medicine men later broadened their horizon and their market by producing these liquids under patents and stocking the shelves of country drugstores. The A.M.A. exposed many of these "patent medicines," but one incident in particular dramatizes the protective aspect of the A.M.A.'s efforts. A remedy known as Nature's Creation was advertised as containing an ingredient, unknown to medical science, that would cure tuberculosis and "weak lungs." It sold for $5 a bottle and produced a profit of 1,800 percent for the manufacturer. Upon investigation the A.M.A. discovered that this same medicine had also been sold by the manufacturers as a cure for syphilis. It was further discovered that glowing reports by "cured" people were false and that many of these people had died of various causes by the time of the investigation, within two years of the publication of their statements.[2] The ensuing legal actions were long and costly for the A.M.A., which in its early years was not wealthy. A legal fight with a patent-medicine company in 1916 cost the A.M.A. $125,000, with the result that it operated in the red for about twenty-five years.

A three-member committee on national legislation was formed at the 1899 A.M.A. convention to present the association's views to Congress and to report back to the membership.[3] It eventually became necessary for a lobbyist to assume these duties, and the A.M.A. now employs a full-time lobbyist in Washington, D.C. It is his responsibility to keep the association informed of any legislation touching on the field of medicine and to press for acceptance of the views of the A.M.A. among legislators. The A.M.A. has taken the lead in proposing, reviewing, criticizing, and promoting much of the legislation that ultimately affects public and mental health.

The A.M.A. is not always able to muster the necessary support on issues that it favors. An example is its opposition to Medicare, an amendment to the Social Security Act granting certain medical-care benefits to the aged and the poor. During the various stages of preparation and proposal, the association actively campaigned against Medicare. The program has since become a fact, and, although the A.M.A. has been reluctant to accept it fully because of restricted fee payments, nevertheless it has cooperated in its implementation.

The A.M.A. is one of the nation's largest publishers. In addition to nearly a dozen monthly journals on such medical specialties as psychiatry, dermatology, and surgery, it publishes the *Journal of the American Medical Association, Today's Health,* and *New Drugs,* which reach a combined circulation of more than 250,000. The *Journal* first appeared in 1883 and had a circulation of 5,000. Within seven years the circulation had jumped to over 17,000.

It is interesting to note that the A.M.A. did not split over the issues in the Civil War, as did many groups of similar nature. Nor did the A.M.A. take any political position on such other issues as child labor, Prohibition, abolition of slavery, and public education.

One of the most significant areas in which the A.M.A. has moved to protect the American public is food and drug advertising and exploitation. Everything from vitamins to cosmetics has been evaluated. A.M.A. efforts to safeguard the citizen from false claims and misrepresentation have been unceasing and have greatly reduced the chances of his being sold products that claim to "work wonders" without scientific research to back them up. The American public's vulnerability to quackery and nostrums has netted manufacturers millions of dollars. The continued efforts of the A.M.A. will help in protecting future generations from this type of exploitation.

Medical Foundations

The American Medical Association, although active and available to assist with many problems that arise, cannot devote sufficient time to pressing questions without the aid of other interested groups. As a result, national foundations have been established to direct concerted attacks on various medical problems by underwriting research, education, and other philanthropic endeavors related to national health. There are more than 5,000 such organizations in the United States, with combined assets of more than $5 billion.

Although private foundations fall into different categories, the type with which we are concerned here limits its efforts to a particular disease or problem. Examples are the Arthritis Foundation, the American Cancer Society, the National Cystic Fibrosis Research Foundation, the Heart Fund, the National Hemophilia Foundation, and the National Tuberculosis Association.

As the specific disease or problem with which the foundation is involved is conquered, a change in emphasis usually takes place. For example, the March of Dimes, redirected its efforts to work with birth defects after its crusade to control polio had been successful. Rather than dissolve one organization and create another, it is more expedient to shift emphasis. Social-welfare institutions thus perpetuate themselves.

Organizations like the National Rehabilitation Association are not included in our list of examples because their range of concerns is broader, but they often help clients referred by one of the foundations mentioned. The National Rehabilitation Association conducts extensive research and training in the rehabilitation of handicapped people.

So far only physical problems have been discussed. The medical profession has long been concerned with emotional problems and mental illness as well. Psychiatrists, who treat mentally ill patients, are medical doctors. In addition, they have taken special training and examinations for certification. It is not uncommon for laymen to confuse psychiatrists with psychologists, who are rarely medical doctors. Psychologists, usually specializing in psychometrics, clinical practice, or research, receive academic training and degrees. As members of a helping profession, psychologists are functional members in the team approach to the study, diagnosis, and treatment of mental illness.

The Mental-Health Movement

Methods of treating mental illness have evolved from very primitive procedures to more sophisticated practices. Demons have been blamed for "madness" since early recorded history. Jesus Christ is described as having cast out the devils plaguing a man and putting them into swine, which "ran violently down a steep place into the sea" [*Mark* 5:1–13]. Flogging, starvation, and other forms of torture were long used to make the body such an unpleasant place that the evil spirit would leave it.[4]

Western beliefs about mental illness underwent a major change in the fifteenth century. Although mental illness was still considered the work of the devil, some measure of compassion for its victims developed. Most "treatment" was left to clergymen, who resorted to the "laying on of hands" and other soothing methods. Later in the century it came to be widely believed that the mentally ill had made pacts with the devil and were actually responsible for their condition. They were feared as witches and demons with "unnatural" powers harmful to society. Torture, burning, and death were once again used to rid the populace of these tormented souls.

Beginning in the sixteenth century many countries began to establish special asylums for the insane. In England the monastery of St. Mary of Bethlehem was converted into a mental hospital in 1547. Its name was contracted to "Bedlam," which has come to mean confusion and noise. Some of the inmates were forced to beg on the streets and the public was charged to see the more violent patients. Similar institutions were established throughout Europe. Most were modified penal institutions, and the inmates were treated like wild animals. They were generally chained to the walls of their cells, and no attention was paid to diet, sanitation, and treatment.

In the eighteenth century scientific inquiry about mental illness began. One of the reformers of this period was Philippe Pinel (1745–1826), who shortly after the French Revolution was placed in charge of a mental hospital on the outskirts of Paris. One of his first acts was to strip the chains from some of the inmates. His kindness brought calming results, and the hospital became a place of relative peace and quiet instead of "bedlam."

An important figure in the mental-health movement in the United States was Dorothea Dix (1802–1887), who crusaded to change conditions in mental hospitals throughout the country. Through her efforts millions of dollars were raised to build more suitable hospitals. She is credited with helping to establish about thirty modern mental hospitals.

Another important figure in the American mental-health movement was Clifford Beers, whose famous book *A Mind that Found Itself* was published in 1908.[5] He described his own mental collapse and his inhuman treatment in the existing hospitals. Through his efforts the first Society for Mental Hygiene was founded in 1908; this organization became worldwide in 1919.

Neuroses and Psychoses

The brief descriptions of the major categories of mental illness that follow are designed to help clarify the special concerns of each of the helping professions. More comprehensive discussions are listed in the Suggested Readings at the end of this chapter.

The diagnosis of mental illness is complex, for many factors enter into consideration; furthermore, specific symptoms are seldom restricted to specific illnesses. For instance, a mentally ill person may exhibit symptoms that characterize two or three different types of mental illness.

Nevertheless, the student should have some simple classification system to which he may refer. Illnesses may be categorized along a continuum from mild neurosis to severe psychosis. An individual suffering from a neurosis has made an adjustment to life that incorporates frustration, hostility, compulsiveness, general anxiety, or similar painful consequences, but his neurosis involves less personality disorganization, with a greater capacity for social functioning, than does a psychosis. The neurotic person is able to cope with reality by and large, despite having more than his share of problems. A person who habitually eats and drinks far beyond what is necessary, stutters, or continually loses his temper over small things, may be neurotic. There are four general categories of neurosis: hysteria (exaggerated excitability); compulsiveness (irresistable, repetitive impulses to act); neurasthenia (nervous exhaustion due to excessive expenditure of psychic energy); and anxiety (overwhelming feelings of impending disaster).

Because of its extremely complex construction, orientation, and presentation, psychosis is often more difficult to understand and treat. Psychoses are classified as functional and organic. The organic type results from medical trauma, disease, or toxic reaction. A severe head injury, an advanced stage of syphilis, or excessive alcoholic consumption or drug use over a long period of time could produce an organic psychosis. Functional psychosis comprises the greatest incidence of severe mental illnesses, and results from negative interpersonal relationships as opposed to tissue damage or toxic conditions.

Psychoses are further broken down into three main groups: schizophrenia, manic-depressive psychosis, and paranoia. Schizophrenia, the most common type, has four distinct subtypes. Simple schizophrenia is characterized by apathy, lack of "affect," and disinterest in other people. Hebephrenic schizophrenia is accompanied by such symptoms as inappropriate and excessive smiling, laughing, and silliness. In catatonic schizophrenia the patient withdraws from the external world and may remain motionless for hours. Paranoid schizophrenia is characterized by delusions of grandeur, suspicion, and feelings of persecution.

The manic-depressive psychoses include various subtypes, such as manic and depressive. Essentially, the patient is either agitated, depressed, or both; he can also shift rapidly from one to the other.

The individual suffering from paranoia has a rigid organization and is unable to tolerate what he suspects are deliberate attempts to thwart him. His suspicions are almost always unfounded. Delusions are often present, usually localized in one facet of the personality such as mysterious inventions, religious aggrandizement or erotic stimulants.

Other "Problems" Defined as Illness

It took many years for the world to recognize that mental illness is, in fact, an illness and not the work of the devil. Medical practitioners began to understand that the insane cannot be held accountable for their behavior, which is the result of forces beyond their control. This change in attitude began in the late eighteenth and early nineteenth century. It was not until recently, however, that drug addiction, and sexual perversion were acknowledged as symptoms of mental illness and not of "poor moral character." During World War II these "problems" were dubbed the "character disorder." This term has been used to designate a wide variety of symptoms such as extremes in impulsiveness, immaturity, unreliability, conflict with authority, and the inability to postpone immediate gratification. The term has been used synonomously to designate both the sociopathic and psychopathic personalities.

The fury of the temperance movement bears witness to strong emotions toward drink that once prevailed. Alcoholism is now recognized as a symptom of underlying problems. Alcoholics can be treated in a variety of ways, and help is available through Alcoholics Anonymous. Results are encouraging,[6] but new treatments are continuously sought. Alcoholics Anonymous reports success with its program which stresses the need for the problem drinker to stay "dry" on a day-to-day basis; A.A. claims only to help the alcoholic to arrest his drinking and not to solve his underlying problems.

Drug addiction has grown to alarming proportions in recent years. Drug use is illegal, and society still regards it as immoral as well. The mental-health professions have become increasingly interested in the problem. There are two Federal hospitals that treat only drug addicts, at Lexington, Kentucky; and at Fort Worth, Texas. All major psychiatric hospitals have drug units, and addiction is regarded as a major health problem. In the late 1960s there has been increasing use of drugs—including marijuana, lysergic acid diethylamide (LSD), methedrine methyl benzedrine, a type of amphetamine, and other "psychedelic" drugs—by young people. One important aspect of this particular trend is that the "typical" drug user of the 1960s was white, educated, and affluent compared to his counterpart of the 1940s, who was nonwhite, uneducated, and poor. Synanon, an organization of former drug users parallels A.A. in its attempt to help each other refrain from self abuse—in this case, harmful drugs.

Homosexuality is as old as history. During the golden age of Greece it was not only accepted but often a luxury reserved for the rich. In our society for many years homosexuals have had to keep their activities hidden, for they are liable to arrest, scorn, and even physical abuse. Many prominent men have been homosexuals, but because of the intense negative reaction of the public the matter is seldom openly discussed. In more recent years, thanks to increasing public awareness and sophistication, homosexuals have become more visible and have even formed fraternal organizations.[7] The new professional view of homosexuality is that it is an acceptable sexual variation rather than a mental-health problem. Generally, therapy for homosexuals focuses on their loneliness and guilt rather than on homosexual behavior itself.

We have examined three specific types of character disorder, or "sociopathic personality." It should be noted that these "problems" have long been associated with violations of the law and, in fact, still are. Until recently the only form of treatment was incarceration; we now recognize that they are associated with emotional problems, and hospitalization and psychiatric care may be alternatives to incarceration.

Agencies Providing Mental-Health Services

Many social agencies have become involved secondarily in mental-health problems. The Veterans Administration (V.A.) now has extensive programs, although they were not originally envisioned. The Family Service Society of America (F.S.S.A.) must, of necessity, include mental health in its diagnoses and treatment of family dysfunctioning. Such other organizations as Catholic Charities, the Jewish Welfare Board, and public-welfare departments are confronted with such a wide range of interpersonal problems that, in order to perform their primary functions, they must also deal with the mental health of their clients.

Many communities have mental-health centers or state mental hospitals. Most public and private hospitals offer psychiatric services on both in-patient and out-patient bases. Leading universities offer mental-health services through their psychology or psychiatry departments, counseling divisions, or schools of social work.

The current national trend is toward comprehensive local mental-health programs designed and partially funded by the Federal government. These services include out-patient care, hospitalization, day care, twenty-four-hour-emergency service, and training and consultation. They are designed to replace often inaccessible mental hospitals, and could well signal the decline of such hospitals in their present form. Such comprehensive mental-health programs enable more people to receive care as out-patients, thus avoiding the stigma associated with hospitalization in mental institutions.

Most mental-health services are offered at the request of the client, but the person suffering from an emotional problem does not always know where to seek help. Consequently a helping professional may assist by referring him to an agency or person trained to help with his specific problem.

Whether he works at a welfare department, in the Red Cross, at a hospital, in a university, or in any other social-welfare institution, a professional will frequently have to refer clients for help with their problems. It appears a simple matter to provide a client with a name and telephone number and to let him make the initial contact. But it is often difficult to "let go" of a client. It is also sometimes difficult for a client to take the first step in forming a relationship with someone else. Often the symptoms that prompted the referral will disappear, and the referral will be ignored. Some workers may be reluctant to make referrals for fear that other workers will judge their preliminary work with the client. These and other problems make it necessary to think through each referral very carefully, especially if a professional relationship with the client has already been established.[8]

A few simple rules help to make the referral process both more comfortable for the worker and more beneficial to the client:

1. Discuss the referral with a supervisor and, if possible, with someone at the agency to which the client is being sent.
2. Discuss with the client the reasons for referral, making sure that he does not feel rejected or helpless.
3. Be available to accompany the client to the new agency if this practice is acceptable to your agency.
4. Provide the receiving agency with all the information you have on the client in writing as soon as possible.
5. After the referral *do not* continue to involve yourself in the treatment plan unless the new agency requests your cooperation.

If these rules are kept in mind, it is possible to help people and at the same time to maintain professional working relations among agencies.

Current Treatment Types

Current treatments for mental illness are quite diversified. We shall describe the more traditional approaches first and then the more recently developed techniques, some of which have not been in use for long. We do not intend the discussion to be exhaustive, nor do we imply that wide acceptance will necessarily be found for all the approaches mentioned.

Psychotherapy

The term most commonly used to describe psychiatric treatment is "psychotherapy." The word has become generic and its definition somewhat nebulous. In its broadest sense it includes anything done to or done in behalf of a patient that is meant to be beneficial to him psychologically. More technically "psychotherapy" means treatment based upon either verbal or nonverbal communication with the patient. This definition excludes drug, surgery, insulin, or electroshock therapy.

There are different types of psychotherapy. Clarence Rowe distinguishes four: supportive, intensive, group, and family.[9] In supportive psychotherapy emphasis is on conscious material, to which the patient has immediate access, and through the client–therapist relationship focuses on behavior modification, reassurance, and consideration of alternatives. Intensive psychotherapy, known also as "insight therapy" or "uncovering therapy," attempts to uncover conflicts that are primarily unconscious and thus to help the patient deal with them more effectively. In group therapy the techniques are those used in individual therapy, but three or more patients take part, and benefit additionally from the interaction of the group.

Family therapy has been developed since 1960 to deal with the mental health of the family unit as a distinct entity. Family therapists argue that the emotional problems of family members result from intrafamily conflicts. Family therapy is closely allied to group therapy; the therapist often employs similar techniques.

Somatic Therapy

Somatic therapy is a broad term that includes all therapy administered to the body. Insulin-coma therapy, electroconvulsive therapy, regressive electroshock therapy, nonconvulsive electrostimulation, water therapy and psychosurgery are examples of somatic therapy. Negative side effects are associated with some of these procedures, and, as they do not always accomplish their ends, they are employed on a very selective basis. An example is the lobotomy, a "last resort" form of psychosurgery in which certain connecting brain tissues are severed to relieve some symptoms of mental illness. As the surgery is irreparable, it may leave the patient impaired.

Operant Conditioning

The technique of operant conditioning is gaining acceptance as a method of therapy for chronic cases of brain damage and autism. It is based on the assumption that behavior patterns can be changed through behavioral reinforcement and that the intrapsychic forces are relatively unimportant. Basically, a patient is rewarded, or rewards are withheld, according to whether his behavior is acceptable or unacceptable to the therapist. In theory unintentional learning on the part of the patient will take place and he will "automatically" respond to the rewarded behavior.

Pharmacotherapy

Psychotherapeutic drugs have become an increasingly popular form of treatment since 1954, when phenothiazine derivatives were first introduced into the United States from France. These drugs include antidepressants and tranquilizers. The antidepressants make the extremely depressed patient more amenable to traditional psychotherapeutic approaches. Tranquilizing drugs, used for the same purpose, have a quieting and soothing effect on patients suffering from extreme anxiety. Drug therapy is considered primarily a supplement to other forms of treatment and is seldom chosen as the major technique to be employed.

Management Therapy

Two types of "client activity" therapies fall into the classification of management therapy, so called because the patient engages his energies in something other than interaction with the therapist. Occupational therapy, involving creative tasks such as wood and metal working that are physically demanding, is most effective with hostile, aggressive patients. Recreational therapy is similar in that much energy is expended by the patient, usually in games in which release of aggression is a prominent factor, like football.

The Team Approach

The helping professions have initiated a team approach, so that the professional expertise of various disciplines can be focused at once on the problems of emotionally disturbed patients. An ideal team would be composed of one or more psychiatrists, social workers, psychologists, nurses, physical therapists, and other physicians. As indicated previously, psychiatrists are medical doctors by training; other physicians on the treatment team direct their attention to physical problems.

The advantages of the team approach are most apparent during the intake process, when primary responsibility is assigned to one member of the team, who consults with his colleagues. The team approach can best be described by outlining the duties of the members of the team.

The social worker is the professional person who has the longest and most direct involvement with the patient. During the intake process he gathers the client's social history for presentation to other members of the treatment team. During early phases of the treatment and in follow-up contacts the social worker deals most directly with the patient.

The basic concern of the team psychologist during the intake process is the administration and interpretation of psychological tests. The information thus obtained aids the team in understanding and diagnosing the problems of the patient and in formulating the most appropriate treatment plan. Certain clinical aspects of the treatment plan, such as counseling, interviewing and obtaining further diagnostic impressions may be assigned to the psychologist after the team evaluation.

Theoretically, the psychiatrist is the head of the treatment team. Because the setting is usually a hospital, the psychiatrist is most likely legally responsible for the patient. He diagnoses the patient's problem and assists the patient in understanding the anxiety and behavior associated with the illness.

As more people receive training in these areas, at both the graduate and undergraduate levels, their services will be sought as members of the treatment team. This will particularly apply to the psychiatric nurse, the case aide and the non-salaried volunteer.

The team approach functions best when each member of the team has been graduated from an accredited professional school. Some social workers may not have, however, received graduate training. There is a great need for more professionally trained workers in the helping services. Originally recruiting was restricted to applicants holding the master of social work degree, but the number of available people has not been sufficient to meet the demand for their services, and as a result all states hire people with only bachelors' degrees as caseworkers. Any such person is called a "preprofessional" worker.

The use of preprofessionals would not be cause for concern if their undergraduate training were oriented toward the helping services. Most states, however, regard the major field of undergraduate study as immaterial when hiring preprofessionals. Applicants who have majored in such divergent fields as animal husbandry, accounting, and modern dance may take examinations and be certified as caseworkers. Considering the variety in their backgrounds, caseworkers have to be trained by the agencies hiring them. In public-welfare departments there is usually a division staffed by specialists, whose main task is to prepare new caseworkers for their jobs. It is called a "staff-development division" and handles both in-service and preservice training.

Staff-development divisions must offer training that is both general and elementary; this problem would be less severe if newly appointed caseworkers had more background in the social and behavioral sciences.

Until recently, no national program of preprofessional training for the helping services existed. But under the guidance of the Council on Social Work Education (C.S.W.E.) standards have now been set for such programs in colleges and universities in all states,[10] which are collectively called "undergraduate programs in social welfare." A school must meet certain requirements before it can be affiliated with C.S.W.E. The broad objectives of such programs are recruitment for the helping services, preparation of students for entrance into graduate schools of social work, and training for employment immediately after graduation. There are approximately 1,000 schools in Canada and the United States and its possessions now operating such programs.

As these programs become more effective, they will produce changes in the helping professions themselves. Eventually all social-welfare agencies will offer higher starting salaries to graduates of these programs than to other preprofessionals. Furthermore, trained social workers will supervise the preprofessionals. Not that agencies will permit only professionally trained social workers to assume supervisory responsibilities; many capable supervisors do not have the M.S.W. degree, but more often than not their appointments as supervisors are contingent upon their obtaining graduate degrees within a certain period. Preprofessionals in most cases will be dealing directly with the clients. The better trained they are, the more an agency can expect of their performance.

Religious Counseling

Even though knowledge of mental illness is available and specialists in mental health are developing more sophisticated techniques, people do not always trust these experts. A growing realization that many people confide their problems and suffering to religious counselors has highlighted the importance of pastoral counseling. This area is so important that an entire bibliography on the subject has been published.[11]

The concern of clergymen for the health and well-being of their parishioners is religious in orientation, but involves more than religious problems. The need for their counsel is such that they are in contact with all segments of society and not just people of their own faith. Because of the diverse nature of the problems they encounter, their particular church affiliation is often not an issue in counseling.

People with problems had access to the clergy many years before they had professional social workers, psychiatrists, and psychologists to consult. Pastoral care, as counseling is known in the Christian ministry, has been exercised in every imaginable human situation. Much as do the other helping professions, the ministry works to relieve problems of people of every age, class, and condition.

In the following example of activities performed by the clergy, as elsewhere in this text, the term "clergyman" refers to an ordained representative of a particular faith who has had professional theological training. This operational definition, understandably, eliminates many religious practitioners but does not imply that they lack compassion, knowledge, interest in human problems or counseling skills.

Marriage Counseling

The clergyman offers premarital guidance and instruction to prepare couples spiritually and socially for marriage. He sees to necessary paper work to secure the marriage license and completes other records; advises on finances, sex, contraception, and in-laws; explains marriage as a religious sacrament; and supervises the rehearsal and wedding arrangements.

There are vast differences in attitudes toward divorce among the many churches of the United States. Some take a "hands off" approach and offer no guidance. Others take a legalistic approach and forbid any divorce. Regardless of the position of the relevant church, an unsatisfactory marriage is distressing to the couple, who may need help. If the couple cannot discuss this problem with a religious adviser, it will have to seek advice elsewhere.

When marital problems come to his attention, the religious counselor is guided by the situation and his own religious commitments. He examines the situation and communication between the partners and brings his skills to bear when possible.

Adoption

Many couples who desire children but cannot have them consult their clergymen. A religious adviser is usually familiar with the agencies and procedures involved in the adoption process and makes proper referrals. He can advise couples about various problems of which they may be unaware, like the "gray" and "black" markets dealing in children. The gray market places children for adoption through third parties (usually attorneys or physicians), rather than through properly licensed agencies. The black market places children for exorbitant amounts of money through other than licensed agencies. After an adoption, the minister can assist with plans for baptism and other religious elements in the child's upbringing.

Members of the clergy are not usually among the first in the helping professions in touch with mothers or expectant mothers who wish to release their children for adoption, and thus they do not have an opportunity to perform a significant service.

Death

Religious faith can provide direct and meaningful support in the event of death. The clergyman stands ready to comfort the bereaved. Some clergymen participate in funerals only for members of their own faiths, but increasing numbers of them recognize an obligation to serve *all* mankind, and fewer restrictions regarding funeral services are imposed.

Institutional Service

Veterans' hospitals usually have professional clergymen assigned to the duties of chaplain, serving all patients, regardless of faith. Each hospital maintains a list of clergymen of various faiths who will visit patients.

State and Federal prisons often also have staff chaplains, whose salaries are paid by local church councils. Particularly for people who are not free to seek out advisers of their own faiths chaplains make themselves available in times of crisis and need, regardless of the referral source.

Family Problems

Although ordinarily serving his congregation through preaching and counseling, the clergyman can also refer troubled parishioners for professional help available in the community in such areas as finances, health, and education. Professor Wayne E. Oates has called such referrals the "ministry of introduction." [12]

The clergy was once largely responsible for caring for the disabled. Today, however, its responsibility consists mainly of referring these people to other sources, public or private, that are better equipped to help with their problems. An example of a social-welfare institution dealing with physical and emotional problems is the Office of Vocational Rehabilitation.

The supportive role of the clergyman is important even after he has referred a family elsewhere. The family may return to him because of disenchantment with the professional helper, because of emotional involvement with him, or for some other reason.

Birth Control

The issue of birth control has been controversial for all faiths. Sophisticated techniques for family planning have become available, but not all of them are acceptable to different faiths. A religious adviser is expected to follow the position of his church on this matter.

Social Action

More and more clergymen are realizing that individual problems cannot be dealt with in a vacuum but must be considered in the context of social issues. Many clergymen believe that to minister fully to people they must minister to society, and thus they have become involved in social action, particularly on the issues of equal opportunity in employment, open housing, race relations and the draft. The degree of each minister's involvement depends on his own commitment and understanding and on the characteristics of his congregation and religious organizations.

Some religious organizations restrict their clergy, either by official order or by withholding financial support. Even in the face of such restrictions many clergymen feel a moral obligation to oppose social ills. Their commitment to justice as they see it is stronger than is their commitment to authority. As a result they may face censure or dismissal, as was demonstrated in 1968 when fifty-one Roman Catholic priests were threatened with disciplinary action by Patrick Cardinal O'Boyle of Washington, D.C., because they had voiced liberal views on birth control following Pope Paul's anticontraception encyclical.[13]

Another test of a clergyman's commitment is exemplified in the experience of Reverend Joseph Schneiders, pastor of the First Unitarian Church of South Bend, Indiana.[14] Following his active participation in antiwar protests, sit-ins, and civil-rights demonstrations, his church was partially destroyed by arson. More than a dozen insurance companies rejected his application for insurance on the church. Other churches have faced this problem after their ministers have participated in controversial social action, and in some cases existing insurance policies have been canceled.

There are many social issues in which the church can involve itself, among them capital punishment, poverty, war, and race relations. Each generates controversy, as suggested by the word "issues." Often sharp differences of opinion exist among different churches and among members of the same church. Establishing approaches to these problems is agonizing and difficult, but they are important to the churches because they involve the lives of people. The churches are concerned when people suffer at the hands of government, or from war, prejudice, poverty, or other social evils.

There is no doubt that individual clergymen face dilemmas arising from their personal feelings about social inequality and injustice. The decision to speak out or to remain silent is one that cannot be taken lightly, yet the "new breed" faces such decisions daily.

Members of the clergy are interested in public and mental health. Such interdenominational groups as Councils of Churches and the interfaith ministerial associations make concerted attacks on many problems. Membership in these groups is open to all faiths, although the Southern Baptist Convention discourages its ministers and members from participation.

Vocational Rehabilitation

In the United States today about 250,000 men and women become seriously disabled each year. To develop their potential abilities and skills the Federal and state governments initiated the Office of Vocational Rehabilitation, whose branches provide grants-in-aid, technical assistance, national leadership, and other Federal aid to help handicapped men and women earn a living. Through the services provided by this arm of the U.S. Department of H.E.W., now officially the Office of Rehabilitation Services (O.R.S.) more than a million people have returned to useful occupations and more rewarding lives through vocational rehabilitation.

For centuries many physically and mentally disabled people were placed in asylums or destroyed. They were considered useless and therefore a burden on society. It was not until the eighteenth century that institutions were devoted to the physical care of disabled persons, but the total needs of the handicapped individual were still not considered.

In the nineteenth century certain agencies began to take account of the total needs of the person, providing both physical care and educational facilities. During this period public and private schools for the handicapped began to appear in the United States and throughout Europe. In 1907 a school was founded in Belgium for the vocational training of people who were too disabled to be admitted to existing apprenticeship programs; it was one of the first signs of recognition that handicapped people can contribute to society.

Immediately after World War I two important events clearly indicated national concern for the handicapped: passage of the Smith-Sears Act of 1918, which offered assistance to disabled veterans of World War I, and of the Vocational Rehabilitation Act of 1920, to aid disabled civilians. A primary purpose of the 1920 act was to encourage states to undertake rehabilitation programs of their own.

Public Law 113 of 1943 liberalized the provisions of the Vocational Rehabilitation Act and extended service to the mentally ill. At the same time the basis of the program changed from one of scholastic training only to one based on the total needs of the client, especially the emotional problems.

Eligibility Requirements

The minimum age of eligibility, with few exceptions, is sixteen years, regardless of sex. The main exception is corrective surgery for a younger person. To receive assistance the client must demonstrate that he cannot provide financially for his own needs, and his disability must be incapacitating in terms of obtaining or returning to work. Qualifying disabilities include amputations; orthopedic deformities; paralysis; impairment of hearing, vision, and speech; emotional and mental illness; lameness; tuberculosis, heart conditions, diabetes, and epilepsy. The client must also be potentially employable after receiving vocational rehabilitation.

How Services Are Offered

Initial referral is made by another agency, or the client himself applies to the rehabilitation office. A comprehensive history is gathered by a team of doctors, social workers, and psychologists, who question the client himself, as well as employers, teachers, and vocational counselors. Upon request of an ORS counselor problem cases may be "staffed," that is discussed in conference with all members of the treatment team. Then the treatment team presents its findings to a psychiatrist and a plan is devised for the client.

Future

The Federal government, presently involved in comprehensive mental-health planning, will continue to channel funds into the mental health field. Many social problems such as civic disorders, will be alleviated to some degree by the expansion of facilities and staffs in the helping professions. Increased use of indigenous persons in the expansion of mental health programs will give a purpose and "reason for being" to some of the formerly prospective clients.

One of the greatest single advances we anticipate in the public health field is the emphasis to be given research. Air pollution, emphysema, cancer, headaches, and the common cold will receive financial support for extensive research.

The AMA will continue to be a powerful economic and political force, but the prestige, status and respect formerly afforded the physician will gradually dwindle. More frequent contacts with physicians by the public, as well as the removal of much of the mystery of medicine —both of which will continue to increase—will account further for this depreciation of the role of the physician.

Training in the helping professions will become more community-centered, as opposed to client-centered. Schools sponsoring graduate programs, especially, will demand that their students get more field experience than before. Monies presently being used on Vietnam and the space (moon) programs will be diverted to such programs as those offering financial assistance to students in psychology, social work, medicine, and sociology.

With new administrations on a national level will come realignments of departments, offices, bureaus, and divisions of government. Political campaigns of the future will ask questions about governmental services on important issues. The American public, through these campaigns, as well as the public relations work of the individual subdivisions of government, might better understand the services for which the government exists. As a result, broader public support should be forthcoming for expanded mental and public health programs.

Mental illnesses will not disappear, but through experimentation innovative techniques will be developed that will more closely realize the goal of alleviation of emotional suffering. The "back wards" of mental hospitals are already fading from the current scene, and will become even less of a stigma in America.

NOTES

1. James G. Burrow, *AMA, Voice of American Medicine* (Baltimore: Johns Hopkins University Press, 1963), p. 9. This book is a history of the organization.
2. *Ibid.*, pp. 119–120.
3. "Editorial," *Journal of the American Medical Association*, 32 (June 10, 1899), p. 1337; "Editorial," *Journal of the American Medical Association*, 34 (June 16, 1900), p. 1547.
4. James C. Coleman, *Abnormal Psychology and Modern Life* (2d ed.; Chicago: Scott, Foresman, 1956), pp. 36–37. This standard textbook on abnormal psychology discusses illness and treatment from a multidisciplinary point of view.
5. Clifford Beers, *A Mind That Found Itself* (Garden City, N.Y.: Doubleday, 1925), pp. 46–180 and pp. 372–388. An autobiographical account of the treatment of mental patients.
6. Sidney Harber, Aaron Paley, and Arnold S. Black, "Treatment of

Problem Drinkers at Winter Veterans Administration Hospital," *Bulletin of the Menninger Clinic,* 13 (1949), pp. 24–30. A report of experimental work with alcoholics in two hospital settings.

7. Samuel B. Hadden, "A Way Out for Homosexuals," *Harper's,* 234, March 1967, pp. 107–120.

8. Bruce Goates, "The Referral Process," (unpublished paper, Community Mental Health Center, Salt Lake City, Utah, 1966). Offers a discussion of dynamics and problems in the referral process from the point of view of each person involved.

9. Clarence Rowe, *An Outline of Psychiatry* (Dubuque, Iowa: Brown, 1965), p. 157. This book is a concise description of mental illness and its treatment.

10. Herbert Bisno, *The Place of the Undergraduate Curriculum in Social Work Education* (New York: Council on Social Work Education, 1959), pp. 205–214. A project report on the council's curriculum study, which ultimately appeared as a thirteen-volume work.

11. U.S. Public Health Service, *Bibliography on Religion and Mental Health 1960–1962.* Publication No. 1599 (Washington, D.C.: Government Printing Office, 1967).

12. Wayne E. Oates, *The Christian Pastor* (Philadelphia: Westminster, 1963), p. 221. Oates views the pastor as a "man of crisis" and describes conditioning and influences in pastoral relationships.

13. "Roman Catholics," *Time,* September 13, 1968, p. 58.

14. "The Risks of Protest," *Time,* October 11, 1968, p. 49.

SUGGESTED READINGS

Ackerman, N. W. *The Psychodynamics of Family Life.* New York: Basic Books, 1958.

Develops a conceptual definition of the relationship between an individual's emotional functioning and the psychosocial functioning of his family.

English, O. S., and G. H. J. Pearson. *Emotional Problems of Living.* New York: Norton, 1963.

A clear description of how, when, and why emotional conflicts arise and how they may be resolved.

Chapter VIII

*The social problems arising from leisure
are discussed, with emphasis on the
implications of extended
life expectancy.*

Leisure has a different meaning in the United States today from that of yesterday or in other countries. For purposes of this discussion, leisure is defined generally as time during which an individual is not involved in any activity directly related to providing a livelihood for himself and his dependents. It is distinguished from "free" time, which implies total lack of restriction, external control, or planning. Leisure implies subjectively defined activities determined by time, space, money, and available equipment or materials. A distinction between productive and unproductive leisure is useful. Unproductive leisure produces no gain, material or psychic, to the individual.

It is difficult to define leisure to fit all circumstances. If a person switches from one task to another simply to relieve the monotony of his job, he would not be enjoying leisure. A salesman who is entertaining prospective buyers on the golf course is not at leisure. Military personnel, who are technically on duty twenty-four hours a day and whose behavior is regulated by external authority, nevertheless enjoy periods of leisure. But what about the homeowner who engages in projects to improve his property that he could easily hire someone else to do? This chapter deals primarily with leisure time after retirement but includes material on labor-saving devices, the short work week, and the effects of vacations on society.

History and Controlling Factors

In early Christian times manual work was glorified as a means of spiritual uplift for the masses. Very few people attained the exalted position of the philosopher, for philosophizing requires time, and time was not available to those engaged in the struggle for survival. The affluent classes converted free time to leisure and enjoyed themselves in a variety of pursuits while slaves performed the work necessary for the survival of both slave and master. Slaves of pre-Civil War days in the United States also devoted their lives to work. Their masters, largely plantation owners, spent much of their lives in the pursuit of leisure activities.

A similar division of labor and leisure existed in this country until World War II. Until then the rich and the professional classes were the only ones who enjoyed the luxury of leisure. But today more and more leisure is available to the masses. As larger numbers of people find it unnecessary to spend the vast majority of their waking hours in the struggle to survive, society feels the impact, particularly among two major groups: retired individuals and younger adults who find more time on their hands due to automation and technological advances. At present approximately one-third of the American population is over sixty, one-third is between twenty-one and sixty, and one-third is under twenty-one. Workers have more free time than ever before. Whether or not they use this free time for productive leisure activities is a social problem of less moment than whether or not retired people do. Retired people often feel that they have too much free time. Social-welfare institutions take an interest in whether older people use their leisure productively or unproductively. The younger worker is meeting social expectations by working. The retired worker also meets social expectations—by not working—but he must make an adjustment that is often difficult. It is not easy to alter such a pattern of behavior as going to work each day. If this pattern has been established for a thirty- or forty-year period, it cannot usually be successfully discarded or replaced without some planning. An individual's choice of leisure activities reflects his health, preferences, and resources.

Leisure activities are not dictated by survival needs, but neither are they entirely free of external restrictions and demands. Few people are essentially free to do what they want when they want. Nature, in the form of weather and the seasons, forces certain limitations. Fishing, for example, is not a likely activity in cold climates. Schedules of television shows, concerts, movies, and other forms of entertainment narrow the choice considerably. Vacations must often be planned to coincide with summer recesses for school children, fairs, commercial trips, cruises, tours, conferences, celebrations, or the plans of friends.

A very significant limiting factor for both young and old is money, which is necessary for most leisure activities: to pay baby sitters or nurses, to buy tickets, to purchase equipment. A person's finances determine how far he can follow his preferences.

An interesting commentary on values was made during the Poor People's March in Washington, D.C., in June 1968. Television news programs showed one of the early arrivals watching television in the hastily constructed shantytown. A television set, which was once considered a luxury, is now a commonplace. This source of entertainment represents the total leisure activity of some families. It may substitute for street-corner gangs, baby sitters, and other social resources.

Commercial promotion of the "great outdoors" has influenced many people, both young and old. Marion Clawson showed a decade ago that attendance at Federal and state parks had risen 10 percent annually for many years,[1] five times faster than the population had increased. Clawson was writing before the advent of the "camper," which revolutionized outdoor living and traveling. This self-contained living unit can be carried on a pickup truck and removed for storage. In 1967 Yosemite and Yellowstone National Parks combined had more than 2 million visitors. In 1967 an Associated Press release noted that, although tourist business at Yellowstone Park had risen 7 percent, lodge business had declined 27 percent, which was attributed to a greater use of campers and trailers.[2]

The Formative Years

A child's point of view on leisure is different from that of an adult. During their formative, dependent years, children use their time in a variety of ways. Playing with others is a source of much information and pleasure. The preadolescent typically spends much time "no place," doing "nothing," but is in fact learning adult expectations, including those on how to spend time, as he ponders the world outside his own limited realm. Although leisure is thus a meaningful concept only when applied to adults, who must also devote much of their time to working, values and attitudes connected with work and leisure are developed during the childhood and adolescent years. Society conditions its children through an array of programs, generally oriented toward building character. Such programs include the Boy Scouts, Girl Scouts, 4-H clubs, and Future Farmers of America, as well as religious youth groups.

Most of these groups emphasize accomplishment. The child can progress through series of challenges, each more difficult than the last and offering corresponding rewards for success: merit badges, attendance prizes, or an elective or appointive offices. All reflect the value that society places on work and achievement. When participation produces enjoyable learning experiences for the child he associates pleasure with conformity to the basic value system of society. Dependability, co-operation, and industry are components of this system; youth organizations would be suspect if they did not promote such values.

Employment and Leisure

The working adult's work periods are usually spelled out in detail by his employer. Although the forty-hour work week still predominates, some employers require slightly different hours. City, state, county, and Federal employees can expect two-week vacations with pay after six to twelve months' employment. The Federal government is the most liberal in paid vacation time, followed by municipal and state governments.

Governments pay employees salaries while they are fulfilling annual military obligations. Many private employers, especially those that do not have government contracts, do not assume this burden, and employees may be required to use their paid vacations for this purpose.

After quitting time, most employees have fifteen or sixteen hours before reporting to work again. It is commonly assumed that an employee has *earned* the right to spend his time off the job as he sees fit. Aside from sleeping and commuting, the worker may use his time in various ways. We are interested in these ways. The worker often considers demands of his employer outside working hours an infringement on his earned privileges. Organizational policy is usually quite clear on working hours and demands on the employee's time. Most privileges are either automatic or must be earned under specific regulations. Vacation policy is an example of a privilege that may vary from one employer to another.

In addition to paid vacations, employees may have a number of paid holidays, ranging from the traditional New Year's Day, Memorial Day, Fourth of July, Labor Day, Thanksgiving, and Christmas Day to various other city, state, and Federal holidays.

Many organizations like hospitals and prisons must be staffed during holidays. Several plans have been developed to solve problems arising from this requirement. They include the following:

1. Compensatory time—equivalent time off the job at a later date.
2. A skeleton crew—reduced staff on holidays, with employees taking turns at such duty.
3. Overtime pay—usually computed at one and one-half times or twice the normal rate of pay and thus serving as an incentive to work on holidays.
4. Rotation—shift assignments so arranged that employees must work on certain holidays but will be free on others and can know their schedules in advance.

Gertrude Bancroft estimates that about 4 percent of all workers "moonlight," or hold second jobs.[3] These jobs may entail from one or two hours to forty hours a week. The significant point is that what would otherwise be leisure time is spent in a second occupation.

There is a wide variety of policies on moonlighting. Some employers prohibit outside employment; others encourage and expect it. A person who is allowed outside employment can still be faced with a conflict of loyalties between his primary and secondary employers. Advertising agencies do not permit most employees to do free lance work for other ad agencies on the grounds of secrecy relative to their own campaigns. Usually employees are discouraged from seeking employment with competitors or with organizations performing basically the same task as the primary employer. A social worker could accept a part-time position in a department store with less chance of a reprimand than he could see clients from his parent unit on a private-fee basis.

In the past most women were homemakers for life and did not venture into the labor market. This pattern has undergone an interesting change; many women now work to supplement family incomes, "retire" to rear children, and then return to the labor market in their forties and fifties. In addition to being attracted by the additional income, these women want to remain active outside the home, to work in what would otherwise be leisure time.

Most housewives today do not expect to bake bread, wash dishes, scrub floors, mend, iron, sew, and clean without the help of such household appliances as mixers, dishwashers, washing machines, dryers, sewing machines, steam irons, and vacuum cleaners. They expect to enjoy neighborhood coffee breaks, play bridge, join bowling leagues, or enjoy themselves in other ways. They often insist that time spent this way is not really leisure time since this is time not shared or spent with their husbands, hence domestic quarrels may result from the differing views of man and wife on such activities.

No single description applies to members of the national labor force, for it encompasses age groups from youth to old age, those who have gainful employment as well as those underemployed but it is upon the labor force that the impact of free time is going to be most significant in the future. If men spend less time on the job each week and women have more time- and labor-saving devices at their disposal, more free time will be available to working adults. Yet little thought has been devoted to ways that this major group can use leisure most effectively.

Automation, both at home and in industry, is the greatest reason for the increase in free time. Not only can machines do jobs faster, but they also reduce the number of workers required for specific jobs. If a machine does the work of twelve men and it requires only one man to operate the machine, eleven men are going to be unemployed, at least theoretically.

We are at a point at which we can foresee reduction of the work week to thirty or even twenty-five hours, which will cause additional problems for young and old alike. For the aged it will increase fear about loss of work, and the younger person will become anxious about his later years because the work formerly done by others in the standard 40 hour week is not as yet being accepted by full-time employees or shared with the underemployed. The sedentary nature of many jobs is not being sufficiently offset by physical activities during leisure time, and as a result a large segment of the population lacks the physical ability to engage in strenuous activities.

There are those who will sit back until society itself, in the form of its government, does something for them. They will wait until they are directed to some recreation or voluntary activity. The question of who should be responsible for finding something for these individuals to do arises. Others will take initiative and find activities for themselves. A bright side to the problem of enforced leisure is discovery by large numbers of people of talents that they had not previously recognized. But most people will probably fall between these extremes. Individuals may have to make the effort, but various programs and activities must be available to them. Increased education of retired workers will not only enable them to sharpen their skills and remain abreast of the times, but also has a value of its own in maintaining mental alertness and emotional stability.

A major problem is necessary reassessment by society of its attitudes toward work and leisure. American society places strong cultural emphasis on personal initiative and productive activity, a heritage from the Protestant Ethic of the colonial settlers. As achievement and financial success produce prestige, we tend to concentrate our efforts on material goals and to lose sight of other purposes in life. Hobbies, sports, reading, and the arts are often underrated or neglected. If a man takes any time from his career for hobbies, recreation, or other personal pleasures, he is regarded as shirking his duties. Although this strong cultural emphasis on disciplined work is gradually shifting, it is moving toward other patterns of achievement and success rather than toward assigning greater value to pleasurable activities.

More stress is being placed on activities by the elderly through which one can serve others or obtain financial rewards, for example, volunteer work or capitalizing on hobbies. Time is often regarded as a more precious commodity than money by the retired person, for he has less of it than does the younger person. Consequently he views it in practical terms. Maurice C. Linden classifies leisure activities of the aging, describes the dynamics involved, and recommends ways to prepare for leisure.[4] His article offers a new perspective on productive leisure, based on recognition of a wide range of motivations, limitations, and resources.

Adults need play, although many do not think so. We have all heard the busy executive proclaim, "my work is my recreation." Work and play are complementary pursuits, however. If they get out of balance, the individual may suffer depression and anxiety. The mature individual must have interests in work, recreation, his community and other people. He must reap satisfactions not only from his job but from his free time as well. The younger a man is, the more ambitious and concentrated on work he is expected to be, yet during this period he could spend time with his children, guiding them and serving as a role model. The older man, having achieved most of his career goals, can concentrate less on work and become more involved in community affairs.

Many employers are coming to recognize that leisure activities can affect job performance; they know that the person who has outside activities is likely to be a much more efficient employee. Some employers provide leisure activities and recreational facilities for their workers at company expense, others recognize the need but make no provision for it, and still others make only occasional haphazard attempts at sponsoring activities but are unsuccessful. The necessary element in any successful program is workers' interest. If they are motivated, they can be helped to make productive use of leisure time, regardless of budget considerations. The range of possibilities extends from discussion groups to team sports like softball and bowling.

An important aspect of company-sponsored leisure activities is social contact, getting to know fellow employees better, which can stimulate interest in the job, open channels of communication, and aid in future planning of employee needs, vacations, complaints, suggestions and company policy. Workers produce better if they believe that their individual attributes are recognized and appreciated—before presentation of the traditional gold watch after thirty years of faithful service. When a person learns more about a colleague at a retirement dinner or a funeral than he did throughout his working years, it seems clear that communication could be improved.

Retirement Problems and Some Solutions

For many years it was common to see elderly people working at jobs with low physical demands. Although they by no means had a monopoly on this kind of job, they were usually paid so little that competition from younger workers was not great. One job formerly in this category was that of elevator operator. With the advent of automatic elevators, older people suffered a considerable employment setback. Most new buildings have automatic elevators, and many older buildings have converted to them. This problem is but one example of how automation has forced leisure on some of the elderly—by causing loss of jobs.

Such a situation places a burden on industry to use the older worker productively, and on the older worker to meet industrial demands. If there is no place for the older worker in industry, he will become economically dependent on those people who are employed in the industry that treats him as expendable. Instead of a potential asset he becomes an economic liability. As an example, consider the concomitant raise in pensions that often occurs with a negotiated raise in salaries and wages. If the pensioned individual were employed at some task for a nominal wage his financial contribution could help sustain both the pension system and the general economy. The income of the retired person usually comes from pensions, insurance, social security, and similar programs, and it is usually fixed. Planning around such a fixed figure can be simplified in relation to regulations restricting the amount of income that can be earned. Wage adjustments could be made by employers for the elderly worker in order for him to retain eligibility for his fixed income. Under social security regulations a person could have his benefits reduced or be disqualified if his earnings were more than $1,200 per year at the present time. Social security is one of the few retirement benefit plans that may be withdrawn for reason of higher income.

Quite often a retired person is only too willing to return to work after having experienced the so-called "luxury" of doing what he pleases. A person nearing retirement more often than not plans to do the things that he did not get done on past vacations. Then he discovers that they do not take as long as he had expected. Americans are used to crowding "ten fun-packed days" into a one-week vacation. Having caught up on what he thought he has missed, the retired worker now faces a future for which he may not have planned adequately.

Planning for retirement leisure itself requires leisure. A person may have many skills that are in demand outside his own field. A tradesman, for instance, may possess a gift for dealing with people and may arrange to participate in such programs as Volunteers in Service to America (VISTA), the Peace Corps, or the Salvation Army. We shall discuss the Peace Corps and VISTA in more detail later in this chapter. To see how a retired person can fit into such an organization, we shall use the Salvation Army as an example here, for it has found the services of older citizens valuable in its work.

The Salvation Army, which was established in 1865 through the efforts of William Booth, needs commissioned officers (in full-time service), soldiers (members of local corps), and adherents (people who base their religious faith on its teachings). Members of the

Salvation Army pray in 167 languages in seventy countries and maintain more than 19,000 religious and charitable centers; the need for experienced people of retirement age will thus persist for some time. One possible deterrent to involvement in this organization is the nature of the religious commitment.

The opportunity to view one's life in retrospect comes only with age. The mature citizen with a talent can still put that talent to work. A word of advice to anyone, and especially to an older American, in search of a useful leisure pursuit: Volunteer! Almost all nonprofit organizations have use for volunteers.

Various organizations provide on-the-job training for volunteers, with the added incentive of possible promotion to more challenging jobs. The financial risk involved in using older workers is not paramount in nonprofit organizations and thus they unhesitatingly offer the kinds of programs that industry should offer: training for immediate tasks, orientation to higher-level tasks, retraining, continuing instruction reflecting change, and assessment of potential and performance regardless of age.

One of the most significant factors in the leisure of the elderly is health. The natural process of aging brings with it functional troubles in the vital organs and decline in the body's ability to repair itself. Malnutrition is also common among older people because of meager income, ignorance, or poor eating habits.

National concern about the health of the aged was aroused when it was found that a great many people were in dire circumstances despite the most careful planning. As medical costs have grown disproportionately to retired people's incomes, many have depleted their financial reserves. Recognition of this problem was voiced by President Lyndon B. Johnson: "No longer will illness crush and destroy the savings they have so carefully put away over a lifetime so that they might enjoy dignity in their later years." [5] Largely thanks to Medicare, the elderly can now plan their leisure without fear of financial ruin. The older person wants to maintain his self-respect and to feel that he is still making a contribution to society, a desire expressed rather vividly in the motto of the American Association of Retired Persons (A.A.R.P.): "To serve and not be served."

Two other expressions of national concern for older indigent Americans are the food-stamp and commodity-distribution programs. Food stamps redeemable at grocery stores, as well as some surplus commodities, have long been available to elderly people with low incomes. In addition to supplementing the food budget, they make nutritional foods more readily available.

One problem that confronts many elderly people is their physical inability to take advantage of such programs. If a person is living alone and is unable to leave the house, he often cannot avail himself of these opportunities unless some volunteer organization assists him. The "Meals on Wheels" program helps such people in many communities. This program makes at least one balanced meal available daily. For a nominal fee a specially equipped truck delivers meals to the homes of people who are unable to prepare their own meals.

Even though the science of medicine has helped to extend life expectancy, maintaining good health in old age is difficult. As noted in the President's Report on Physical Fitness, maintaining health in today's society, when many jobs are of a sedentary nature, has become a national problem for all ages.[6] Medical advances that prolong life also mean additional health problems connected with age, although there are some indications that many of the retired individual's health problems are psychosomatic in origin. When a person has no mental challenges, his brain begins to "rust." As mental agility decreases, so does physical health, for without mental alertness, the body loses its resilience.

The problems of aging affect not only older people themselves but the entire society as well. As more people live longer and possibly retire earlier, the balance of industrial input and output will become lopsided. If the situation develops to a point at which more people are retired from the labor force than are gainfully employed in it, a crisis will develop. Productive time, whether at work or at leisure, will have to be found for most people. The types of activities in which the elderly can be productive remain problematic. Some people advocate that employment be open to all and that hiring be determined by ability with no attention to age, but this suggestion does not entirely solve the problem because there are already too few jobs available and automation may reduce them proportionally even further. If additional employment were to be found for older workers at the present level of economic activity, it could only be at the expense of other groups. At present such a scheme is therefore impractical, even though it is recognized that many retired people possess the necessary qualifications for continued employment.

The arbitrary retirement age of sixty-five, which has been widely adopted, often deprives business concerns of the services of a qualified individual who cannot adequately be replaced. The disadvantages to the worker who is retired involuntarily are, as we have already shown, greater.

Another suggestion is that retired people should become more involved in voluntary service to the community. This suggestion has a certain merit and, as we shall see, has received national attention. The Federal government in particular has taken an active interest in the problems of aging.

Age per se is not a barrier to employment with the Federal government. All types and levels of jobs are open to older people. Nondiscrimination in Federal employment is fully supported by both legislative policy and personnel practice. The Federal Employment Act of 1946 did much to eliminate age as a barrier to employment.

For many years the number of retired people in the population was relatively small. Because of the growth of our aged population thanks to medical advances, however, society has become more aware of its needs. There is concern not only about employment but about other activities as well. Change will come about as older Americans speak out in their own behalf and as other groups take an interest in problems of the aged.

Historically, society looked upon the retired father as the "patriarch" of his family and community. He was expected to relax after a life of hard work and to pass on his experience and wisdom to guide the destinies of the upcoming generations. This patriarch of the past remained "on the job" as long as he was physically and emotionally able. But there is little place for the patriarch in the society of today.

Often the retired individual has nothing to do. As this problem develops, society attempts to find a panacea, one that will require the least effort and expense. Related to this apathy is the thinking of many workers who do not understand the problems of retirement. Those who remain on the job usually envy those who are retiring their freedom from work responsibilities. There is even less understanding of the limitations that age itself imposes.

Immediately upon retirement workers usually immerse themselves in recreation. Some people travel frantically; others play until play becomes work. Many then lapse into idleness, for life has ceased to have meaning for them. Retired couples often reach a point where they have seen so much of each other that they exhaust channels of communication other than quarreling. The overriding reason for unrest among "senior citizens" is not lack of health or money but the absence of purposeful activity.

At the present time there is no model plan for living after retirement. There are three characteristic sets of conflicting feelings common among older people that should be considered in any attempt to develop such a model plan: success and failure, novelty and monotony, and harmony and disharmony (reflected in values and attitudes). An individual may have been a success at work but a failure in retirement. If his organized routine of past years is not satisfactorily replaced, he will be adrift in strange surroundings. It is also possible that a man can be successful in retirement even though he was quite unhappy during his working years. But he does not present a problem and is therefore not considered in this discussion.

Generally both industry and workers plan for the use of leisure time. State and national organizations are trying to involve the more than 19 million people over sixty-five planning for the future. The National Retired Teachers Association (N.R.T.A.), the President's Council on Aging, the A.A.R.P., and the senior citizens' centers throughout the country are examples of such organizations.

The experience gained in a long life is increasingly being used. Older people can and do win recognition through community service. Many success stories have been written about people who began new careers in their later years. Seven Presidents were elected near "retirement" age, and another twenty-two were inaugurated after they had passed fifty.

"To retire" has been defined as "to withdraw, retreat, go away." This definition does not apply here, for efforts by employers, communities, and older citizens themselves are directed toward something more than "dropping out." Older people want, on the contrary, to "drop in." Many people have the creative ability to continue being active for many years after their enforced retirement, and they engage in many activities, religious, civic, fraternal, and even business.

In many communities there are "retirement villages" for people who can afford the luxuries offered. An elderly couple with enough income can live in a contemporary home without the worry of lawn upkeep, trash disposal, or snow removal. Some establishments provide resident medical staffs, recreation directors and gatekeepers, the latter protecting against bothersome peddlers and unwanted visitors.

The Administration on Aging

The Administration on Aging (A.O.A.) was established within the U.S. Department of Health, Education and Welfare to coordinate efforts relating to problems of older people. Its scope includes public and private agencies working primarily with the aged, as well as organizations in any way involved with the aged, for example, universities and other institutions interested in developing new programs and collecting and publishing relevant data. Consultation is available at A.O.A.'s nine regional offices on any program dealing with aging. Grants are given to strengthen existing programs or to help initiate new ones.

This list, excerpted from the Older Americans Act (Title I) describes the objectives of the A.O.A.:

1. An adequate retirement income, in accordance with the general American standard of living.
2. The best possible physical and mental health that science can make available, regardless of patients' economic status.
3. Suitable housing, designed and located with an eye to the special needs of the elderly, at costs within their means.
4. Services concerned with preservation and restoration of functioning for those people who require institutional care.
5. Opportunities for employment without discrimination because of age.
6. Retirement with health, honor, and dignity after years of contributing to the economy.
7. Pursuit of meaningful activities within the widest range of civic, cultural, and recreational opportunities.
8. Efficient community services that provide social assistance in a coordinated manner and are readily accessible.
9. Immediate application of new research knowledge to sustain and improve health and happiness.
10. Autonomy and free exercise of individual initiative in planning and managing one's own life.

Some avenues open to older Americans who wish to serve both themselves and others will be discussed at this point. Whether just to keep busy or to earn needed income, older people do attempt to return to the labor market. The U.S. Department of Labor, the Office of Economic Opportunity (O.E.O.), the U.S. Department of Health, Education and Welfare, the Civil Service Commission, and the Small Business Administration are all interested in developing employment opportunities for them.

Peace Corps

The Peace Corps, which was established in September 1961 by President John F. Kennedy, has taken advantage of older Americans' skills in its attempt to promote world peace and friendship. On August 30, 1962, President Kennedy acknowledged the efforts of twelve volunteer teacher trainers between the ages of sixty and seventy-six who were on their way then to serve in a number of foreign countries.

Several programs for the elderly have also been developed within the O.E.O., and a few of them will be discussed here.

Foster Grandparents

Tender loving care is needed by people of all ages, especially children. Children who are neglected, deprived, mentally retarded, or sick are more in need of such care than are others. Under this program older men and women have been recruited and trained for such tasks since 1965. Its original intent, announced by the White House on August 28, 1965, was to eventually offer employment to 5.5 million people over sixty-five at an average wage of $1.85 an hour. Because of its immediate acceptance by the elderly it was placed under the administrative supervision of the Community Action Program. More than sixty such projects employing over 4,000 foster grandparents were in existence by 1967, benefiting more than 8,000 children. The program should continue to expand because of the need it fulfills for both the elderly and the children.

Operation REASON

Begun as a demonstration project in 1965, Operation REASON (Responding to the Elderly's Abilities and Sickness Otherwise Neglected) is designed to help people over sixty who want to work and are physically able to do so. It also assists the chronically ill elderly person in acquainting himself with appropriate health and social services in his community. The success of the program has been such that it will be moved from the temporary demonstration project status to a direct community action service with permanent staff and budget.

Project Green Thumb

Project Green Thumb, initiated in Minnesota, New Jersey, Arkansas, and Oregon, aims at community beautification. Three hundred older men with farming backgrounds were originally selected to work with highway departments, park commissions, and soil-conservation districts. Six states have now joined in this project, and others want to participate but are hampered by budget restrictions.

Medicare Alert

This program, designed to inform elderly people about new benefits available to them under the 1965 Social Security amendments, was rushed into existence in February 1966. Before the registration deadline on May 31, 1966, more than 14,000 older people had notified more than 4 million persons of their rights to participate in Medicare. Incidentally, it was because of this crash program that many inequities and austere circumstances of the elderly were uncovered and through which remedial programs were initiated.

Project FIND

Project FIND (Friendless, Isolated, Needy, Disabled) was founded on March 8, 1967, with $1,251,580 granted through the National Council on Aging to assist older people to participate in housing, health, employment, financing, nutrition, and recreation services. Intensive two-week training is offered locally, and the number of those who complete the course has been high.

VISTA

Volunteers in Service to America (VISTA), the domestic counterpart to the Peace Corps, has made special efforts to recruit older Americans. After a four- to six-week training period, volunteers spend a year in slums, migrant work camps, Indian reservations, or wherever in the United States their services are requested. Requests for volunteers have come from such sources as the Kentucky Department of Corrections, which needed tutors for inmates awaiting release, and a Minnesota nursing home, which requested volunteers to work with elderly mental patients.[7]

Volunteers work directly with the "disadvantaged" in their own communities. They receive no pay except a subsistence allowance plus $50 a month paid all at once at time of termination. They help to provide hope, dignity, skills, and knowledge from their own funds of experience, in order to help people rise from the depths of poverty.

VISTA has no minimum educational requirements, and couples can serve if both are eligible. Anyone eighteen years of age or older may apply, but for the retired person VISTA offers a special opportunity to make a contribution to the younger generation. This work can prove rewarding and inspiring to any older individual who seeks to recapture his sense of usefulness and self-confidence.

SCORE

Initiated by the Small Business Administration, the Service Corps of Retired Executives (SCORE) meets two important needs: It keeps retired executives busy after retirement, and it gives small business-men expert counseling on marketing, management, and business meth-ods. Here is another demonstration of wise use of leisure time by older people.

Politics

The older American has retired from a work-oriented society in which status and prestige are attached to the job holder. Unless he remains active, it becomes difficult after a short time for him to discuss the business world in current terms. An interest in current events keeps the older American in contact with what is going on around him and helps him to dwell less on his past life. One area in which retired people often find personal satisfaction is politics. If this group of more than 19 million voted as a bloc, its political strength would be felt at all levels. An interest in politics carries with it the responsibility for keeping informed about what is happening in all areas of society.

The Future

All too often the United States postpones attacks on its problems until a crisis occurs. Then there is a frantic effort to mobilize resources to combat the problem: This complacency is especially characteristic of both the physical sciences and applied social science. National concern over the moon race appears to be as great as that over civil rights. Both were precipitated by crises, even though the nation had long been aware of the conditions leading up to the crises. The Russian launching of *Sputnik* on October 4, 1957, and the Watts riot in Los Angeles in 1967 are specific examples of such crises.

It is to be hoped that the problems of leisure will receive enough attention to avert a major crisis. Many industries have initiated forms of retirement counseling and have experimented with gradual retirement, which involves cutting down the work week gradually so that the employee can make the transition through a series of adjustments in his routine.

Future planning for constructive use of leisure will involve many existing institutions and perhaps entail the creation of others. For example, in April 1962 the Bureau of Outdoor Recreation was created within the Department of Interior to coordinate about twenty existing agencies dealing with outdoor recreation. It was one step in the direction of overall coordination of programs connected with leisure. An all-encompassing bureau with the word "leisure" in its title could offer consultation, financial assistance, new programs, and technical assistance to existing programs.

Educational institutions will continue to initiate and develop leisure programs. Secondary schools will make their equipment and space more readily available. Institutions of higher learning will become more involved in research on leisure time and will develop curriculum materials for community programs. People will eventually have the opportunity to prepare for retirement as they now prepare for professions. Schools will administer aptitude tests in leisure activities and will offer instruction to those with newly discovered talents, thus enabling people to capitalize on their skills and relieving the problems of boredom and inactivity among retired citizens.

Contributions to the welfare of older people will be made by a variety of professions, including architecture. Many of the undesirable features of cities will be eliminated, and architects will be instrumental in this improvement. There are already many examples of homes designed for older people, ranging from single-dwelling units to nursing homes and self-contained apartment cities, that include features attractive to older people, like ramps instead of steps, hand rails, good lighting, draft-free heating, and specially designed furniture. In the planned communities of the future such features as swimming pools, clubhouses, and golf courses will be available on a shared basis.

Religious organizations will expand their services to older members and incorporate activities, conceivably ranging from square dancing to literary-discussion groups, into programs that coincide with the philosophy of each particular church.

We can expect a quickening pace in the promotion through the mass media of glamorous vacations, elegant dining, recreation and sporting equipment, and mechanized leisure activities. It will be rare to hear the almost extinct pleasure of idleness exalted by anyone other than the poet or the social dropout.

NOTES

1. Marion Clawson, *Statistics on Outdoor Recreation* (Washington, D.C.: Government Printing Office, 1958), pp. 25–27. A prolific writer on outdoor recreation, government land, and natural resources presents valuable information for planning leisure activities.
2. *Salt Lake Tribune*, July 6, 1967, p. 6C.
3. Gertrude Bancroft, "Multiple Job Holders in December, 1959," *Monthly Labor Review*, 83, No. 10 (October 1960), pp. 97–121.
4. Maurice C. Linden, "Preparation for the Leisure of Later Maturity," in Wilma Donahue, Woodrow W. Hunter, Dorothy H. Coons, and Helen K. Maurice, eds., *Free Time* (Ann Arbor: University of Michigan Press, 1958), pp. 65–82. Report of the University of Michigan Tenth Anniversary Conference on Aging. It presents challenges to discovery and use of leisure time in late maturity.
5. *Health Education and Welfare Indicators*, August 1965, p. 2. Comments made by President Lyndon B. Johnson, on the occasion of signing the 1965 Social Security amendments.
6. President's Council on Physical Fitness, *Four Years for Fitness—1961–65* (Washington, D.C.: Government Printing Office, 1965).
7. Office of Economic Opportunity, *The First Step on a Long Journey* (Washington, D.C.: Government Printing Office, April 1956).

SUGGESTED READINGS

Harrington, Janette T. *Who Cares?* New York: Friendship, 1962.
    A project guidebook for church work with elderly people.
Koller, Marvin R. *Social Gerontology*. New York: Random House, 1968.
    This book comprises a "distillation" (the author's term) of much current thinking on the impact of the aging process on society.

Chapter IX

EVOLUTION OF

CORRECTIONAL PHILOSOPHY

IN THE UNITED STATES

The correctional philosophy of the United
States, as revealed in the evolution of both
state and Federal prison systems,
is reviewed.

The loss of liberty is the most common form of punishment for law breaking today. Much has happened in the history of penology (from the Latin *poena,* "punishment") to bring us to the present rehabilitative emphasis in treatment of offenders. By the time that rehabilitation of the offender was first considered, almost every other approach had been exhausted.

As long ago as 1669, sixty-eight years after the passage of the English Poor Law, houses of correction were being established in Europe that were to affect English and American correctional philosophy in the nineteenth and twentieth centuries. For example, London's Bridewell (a prison founded in 1557) housed minor offenders, family deserters, prostitutes, children, and vagrants together, providing them hard work as an important part of their sentences. This last element was a throwback to correctional philosophy of the fourteenth century, when servitude in the galleys had been the most common punishment for offenders. Our present concept of "hard labor" had its roots there and has been an integral part of American correctional philosophy, even to the exclusion of treatment, which appeared much later in our history. Although the hard-labor concept was very popular, there were many other devices for dealing with offenders. Physical torture, branding, maiming, the pillory, and deportation to prison colonies were common. Many of these earlier types of correction still form integral parts of our modern system. For example, the warden of the state prison at Wilmington, Delaware, administered floggings to four inmates in 1949, and several states still have in their statutes provision for use of the lash to enforce institutional disciplines.

Since before the time of Christ, attempts to deal with violators of the law sought to isolate them from the rest of the society: through public announcements, brands, public floggings, the pillory, banishment, or execution. These devices served to warn other citizens of the presence of the offender. One present-day version of society forcing the criminal to be accountable for his actions is the notion of restitution, restoration to the injured party of stolen or damaged property or replacement either directly or through cash payment. Historically when such restitution was not possible it was considered equitable to "take it out of his hide" or to resort to some other form of corporal punishment.

The concept of rehabilitation of offenders was not firmly established until punishment had been tried in many refined forms. People were more interested in extracting their "pound of flesh" than they were in developing the potential strengths of an offender. In fact sometimes the victims of theft thought that the branding (literally) of thieves was more important than recovering their own property.

The idea of branding has undergone an interesting evolution as different meanings have been attached to it by society. A refinement was introduced in the early American Colonies: Convicted offenders were required to wear cloth badges for the duration of their sentences. This type of public marking was used by the Nazis in Germany during their persecution of the Jews; arm bands had to be worn by those designated as Jewish. Such signs served to identify Jews as "criminals," to be avoided by society, even though there was no legal basis for such definition.

The Growth of Prisons

Prisons as we know them did not exist in Europe for many years because of the problems associated with construction and maintenance of such facilities. Only recently has any serious attention been given to trying to "correct" criminals. Prisons before the eighteenth century simply detained people who were awaiting trial or debtors until they could pay their debts. As late as 1951 there were still twelve states in the United States with laws that made it possible to imprison a debtor and to hold him until his debt was paid.

Two factors in particular made the trend toward incarceration practical. The first was use of the manpower of the prisoners in the financial interest of the state or powerful individuals. This factor was particularly important early in the Industrial Revolution, when labor was badly needed. Second, members of the elite occasionally became victims of the system; as a result of reform pressures from their families and friends, physical mutilations were replaced by periods of forced servitude.

Many people were held because of the popular attitude that a wrongdoer was responsible for his plight and should suffer the consequences, regardless of how severe they may have been or of any extenuating circumstances. This is known as retribution, recompense or revenge. Scholars of the day rejected this simplistic view [1] and advanced the notion of repentance as a "higher idea" than that of revenge, but they still considered an offender's recognition of the adverse consequences of his actions a prerequisite to his repentance.[2] Two major problems are associated with this philosophy, however: the difficulty in deciding how long and in precisely what way an offender should "repent" and the overcrowding of prisons that soon developed.

It became obvious after a short while that the jails and houses of correction were not adequate to provide for long-term offenders. For these "hardened" criminals, solitary confinement was initiated as a substitute for costly supervised work programs. John Howard, who was instrumental in the building of the Wymondham jail in Norfolk, England, in 1784, is generally credited with helping to implement this notion. In his travels to Italy, he had been impressed with an institution in Rome, the Ospizio (Hospice) di S. Michele, which had been practicing the solitary confinement and segregation of boys for many years. This institution had been founded by Pope Clement XI in 1703 for the correction of youths. Isolation was an advanced concept at that time. Each boy had a private room and engaged in work projects during the day. At a time when capital punishment was common in children's cases Howard's foresight was amazing.

Wymondham jail, founded upon this Italian model, was in turn the model upon which the Pennsylvania correction system was developed. The two most important elements of the Pennsylvania system, the first prison in America, were solitude and silence. Howard's book exposing prison conditions of the mid-1700s [3] probably set the stage for prison inspection, discussed later in this chapter. His appeal was an emotional one, laden with biblical quotations, which were popular at the time.

In 1786, primarily at the instigation of the Quakers, application of capital punishment in Pennsylvania, which had previously been used widely and often injudiciously, was restricted to treason, murder, arson, and rape. Four years later, in 1790, the Walnut Street prison in Philadelphia instituted a change in correctional philosophy that influenced other countries with similar problems. It was, unmistakably, the first modern prison. The inmates, observing almost constant silence and living in solitary confinement, were able to earn small amounts of money for what were then considered reasonable working hours. Some inmates served sentences of several years without ever seeing or hearing the voice of anyone but the warden, guards, chaplain, or "official" visitors of politically dominated organizations. There was no reading material except the Bible, and no correspondence between inmates or between inmates and the community was allowed. The idea was that the inmates' entire time should be devoted to thinking about their own transgressions and eventual reformation.

Even that early the role of the prison chaplain was envisioned much as it is today. There has always been a close connection between religion and correctional philosophy. Essentially, religious bodies have favored a correctional system rather than the cruel and unreasonable corporal and capital punishment emphasized in the past. Paul W. Tappan provides a collection of articles on the influence of ecclesiastical bodies on penology and examines the role of the chaplain with precision and comprehensiveness.[4] This book provides the interested student with a complete survey of one important phase of evolving correctional philosophy in this country.

Thirty years after the Walnut Street prison had begun operation the next significant step in the evolution of correctional philosophy occurred—in the Auburn, New York, penal system. Two "advances" are associated with Auburn prison, where in 1819 inmates were first allowed to congregate for work under a rule of silence: the inside cell block (two rows of cells back to back within another building) and the electric chair.[5] The opportunity to leave the cell, although for the purpose of work and not recreation, nevertheless relieved the severe monotony of confinement.

Another major aspect of modern correctional philosophy was born in Australia, which was used by Great Britain as a penal colony. Captain Alexander Maconochie devised a system of "good" time, indeterminate sentences, and parole. "Good time" was the term used to designate the number of days an inmate could be released from prison prior to expiration of his sentence. It carried with it the obligation of causing no trouble within the institution or one would suffer the loss of days earned toward early release. Upon release the former prisoner would be free since his total sentence was considered as having been served. Under an indeterminate sentence a man could by his conduct determine his own release within upper and lower limits set by the court.

The most significant characteristic of Maconochie's system, also called the "Irish system" was the stages through which a prisoner moved during incarceration. He was first placed in solitary confinement. Later he was permitted to associate with other inmates, usually at hard labor. The final phase of his sentence was served in an atmosphere of relaxed discipline, during which time he was under the supervision of unarmed guards and was given considerable freedom in moving around designated areas. When he had successfully passed through all these stages, he was released from the institution with the stipulation that he could be returned to finish serving his sentence if he did not make a satisfactory community adjustment. This last phase closely resembles the current concept of parole, release from an institution under some form of supervision or control by proper authorities.

Prisons in the United States

As Europe has adopted and expanded on the Pennsylvania system, the United States stayed with a combination of the "Irish" and Auburn systems. Equally interesting, and of major importance, is the fact that no system has yet been able to demonstrate consistently any marked degree of rehabilitation of its inmates.

By 1926 nine states had prisons constructed and in use. In that same year Massachusetts modified its system by separating adult and juvenile offenders. An honor system that permitted some inmates to go outside prison walls for selected duties during the day existed in

Connecticut as early as 1827. In 1844 prisons and mental hospitals were cooperating in the transfer of insane prisoners to the latter for "treatment." The interrelatedness of these social-welfare institutions became more obvious as their services began to expand. First, recognition of the expertise of other disciplines and institutions had to exist. Then, a willingness to involve other people in the helping process had to be made into policy and implemented.

Several strides were made toward a more reasonable correctional philosophy with the establishment of the Elmira, New York, reformatory in 1876. At that time parole was adopted in the United States for the first time, the indeterminate sentence was instituted, and an attempt was made to move away from repressive imprisonment. By the turn of the century an evolution could be seen in the correctional philosophy of the United States; it was widespread enough to be identified as a trend. The first prison library had been initiated, a prison orchestra had been formed, an inmate school was in existence, a system of rewards for good conduct had been tried, and inmates were allowed to gather on holidays. At the same time this trend was being established, the pillory lost its popularity; it was last used in the United States in Delaware in 1905. No penal system, no matter how open it is to new principles, can be rated successful without assessment of effects on the people incarcerated.

One of the basic principles of correctional work is classification of prisoners. Although no two inmates are alike, any more than any two other people are alike, very few attempts at individualizing treatment had been made before the United States modified and improved its inherited penal system at Auburn, where prisoners were classified in three distinct categories. These categories were the forerunners of the system common in most American prisons today: the use of "maximum," "medium," and "minimum" custody.

Classification today usually is based on an inmate's history and specifies both his custody arrangement and his general treatment plan. His history includes evaluation of such factors as his age, criminal behavior, adjustment to incarceration, and family and social background. His custody arrangement is determined by the estimated risk to the prison community, the individual himself, and society. The treatment plan reflects his attitudes and motivations, the availability of various resources, personnel, and programs; and the overall philosophy of the institution. A man may be assigned to a shop making license plates in medium custody, even though he could function as an accountant under minimum custody; the latter assignment may not, however, be possible because no program or job exists in accounting. It may be that the prison cannot find a job that matches each inmate's talents. Another factor that might control his assignment is overcrowding in the minimum-security dormitory. Quite often an inmate arrives at an institution that has very little to offer him but cannot refuse him admission, transfer him to a diagnostic center or other facility, or create a program to meet his needs. Historically, convicted people have been committed to institutions without thought for a coordinated approach to rehabilitation. Although this situation still prevails, changes are taking place.

A milestone in correctional philosophy was the passage of the Federal Youth Corrections Act of 1950, which first made possible an integrated approach to sentencing, diagnosis, and treatment of offenders under twenty-two years of age. This approach avoids duplication of classification efforts, waste of manpower, and delay in implementing treatment plans. Instead of the court, the probation department and the prison work independently of each other and both compile the same data, making them able to join forces for a more comprehensive study, diagnosis and treatment of the youthful offender.

When we look at our expensive institutions, each of which houses from several hundred to several thousand prisoners at a time, and examine the backgrounds of their inmates, we find that more than half the latter have been in prison before. This discovery is a rather strong indictment of the current system. Any suggested change that promises potential solutions is worthy of consideration.

The most that can be said of various prison systems up to this time is that nothing has proved consistently successful. In Europe, in the past, rapists were castrated, perjurers' tongues were cut out, and thieves' hands were chopped off. These extreme measures did not prove to be effective deterrents. In this country attempts at solving the crime problem have included witch burning, the Ku Klux Klan, vigilante groups, and death penalties often in the form of lynching. Having experienced both legal and extralegal methods of solving the crime problem we continue to build bigger but not always better prisons.

The construction of new facilities has not been the solution. There is one aspect of the problem in particular that requires explanation: Increased reliance on probation, retention in the community under supervision, especially of first offenders, means that prisons are increasingly populated with repeat offenders, many of whom have failed to adjust on probation. It is among this group that rehabilitation efforts are least likely to succeed.

The success or failure of a program for rehabilitation of adult offenders would have to be determined according to the following five standards:

1. Motivation of the inmate to participate and succeed in the program.
2. Social and economic rehabilitation of inmates.
3. Capabilities and limitations of the prison staff.
4. The public's readiness to accept "rehabilitated" convicts.
5. The contributions of other social-welfare institutions.

Retribution and vengeance are giving way to rehabilitation for economic if no other reasons. Rather than having to pay for the care of an inmate, the state would prefer that he be gainfully employed and supporting himself and his family.

Societies have punished themselves ultimately by not recognizing this economic fact. The same nonsensical approach in industry would be catastrophic. If, for instance, a machine on the assembly line were malfunctioning because of lack of lubrication, the engineers would immediately apply oil or grease to the appropriate points. If the lubrication did not correct the situation, other solutions would be attempted until assembly-line production could be resumed.

Using a mechanistic analogy, society does not consider adult offenders with the same logic as it does machines. A piece of equipment is not retired until it is beyond repair and all attempts at restoration have failed. It would be nonsensical to remove, at considerable cost in time, effort, wages, and production, a malfunctioning part for which a repair exists. Yet, instead of applying corrective treatment to the malfunctioning individual, we remove him from the production line, so to speak. But a new idea seems to be growing—that of giving malfunctioning individuals opportunities to become assets to society instead of liabilities, and old penal solutions are beginning to give way to this more logical approach.

Vestiges of our earlier "solutions" remain with us, though perhaps in disguised forms. Sentence to prison today is *as* punishment not *for* punishment. Such punishment has been suspect for years because it is applied only to the offender who is caught, often by people whose own offenses, like cheating on income-tax reports, have gone undetected or unpunished. It is also suspect for a more subtle reason: Offenses have often been of a kind—like murder—that have tempted others in society as well. Even though most people repress urges to succumb to temptation, they may have a certain hidden admiration for some offenders. This accounts in part, we feel, for the demand for severe punishment when the visible manifestation of similar impulses in others is made public.

During the period of incarceration offenders are separated from family, members of the opposite sex, friends, and society in general, yet they are expected to make good "adjustments" before they can return to these contacts. This very separation from other people is the basis for many inmates' complaints and discontent, whether in institutions for men or for women. It is not too difficult to comprehend that inmates develop much bitterness toward the society that punishes them. Regardless of the amount of time served before they have "repaid their debt to society," it is perceived as "unnecessary" by the inmate who often blames his incarceration on his bad luck in getting caught.

The average length of stay in prison in the United States is slightly less than two years, which includes sentences served for all felonies and in some cases certain misdemeanors. A person sentenced to life is usually released in twenty years. In either case the inmate is going to return to the community only *after* being punished. Some inmates "waste" this interval, whereas others put it to use. Some plan their next "jobs" whereas others "mark time" until their releases. A more prevalent attitude is the desire to accomplish something even during imprisonment: to complete high school, learn a trade, or produce economically for the state. Those inmates who are dangerous or totally unwilling to make any effort toward better adjustment to society represent, in our opinion, less than one-fourth of the total inmate population. For them, it seems, our society has so far failed to produce rewards strong enough to induce desired change.

Three institutions, representing three different philosophies, have taken interesting steps toward producing such change: The Federal prison at Seagoville, Texas, the Chino facility within the California prison system, and the maximum-security block of the Utah state prison. Unlike Seagoville and Chino, which allow inmates relative amounts of freedom, Utah has a prison within a prison for its maximum-security inmates. In all three institutions civilian clothes are worn in an attempt to keep reminders of prison at a minimum. Inmates at Chino are made aware of the ease of escape, but at the same time are notified that they will be returned from escape and sent to another institution. Educational-vocational programs are available and visiting with families may be conducted picnic style in areas resembling municipal parks. The current program in Utah is remarkable in that in only a few short months many long-standing prison traditions have been replaced by modern and behaviorally sounder techniques. For example, the system of altering a prisoner's classification from maximum-security to freer status has been put largely in the hands of the inmate. He can seek self-improvement or, as their jargon aptly describes, "vegetate." He can put forth efforts to earn points and move to a less confining classification, remain where he is, or return to solitary confinement. A point system based on operant conditioning is employed: Appropriate behavior is elicited through both positive and negative reinforcements. From a treatment point of view, one of the primary steps toward correction is to bring the offender to awareness of his responsibility for his own overt behavior, be it appropriate or not. Older systems have not been successful in this task because they have been inflexible in the use of time as a reinforcement. For example, the inmate now often faces the prospect of serving at least one year before he is eligible for parole or release. Equally disheartening to the inmate is a wait of from four months to a year before he is eligible for consideration by the classification committee for a change in his custody arrangement. The system initiated by David Franchina at the Utah state prison has eliminated this problem as much as possible, and the time spent in maximum security and, in some instances, in prison itself is determined entirely according to the prisoner's behavior. Custody and treatment personnel complete evaluation forms on each inmate weekly. All inmates are rated on scales of from one to twenty points in the first three areas, and of from one to forty points in the fourth area:

1. Personal appearance and housekeeping skills.
2. Relationships with other "residents."
3. Relationships with staff and prison personnel.
4. Working toward self-betterment, including improving attitudes, educational planning and family and release concerns.

Space is provided on the form for written comments from the prison staff, which have revealed more specifically the kinds of behavior that require modification.

The inmates must work through four progressive levels of custody, each requiring a higher number of points to gain entrance. An inmate *must* advance to and successfully earn points in all four levels of custody before he can be returned to the main population.

The Franchina system has many advantages, but among the most important are, first, acting on the assumption that the inmate is in control of himself and his behavior makes him keenly aware of the relationship between his behavior and its consequences. Second, all prison personnel become involved in the treatment program of each inmate and must become acquainted with him on more than a superficial level. Third, the inmate who feels in control of his own future learns how to earn the privileges that he desires.

It is important to recognize that some states have not yet advanced to the point at which more progressive systems began. For example, the sweat box (a small metal cage with little or no ventilation) and similar instruments are still used in some states. Several hours in the sweat box at 100-degree temperatures can bring the most recalcitrant inmate to terms with his jailers.

In 1873 Indiana became the first state to segregate men and women in separate facilities. This innovation did not receive widespread national acceptance until after 1910. Some prisons have simultaneously housed first and repeated offenders, the old and the young, males and females, the feeble-minded, the mentally ill, alcoholics, drug addicts, and sex offenders. Although it is impossible to define mutual effects precisely, it stands to reason that interaction in such populations would not be generally beneficial.

Incarceration is only one phase of correctional philosophy in the United States. In many instances statutes do not specify rehabilitation. The laws clearly define the function of prisons as to detain inmates under sentence for various lengths of time. When programs aimed at rehabilitation are initiated, they must be administered so as not to conflict with the statutes.

Official organs like boards of Correction implement programs in the facilities under their jurisdiction. These facilities deserve mention in greater detail. There are more than 400 facilities for adult felons in the United States. Twenty-five of them are more than 100 years old, which makes it difficult to create atmospheres conducive to inmate freedom of expression, for the older prisons are characterized by high walls and escape-proof cages for large numbers of men. The cost of abandoning old facilities and constructing new ones is prohibitive. As a result, rehabilitation programs must be geared to physical plants in which the basic intent of the statute is already being met. Although incarceration is only one phase of correctional philosophy, it is nevertheless the cornerstone from which other phases develop.

An "evolution" in American correctional philosophy is recognizable in comparisons of what happens to inmates today and what happened before. In Mississippi, some married convicts are now allowed conjugal visits with their wives. Adequate research is not available to assess the value of this privilege as an adjunct to rehabilitation. Harry E. Barnes and Negley K. Teeters suggest that temporary home visits will be acceptable long before conjugal or sexual visits ever gain any degree of regularity.[6]

Most state prisoners receive no usable vocational training. The principle reason is that private enterprise and labor unions have sought laws preventing competition from inmate labor. As a result, both inmates and administration look upon many work projects as "busy work," which does not offer the satisfaction of accomplishment and fails to teach the value of work as an end in itself. Many inmates have already had poor work histories before incarceration and cannot benefit from further idleness.

Significant strides toward more productive use of inmates' time have been made through work-release programs, in which inmates engage in useful occupations outside prison but return at night or whenever the demands of the job dictate. This does not represent unfair competition on the labor market because the inmate is required to assume responsibilities such as taxes, union dues and other obligations incurred in working and becoming a self-sustaining individual. North Carolina has pioneered work-release schemes in which 12,000 inmates have earned $10 million in less than ten years, working in occupations as diverse as court reporting and truck mechanics. They have partially supported their families and paid for their prison keep as well.

There are several apparent inconsistencies in the goals of prisons themselves. First, they are artificial environments based on enforced conformity to many rules and regulations. Second, they seek to be "models" for those preparing to live in society. Yet the ability of the prisoner to adhere to the prison rules is the determining factor in his eventual release and the distorted social environment of a prison bears little resemblance to the outside world. Third, the prison accepts only those who are "eligible," that is, have committed offenses, regardless of the need for further treatment, and readmission to prison for continued consultation and treatment is denied. Parole is at present the only institutional recognition of the problems that a released prisoner may face in his adjustment to society after release from prison and of the fact that further treatment might help to prevent further criminal acts. As long as the prison is operated only for involuntary inmates, there can be no claim that it is basically a treatment facility. No one becomes alarmed when a patient who has been placed on a diet seeks out his physician before the final results have been accomplished, but this avenue is denied to an "ex-convict," or, in the current professional term, a "former offender." The idea of providing such help is in keeping with preventive medicine and could logically be labeled "preventive criminality." Fourth, discipline is "artificial" and inconsistent, especially in comparison to that found in other institutions. Some prisons are very severe, and others are extremely lax in their discipline. As recently as 1939 corporal punishment was practiced in twenty-six states; it included floggings, stringing men up by their wrists, electric shock, sweat boxes, beatings with canes or with clenched fists, and handcuffing to stationary objects.

In the United States one of the most distressing practices is use of the chain gang in southern states. Historically, inmates had been used in the North for work in various aspects of manufacturing. The South, which derived most of its revenue from agriculture, used inmates largely in farming, as well as in road building and construction work, which entailed being in the open, away from walls and fences. Chains were used to insure against escape. Inmates were usually shackled together by leg irons; or chains about two feet long were attached to irons on each of their legs to prevent them from running. Much public attention has been given to the cruel and inhumane treatment of prisoners in chain gangs, and as recently as June 1968, the American public was made aware of mistreatment of prisoners in Arkansas involving something more inhumane than chain gangs.

Winthrop Rockefeller was elected Governor of Arkansas in 1966 on a platform including "prison reform." Arkansas did not have a prison as such, complete with buildings, walls, gun towers and cell blocks and in February 1967 Rockefeller appointed Thomas O. Murton superintendent of the Arkansas state prison farms at Cummins and Tucker. In December Murton, who had a record of successful prison reform in Alaska, was appointed the first superintendent of prisons for the state.

Just after this appointment a state-police report of deplorable conditions on the prison farms was released. Murton declared that the Arkansas system was the worst in the twentieth century. Prison records showed that the outcomes of 213 escape attempts since 1900 had never been noted. Seventy of 254 deaths since 1936 had resulted from violence, and foul play was suspected in many others.

A grand jury was called to investigate the discovery of several skeletons by inmates digging a foundation for a new building. The jury ruled that the site was that of an old graveyard and branded Murton a publicity seeker. Its recommendation that prison authorities revive the use of the strap to replace isolation cells was perhaps the most revealing: Its rationalization was that long periods of isolation would permanently damage the minds of the inmates.

Walter Rugaber, reported in *The New York Times*, March 1968, revealed some other abuses known to have taken place in Arkansas. After mentioning such "standards" as vicious kicking by guards and thrusting needles under prisoners' fingernails, Rugaber described an instrument of torture invented by a prison physician. It was called the "Tucker telephone" and consisted of a crank-operated telephone with two dry-cell batteries. One lead was attached to the toe of an inmate and the other to his testicles. The current of electricity sent through his body when the crank was wound was extremely painful and often induced involuntary urination and defecation.

It was further reported that brutal killings of inmates were not rare. There was little or no attention to inmates' dignity, future, or well-being. It is difficult to comprehend the inconsistency of those who would worry about a man's sanity in solitary confinement yet would recommend corporal punishment, even to the point of specifics. Indeed it seems more like the love of primitive types of punishment mentioned earlier.

We have given a brief summary of programs, policies, and disparities in state prison systems. To arrive at an understanding of penology in the United States it is also necessary to review the growth and development of the Federal prison system.

The Federal Prison System

The Federal prison system has a history dating back to 1776, when the Continental Congress declared that persons convicted of violating Federal laws would be incarcerated in local facilities. This situation proved satisfactory, and for the next 100 years Federal prisoners were boarded out to state and local institutions; as Federal violations were confined to counterfeiting, piracy, and other crimes committed on the high seas there were few Federal convicts. All other crimes fell under state jurisdiction.

As the population increased and more acts were defined as Federal crimes the boarding system became unmanageable; the Department of Justice then began to acquire prisons of its own. After the transfer of the military prison at Fort Leavenworth, Kansas, to the Department of Justice in 1895, it was decided to scatter other prisons throughout the country. Eventually there were also Federal prisons at Atlanta, Georgia, and McNeill Island, Washington.

Females continued to be boarded out to the states until a facility for women was opened at Alderson, West Virginia, in 1927.

There were more than 12,000 prisoners in seven institutions under the jurisdiction of the Department of Justice in 1930. Half the Federal prisoners were still being boarded out to various states. The Federal Bureau of Prisons had 650 employees without benefit of civil-service status and untrained beyond on-the-job encounters. Prison supervisory personnel were political appointees unschooled in administration. They paid little attention to mandates and orders from the central office, which also had no control over the appropriations or budgets of the various institutions. Because he lacked professional staff, the Superintendent of Prisons was unable to oversee the operations of the various institutions under his jurisdiction. There were no organized plans or programs for rehabilitation of inmates of any age or sex.

The report of a congressional committee established in 1929 to study the Federal prison system was one of the first of its kind to recognize the necessity of rehabilitation, in view of the fact that the vast majority of inmates would return to the community eventually. The committee observed the congestion in both the Federal institutions and state and local facilities boarding Federal prisoners and recommended building more prisons.

President Herbert Hoover signed an act of Congress on May 14, 1930, creating the Federal Bureau of Prisons. From that point on, numerous changes were made, consistent with the philosophy of rehabilitation. Planning for an integrated system of institutions, ranging from maximum-security to "open" facilities was quickly initiated. More than 15,000 prisoners in open facilities were put to work constructing physical plants for the system. Not only did the program include building a penitentiary, a reformatory, a medical center, and facilities for short-term offenders, but it also called for the U.S. Public Health Service to furnish medical services to all institutions and brought the U.S. Probation Service under the management of the Bureau. There were eight probation officers and 4,280 probationers at that time. The administrative office of the U.S. courts assumed supervision of the Probation Service in 1940.

In spite of subsequent improvements in its organization, the Bureau did not lose sight of the two basic parts of its job: protection of the public and rehabilitation of inmates to assist them in more fully realizing their potential as useful citizens.

Early in its existence the Bureau recognized the benefits to both the individual and the community at large inherent in the probation system. Probation had not been used extensively at the time and met with much resistance, for it was looked upon as "coddling" of criminals. Law-enforcement officials regarded their jobs as incomplete until offenders were behind bars.

During the last days of Prohibition, the inmate population of Federal prisons contained kidnappers, bank robbers, and mobsters. These intractables were escape-conscious, and therefore in 1934 the Bureau acquired the island of Alcatraz in San Francisco Bay for an escape-proof maximum-security prison. It housed, however, only a small proportion of all Federal prisoners. Others were screened for classification in programs suited to their needs and assigned to appropriate prisons.

Inmate classification was pioneered on a large scale by the Bureau. It was first introduced into the Federal system in 1934, when inmates were permitted to transfer to institutions that would best serve their individual needs. Its operation mainly took the form of interdisciplinary evaluation of inmates to further their rehabilitation.

The Bureau also attempted to change the rigid routine and regimentation of the old-fashioned prison. Harsh discipline was modified in an effort to deal with inmates' attitudes, individual problems, and future planning. Group discussions, professional lectures, and inmate debate were encouraged. Casework services, counseling, therapy, and advisory services were instituted. Not all the resistance to new methods came from inmates. Many seasoned employees in the prison field were dubious about any change, and as a result it has taken the Bureau, under the directorship of two outstanding penologists, many years to win the respect it now enjoys. Both Sanford Bates and James V. Bennett, former directors, were men of foresight, courage and broad understanding. Obviously they also had vision, for none of the advances during their respective administrations was achieved without opposition.

Today, the Federal Bureau of Prisons is the most progressive system in the field of penology. To achieve such a position it had to develop within its own ranks an esprit de corps of the most dedicated kind. To those who developed the concept of career service, training seemed the most needed commodity. The guard of the past became the correctional officer of the current system. He has not carried a cane, a club, or a night stick among the prisoners since 1938. Instead, he has been instructed in the use of firearms, which are restricted mainly to the gun towers surrounding the prisons; he has been trained in procedures to deal with disorder; he has been given responsibilities in cell blocks, dining rooms, and other parts of the institution, as well as in gun towers. His training is still received mainly on the job, but he is supervised and advised of his own progress. The opportunities for, and paths of advancement are explained to him throughout his training program. In addition to continuing assessment, employees are given opportunities to expose themselves to new programs, policies, and procedures. Every applicant for the position of correctional officer is screened by the Federal Bureau of Investigation, thus eliminating people whose past behavior indicates their unsuitability for helping to rehabilitate inmates. New employees' physical and emotional functioning is assessed by competent professionals, in order to eliminate those whose health and attitudes seem inadequate for working with large numbers of frustrated, discontented, and unhappy prisoners. In the history of penology homosexuals, sadists, and mental defectives have often been employed as prison guards, and the results have been most distressing. Inmates have enough problems without adding inadequate staff to his list. The Bureau claimed in 1960 that it had more than 5,000 well-trained employees.[7]

At the end of fiscal year 1960 there were 23,228 Federal prisoners in institutions maintained by the Bureau, with relatively few being boarded out. By then the average length of stay for a Federal prisoner had increased from twenty-four months in 1930 to thirty-three months, which meant either that more prisons would have to be built, that overcrowding would become severe or—the most logical alternative— greater use of probation, parole, or both would have to be made.

An "experiment" was initiated in 1945, when a former U.S. Immigration Service facility at Seagoville, Texas, was turned over to the Bureau of Prisons. The first inmates were aged and physically handicapped prisoners and Selective Service violators from other Federal institutions. Later the courts began committing prisoners directly to Seagoville. It is a prison "without walls" and the first "halfway house," a concept that had been pioneered by religious groups assisting ex-convicts in finding employment. An important and integral part of the Seagoville program was intensive prerelease training. Through such training at Seagoville and other Federal institutions, the rate of recidivism has been cut by 15 percent or more—one of the first indications of success. It is not to be assumed, however, that prerelease training alone is responsible for such success, which also depends on effective classification, rehabilitation programs, and general institutional atmosphere, coupled with an interdisciplinary and interagency approach to aftercare or inmate problems following release.

The escape rate at Seagoville, as at most Federal prisons, is low, another indicator of success. It is noteworthy that many more unsuccessful than successful attempts are made. When escapes are evaluated, one must therefore also examine the unsuccessful attempts to gain a clear view of the situation. It is usually considered an escape when a prisoner is someplace outside the facility without authorization. Many attempts are thwarted before the escapee leaves the prison property.

In discussing general institutional atmosphere consideration must be given to the gradual change that has taken place in the living conditions to which inmates are required to adjust. From the solitude and silence to which men were formerly committed, a transition has been made to a more "social" environment. Food preparation and service, one of the areas causing the most discontent in prison, is now handled "family style" in many Federal institutions. Instead of seating men at long tables according to their cell-block designations, authorities provide tables seating four or six, and prisoners can elect where and with whom they eat. In some institutions there are tablecloths, and food is even served on china.

Arrangements for visits from friends, families and other interested persons have also changed. At Alcatraz an inmate was brought into a closely guarded room and talked with his visitor by telephone. The visitor sat on the opposite side of a wall with a double glass partition between him and the inmate. Calls could be monitored by the correctional officer on duty in the room. Visiting at Seagoville resembles a picnic in the literal sense of the word. There are tables and chairs on open lawns for picnic baskets brought by visitors. Children are encouraged to accompany other members of the family, and the inmate can be reunited with the entire group, not only his spouse, as was formerly common in other institutions. Conjugal visits, during which the wife stays overnight on the premises, have not yet been authorized within the Federal system. Mississippi is the only state that permits them at this time.

Recreation outside the cells has evolved from ten- and twenty-minute exercise periods to such activities as deep-sea fishing at Lompoc, California. An institution with an adequate budget for supervision and equipment can use recreation in inmate rehabilitation.

The need of the inmate for some activity is evidenced by the large numbers that volunteer to help in fighting forest fires, flood control, and other disasters as an alternative to pacing an eight by ten foot cell. A sense of accomplishment and of being needed result in the inmate viewing this work as a welcome diversion of his routine.

An extremely important aspect of prison life is the relationship between the inmate and the correctional officer. The officer can make prison life extremely unpleasant for an inmate, or he can assist the inmate in working out his problems, through direct counseling or referral to competent personnel. By fulfilling the responsibilities of his job calmly and pleasantly he sets a good example for the inmate, who responds favorably to being treated in a professional manner. It is difficult to imagine how a staff of maladjusted correctional officers can do anything but harm to a group of inmates whose very presence in prison is evidence of personal problems.

Inmates often despair at the dismal prospect of continued regimentation, which, coupled with idleness, deepens their sense of worthlessness. One area in which help can be offered is a constructive educational program. Many school districts provide classroom instruction locally, as well as the opportunity to earn high-school diplomas. Colleges and universities frequently offer instruction for college credits. An inmate sufficiently motivated to take advantage of such opportunities can also be encouraged to make productive plans for his future.

Although by no means unique in the Federal system, professional psychiatric, social-work, and psychological services are vital components of the treatment programs. Of the approximately 150 full-time psychiatrists in American prisons, half are employed by the Federal Bureau of Prisons. Many state prisons employ psychiatrists on a part-time schedule, but utilize their services more on a consultive than treatment basis. States ordinarily use closed wards in their mental

hospitals rather than construct special facilities for severely emotionally disturbed inmates. The Federal medical center at Springfield,
Missouri, houses 600 psychiatric patients who have been transferred
from other institutions or assigned temporarily for presentence investigations.

The presentence investigation, used throughout the Federal system,
is an exploration of the individual's background in order to make a
recommendation for his sentence. This recommendation is not binding
upon the court but is helpful in arriving at a decision in the best
interests of all concerned, especially in sentencing juveniles (ages
seven to seventeen) and youths (ages seventeen to twenty-one). The
Federal Juvenile Delinquency Act of 1938 granted to juvenile offenders the right to informal court procedures and indeterminate commitment that had existed in state courts for some time. The 1950 Federal
Youth Corrections Act granted Federal courts the authority to assign a
person under the age of twenty-two to the custody of the U.S. Attorney
General for a period of time up to the length of the maximum sentence
for his particular offense, depending on how quickly he made a
satisfactory adjustment. He would then be committed to an institution,
and if, after his release he made a particularly good adjustment, the
Board of Parole could discharge him from supervision.

Federal Prison Industries, Incorporated

In 1934 a corporation known as Federal Prison Industries was
formed within the Bureau of Prisons. In addition to employing large
numbers of inmates, this corporation coordinates vocational training
and paid more than $43 million in dividends to the U.S. Treasury
during its first twenty years of operation. It continues successfully to
the present day, involved in the production of self-sustaining needed
items such as brooms, rope, bookbinding and printing within the
Federal system. Even though its programs reflect attention to the needs
of private enterprise and industry, fewer than 20 percent of former
Federal prisoners are employed in jobs related to the training they
receive in Federal Prison Industries. The corporation has contributed
to the war effort of the nation in World War II, the Korean Conflict,
and Vietnam, at the same time providing inmates with funds for
themselves and their families. An inmate is credited with money for
his work on Prison Industries Inc. books, which later bills the particular institution receiving the products. The money thus earned is either
paid to the inmate upon his release or used by him for special

occasions. Although the corporation reimbursed the Bureau for its initial appropriation within three years of its inception, its goal is not to make the prison system self-sustaining. Through such an organization the inmate can be trained to work, develop marketable skills and habits and better prepare for his return to the community.

Jails and Supervision

Because of its policy of boarding inmates awaiting transportation and prisoners awaiting trial or sentencing in local institutions, the Bureau maintains an inspection program. Continuation of Federal contracts has been denied to a large number of jails until changes have been made in conformity with minimum standards. Such contracts are a source of revenue to the states, and changes have therefore been made if only to continue eligibility for funds. It was not through enforcing its standards that the Bureau earned the respect it enjoys, however, but through offers of assistance to politicians, jailers, guards, and other correctional personnel. Requests for inspections, suggestions, training, and consultation come in from other nations, as well as from municipalities and states in the United States.

The greatest single problem that existed early within the Federal system was different sentences for the same offense. The proportion of defendants placed on probation ranged from 64 percent by some judges to as few as 15 percent by others for the same crime. Still others were being sentenced to prison for virtually the same offense. Flexibility in sentencing is desirable, but a degree of uniformity must exist in the development of individual treatment.

The Federal Bureau of Prisons has evolved from rather modest beginnings into the arbiter of a system that has received international acclaim. Its progressive leadership and the individual devotion to duty apparent among its career employees have earned it the highest reputation.

There is no panacea for dealing with offenders. Probation and parole, which account for two-thirds of all offenders (those over whom the court has retained jurisdiction) supervised in the community, are useful. The average cost of supervising an adult felon is approximately $200 a year on probation, compared to more than $2,000 in prison.

By tripling the number of probation officers on its staff in 1963, New Mexico cut its prison population 32 percent and now saves $4 million a year in prison costs and welfare payments to the families of inmates.

Probation

Probation, supervision of offenders living in the community under the auspices of a social-welfare institution, has spread rapidly in this country. It was initially viewed as a way to avoid the stigma of criminality and the trauma of incarceration, particularly for children. It is an alternative plan to incarceration and permits the offender to remain in the community. Although its history goes back to the Middle Ages, it was first applied in the United States when John Augustus, a Boston shoemaker, volunteered in 1841 to supervise drunkards released to his custody. In 1878 Massachusetts passed a law authorizing the employment of one full-time probation officer. England was also using probation by that time, but English supervisors were known as "missionaries" and were employed by another social-welfare agency other than a court or a probation department. In 1900 only six states in the United States had laws recognizing probation, but by 1940 there were such statutes in forty-two states and the District of Columbia, Puerto Rico, and Alaska.

As the practice became more widely accepted, professional standards for probation officers were developed. Most probation officers are selected through a civil-service or merit-system examination, but many jurisdictions still provide that the officers "serve at the pleasure of the court," which means that the judge can select personnel without considering standards.

Probation, as it has been refined to the present time, takes into account the specific needs of the offender. At the request of the adult courts, but as standard procedure within juvenile courts a presentence report is prepared by the probation department containing a recommendation for disposition. This recommendation is not binding upon the court. Determination of the treatment program thus requires large amounts of data, including comprehensive information on the causes of the offender's physical, emotional, mental, or social maladjustment. The circumstances of his family, its economic status, his work record, associates, affiliation, recreational habits, and past arrest record are evaluated. As a consequence, some people are not considered amenable to probation, whereas others seem likely to respond to it.

Not all offenders need psychiatric evaluation, but such evaluations are becoming more and more common, judging from the number of requests for them from the courts. Very few courts or probation departments have the services of psychiatrists available, but other social-welfare institutions can be brought into the treatment plan to accomplish the same ends. The use of psychiatric examinations and evaluations is even more extensive with juvenile offenders. Together with psychological-test results and other reports such evaluations help the court in making decisions and facilitate "treatment" either on probation or in institutions.

There are two main kinds of probation—individualistic and legalistic—each with several subcategories. Individualistic probation involves a relationship between the offender and probation officer; sometimes the latter has such relationships with several probationers. An attempt is made to lead each probationer to understand his situation, to reveal both his strengths and his limitations, and to provide emotional support for him, especially at times of crisis. Legalistic probation involves only a pronouncement by the magistrate that a repeat of the offense or similar misconduct will result in imprisonment. No supervision is prescribed, and the offender is solely responsible for avoiding arrest in the same jurisdiction again. One problem with the probation system is the tendency to overload it. Typically a probation department is set up on the understanding that its services will represent a lower per capita cost to the taxpayer than would imprisonment of all offenders. But the courts come to rely on the system, and soon the number of probationers supervised by each officer is increased; eventually the effectiveness of the program is thus reduced. One solution to this problem would be to budget and plan on a "unit of work" basis. Each of the various responsibilities of the probation officer could be broken down into units of work. When officers in the department reached a predefined maximum workload, new personnel could be recruited. This suggestion is not new, and such schemes have been considered in many places. The real problem seems to arise at the funding level, however, for those responsible for appropriations often assume that officers can absorb the "overflow." Yet seen in proper perspective, an adequate system of probation could represent savings to the taxpayer similar to those achieved in New Mexico. Society would first have to forego its propensity for punishment and vengeance, however.

Parole

Releasing a prisoner before he has completed his sentence, accompanied by provisions for supervision, is known as parole. No institution, adult or juvenile, can possibly hold all its people for their maximum sentences. Ideally, parole is jointly planned by the inmate and his caseworker. A man's final adjustment cannot be evaluated until he returns to the community. If he had served his maximum sentence, he is no longer subject to counseling. The parole officer, however, can offer assistance that would otherwise not be available in times of crisis.

Parole is simply the early release of a man who will return to society anyway sooner or later.[8] We intend here simply to describe parole and not to go into the many problems faced by the parolee, the parole officer, the releasing institution, and the community. The fact that a parolee can be reincarcerated reveals that much depends upon his "adjustment." He is therefore going to make his "adjustment" look as good as possible, perhaps even better than it is. As a result, the parole officer is often forced to counsel with his clients in an atmosphere of distrust and artificiality that would seem likely to impair, rather than enhance, the professional relationship. Although some parolees do make notorious headlines from time to time, most probation and parole officers achieve higher percentages of "success" than of failure.

Youthful Offenders

Little has been said so far about youthful offenders, even though they have aroused much concern over the years. Establishment of the juvenile court of Cook County, Illinois, in 1899 was the first recognition in this country of the need for separate facilities for children.[9] A need for an informal atmosphere and hearings closed to the public was also recognized. The idea was that the court should act in the best interests of the child, as parents *should* act. This attitude eliminated many of the harsher elements of criminal justice for children and allowed a focus on the future education, direction, and guidance of children, as opposed to punishment for their past misdeeds. This philosophy was operant as early as 1869 in Massachusetts, where the responsibility of a "visiting agent" was defined as working for the child's welfare and not for his punishment.[10]

In adult criminal proceedings the defendant is indicted in technical language for a specific crime, and a public trial is held to establish whether or not the defendant has, in fact, committed the crime as charged. The fundamental intent is to identify and punish the wrongdoer. Little, if any, weight is given to such factors as health, family, associates or education, which might suggest alternative approaches to a court "battle." The defendant finds himself pitted against society itself when the indictment is read: "The State of——versus John Doe."

The juvenile court should concern itself with the proper training, education, and reform of the delinquent child. Its proceedings are not open to the public and are supposed to be "in the best interests of" the child. The legal document alleging the delinquent acts, the petition, is prepared in terms simple enough for the child to understand. Informality is still the rule in the courtroom, even though certain elements of due process are disposed of early in the hearing.

These differences illustrate the shift in emphasis from punishment to concern for the welfare of the child. The juvenile court has an obligation to take whatever action it deems necessary to correct the problem that has brought the child before it. In keeping with this obligation the prescribed course is viewed as "treatment" because it is determined with reform of the child in mind. The child or his family may not necessarily agree that the treatment is in his own best interests, but that is the basis on which the juvenile court is supposed to act.

Not all courts live up to these principles. Judges and their probation staffs sometimes react to active public interest and stress efficiency of operation over quality of investigation and supervision. Partly because of untrained personnel in probation departments and mandatory rotation of judges, such courts can become too busy and too indifferent to remember their true functions. Their procedures may become mechanical, and judges may be hearing types of cases for which they are least suited.

Some judges see themselves as administrators. It is our opinion that administration is best left to chief probation officers, for such responsibilities can impair judges' effectiveness in rendering the most appropriate decisions. A judge who concerns himself with the investigation, reporting, and physical arrangements of a case before he hears it in court can prejudice himself and thus be unfit to render a fair decision.

A Supreme Court decision of May 15, 1967, restored to juveniles procedural safeguards that had been ignored.[11] Former Justice Abraham Fortas, author of the majority opinion, clarified juveniles' rights to notice of charges, counsel, protection against self-incrimination, confrontation, and cross-examination. He further stressed that records of juvenile-court proceedings should be kept for use on appeal, although there had not been a specific issue of that kind in the case at hand.

The burden of this decision is a demand for closer adherence to "due process of law," a Constitutional provision limiting the power of government to deprive a person of his life, liberty, or property. Future court proceedings involving juveniles are likely to be less informal, in order to conform to this decision.

The Future

Sentences should be more flexible to account for individual differences among defendants, who respond to situations, including treatment situation, differently. Sentencing should be handled by penal experts relying on presentence investigations. Once a sentence has been imposed, the offender should be remanded to the custody of the appropriate authority. If the defendant is placed on probation, a probation officer should immediately assume responsibility for supervision and implementation of the treatment plan. If he is sentenced to prison, classification experts should determine to which institution he will be sent initially. His subsequent fate should then be determined by a thorough and complete diagnostic study.

Desirable behavior is most effectively induced through positive reinforcement, or rewards, and takes time and effort. Many successes reported by various prisons are traceable to this approach.

Eventually there will be minimum standards of admission, segregation, treatment, training and release for all correctional institutions, as there already are for hospitals, universities, and in the military services. These standards, perhaps set after consultation with the Federal Bureau of Prisons, should be enacted into law by various states wishing to participate in programs involving Federal matching funds.

Correctional facilities of the future should include, in expanded and refined form, many of the progressive features of the Swedish prison system which is still considered advanced a quarter of a century after its reform. We have added little to the list, and edited only where necessary to apply to the United States.

1. Individual states should administer their own correctional systems, with Federal consultation available on an optional basis.
2. There should be wider use of probation, with competent professionals to submit adequate reports.
3. There should be exclusive use of the indeterminate sentence.
4. The parole system should be geared to the individual inmate and

his readiness for release and reabsorption into the community.

5. The classification system for all convicted felons should attempt to fit treatment to the individual.
6. Training programs and educational opportunities should be provided as needed in each institution.
7. Professionally trained career people should be recruited at all levels.
8. "Graded" institutions should include diagnostic centers, minimum- , medium- , and maximum-security facilities.
9. Institutional staff should submit to periodic administrative review and take responsibility for correcting any deficiencies noted by the review team.

We shall continue, at least in the foreseeable future, to have prisons. But prisons must be recognized as only one weapon in the fight against crime, in itself a symptom of social disorganization. Prevention is more likely to solve the problem of crime than is imprisonment. Techniques of prevention can be developed from a body of knowledge both scientific and practical, using the perspectives of the offender and staffs dealing with them, as well as a perceptive, informed and interested citizenry. The inmate is not likely to be helped by anyone who attempts to impose a set of values upon him. The idealist may have had a totally different kind of life from that of the offender and as a result may often think, feel, and act in ways incomprehensible to the latter. The predominating goals should be to protect society and at the same time to attempt to reform offenders who are capable of change. Other social institutions should be involved in this process, even before offenders' arrival in prison. We believe that the halfway house will eventually be used both before and after incarceration. That is, before a person is committed to an institution, he will be housed at an observation and diagnostic facility, and he will also live in an observation center preparatory to his release into the community. The courts will continue to have the sole responsibility for determining guilt or innocence, but upon conviction an offender will no longer be committed immediately to prison. At the diagnostic center, a decision will be made jointly by the offender and the professional team on what course of treatment is best suited to his needs.

By our estimate, as many as 50 percent of the people imprisoned today could have benefited from an alternative to incarceration. Inmates need opportunities to serve society in order to regain their self-respect. When such opportunities are denied and they are isolated from "normal" society, they lose faith in their own future.

Work-release programs, whatever they may be called, should replace much of what is now vast idleness within the penal system. An inmate should be classified, evaluated, and placed in a treatment program that will permit him to be reabsorbed into the community as soon as he can accept the responsibility. Custody, which was once dependent upon guns, iron bars, and high walls, will eventually be almost exclusively handled by professionally trained correctional workers under the direct supervision of competent administrators.

As the community becomes more open to convicted offenders, work programs may begin to change. Private enterprise may find a constructive role in the use of such manpower. Labor unions can assist by sponsoring prison apprenticeship-training courses especially designed to meet existing shortages.

The emerging philosophy, which will inevitably gain public acceptance and support, is based on concern for the protection of society not only in the immediate present but also in future design, construction, furnishing, and maintenance of correctional facilities. In the future, before a person could be incarcerated, the resources of other social-welfare institutions would have to be exhausted.

The prison of the future should be located in or near the offender's community, thus giving him a chance to serve society instead of being a burden to it. There are many men and women in prison today who could perform their present tasks outside the institution with minimum supervision. Furthermore, some of the better-trained prisoners could be employed in higher-level jobs than are common in institutions. For instance, a convicted income-tax evader or embezzler usually has higher-level skills than are required to operate a spray gun in a license-plate plant, yet he has little opportunity for further growth when he is assigned to tasks that offer little or no challenge.

As modern penology expands there will be experiments in "desegregation," involving older, more "fatherly" inmates in the treatment of youthful offenders. Many inmates already have qualifications exceeding those required of nonprofessional workers in juvenile institutions and could assume responsibilities as group supervisors, maintenance supervisors, truck drivers, and other nonprofessional jobs. The results might be similar to those achieved by Alcoholics Anonymous, whose program is based on aid by those who have themselves experienced similar problems. It has long been observed that growing older results in a "mellowing" of active involvement in deviant behavior. Observing and interacting with selected adult offenders may motivate younger boys to want to help themselves and thus choose less damaging forms of behavior in the future.

A network of correctional programs involving detection, apprehension, and detention can better coordinate correctional activities in the future. As specialization outside the system increases, corresponding specialization within the system will be imperative. Better public relations will be required, for one thing, to help society arrive at a consensus on treatment of offenders. Many people will remain adamant in favor of corporal and capital punishment, but effective information programs will help to persuade most of the public in a forthright manner of the validity of correctional philosophy over punishment.

In keeping with the goals of rehabilitation, more training should be made available to inmates, thus hastening their return as productive members of society. For those who are unable or unwilling to become involved in self-betterment, custody will have to remain part of the overall program.

Capital punishment as a deterrent to crime is being deemphasized internationally. France and the United States are the main countries that still use it, but even they resort to it less and less frequently.

There are three traditional features of prisons that no longer prevail: silence, isolation, and expectations of "penitence." They have been gradually discarded over the last several hundred years and replaced by more advanced ideas like rehabilitation. In all prisons today, however, there are still vestiges of these old approaches in maximum-security prisons, "special-treatment units," and "adjustment cells." The two latter devices include solitary confinement, darkness, and shortage of food rations.

Perhaps more from necessity than from ideological advancement, the sheer numbers of inmates housed in institutions have already been reduced through probation and parole plans. Other yet unknown alternatives will be developed and used, causing less reliance on incarceration. The elements for such alternatives are probably known to us, but someone will have to put them into a workable plan—the sooner the better.

NOTES

1. M. J. Sethna, *Society and the Criminal* (Bombay: Leaders,' 1952), p. 207. Offers an interesting international perspective on correctional philosophy.

2. *Ibid.*, pp. 208–209.
3. John Howard, *The State of Prisons* (New York: Dutton, 1929). Contains descriptions of appalling conditions that were probably described in a way to obtain a sympathetic audience.
4. Paul W. Tappan, ed., *Contemporary Correction* (New York: McGraw-Hill, 1951), pp. 254–264. Views religious involvement from the point of view of its value to inmates.
5. Sethna, *op. cit.*, p. 269.
6. Harry E. Barnes and Negley K. Teeters, *New Horizons in Criminology* (New York: Prentice-Hall, 1951), p. 712. This book is the American classic in the field of criminology; it contains comprehensive coverage of the subject with a convenient and valuable index.
7. U.S. Bureau of Prisons, *30 Years with the Federal Prisons* (Washington, D.C.: Government Printing Office, 1960).
8. Paul W. Keve, *Prison, Probation and Parole* (Minneapolis: University of Minnesota Press, 1954), pp. 33–35. Explores the interrelations of offenders' status before, during, and after incarceration.
9. Grace Abbott, *The Child and the State* (Chicago: University of Chicago Press, 1938), pp. 31–33. This book offers an analysis of society's involvement with children.
10. Barnes and Teeters, *op. cit.*, p. 321.
11. Re Gault, 387 U.S. 1, 18 L. Ed. 2d. 527 S. Ct. 1428 (1966).

SUGGESTED READINGS

Laurence, John. *A History of Capital Punishment.* New York: Citadel, 1960.
　　A "classic study" first published in 1932 and reprinted because of the renewed controversy over abolishing capital punishment.
Neigher, Alan. "The Gault Decision: Due Process and the Juvenile Court," *Federal Probation*, 31, No. 4 (December 1967), pp. 8–18.
　　Discusses the likely impact of this famous case on juvenile-court proceedings in the future.
Polier, Justine W. *A View from the Bench.* New York: National Council on Crime and Delinquency, 1964.
　　An appraisal of juvenile-court procedures, services, workloads and effectiveness.
President's Commission on Law Enforcement and Administration of Justice. *The Challenge of Crime in a Free Society.* Washington, D.C.: Government Printing Office, 1967.
　　A report on crime and corrections that focuses on setting goals for future detection, apprehension, prosecution, and correction of criminals.
Richmond, Mark S. *Prison Profiles.* Dobbs Ferry, N.Y.: Oceana, 1965.

Written for the lay public on topics usually reserved for professionals in the field of corrections.

Rubin, Sol, Henry Weihofen, George Edwards, and Simon Rosenzweig. *The Law of Criminal Correction*. St. Paul: West, 1963.

A scholarly work on the technical aspects of criminal legislation, correctional administration, and supervision.

Chapter X

EXPANDING CONCEPTS OF
VETERANS ADMINISTRATION
SERVICES

A brief history of the Veterans Administration,
including the events leading to its formation,
its responsibilities, and services
currently available to veterans,
is presented.

The Veterans Administration (V.A.), as it is known today, was established by Executive Order 5398 in July 1930. It was to be an independent agency incorporating the responsibilities of the Bureau of Pensions, the U.S. Veterans' Bureau, and the National Home for Disabled Volunteer Soldiers. In December of the same year the Veterans Administration was assigned the duty of supplying artificial limbs to veterans.

The creation of the V.A. thus merged the services of several agencies concerned with veterans of different wars and focused nationally on medical care and other services available to all veterans.

By the time it was clear that such reorganization was needed, the government had already undertaken one of the most complex tasks ever conceived. The various administrative pressures resulting from many veterans needing services were so great that large numbers of physicians were recruited for the purposes of medical and surgical treatment, administration, and consultation services under the auspices of the Public Health Service. The various naval and military hospitals were not yet centrally coordinated. But Public Health Service facilities, it was soon discovered, were inadequate to handle the patient load, and some hospitals run by the War and Navy Departments were transferred to the Public Health Service. During the 1920 fiscal year there were fifty hospitals, accounting for 11,660 beds, under jurisdiction of the Public Health Service.

England first offered limited assistance to veterans in 1593, but it was not until more than 100 years later, in 1697, that retirement pay was granted by England and then exclusively to officers.

When the American Colonies were faced with the problems of raising armies and providing relief for wounded and disabled soldiers, they turned to taxation. The prevalent sentiment throughout the Colonies was that a person wounded in the service of his government should be "looked after" at the Colony's expense. Crude but workable pension plans were thus provided in this country as early as 1776.

As it was the responsibility of each Colony to raise its own militia, various pension schemes were propounded, to encourage enlistment, as well as to discourage desertions and resignations. In 1778 Virginia offered full pay for life to disabled veterans and half-pay to their widows. Pensions for disabled veterans were $5 a month ($5 was full pay) but were raised to $8 a month in 1816. These promises looked good on paper and probably did a lot to promote recruiting. The new government failed to produce the necessary money for these pensions, however, and few veterans or their surviving families were paid.

In 1818 President James Monroe was instrumental in achieving passage of an act setting the pension for officers at $20 and enlisted men at $8 a month *for life*. In 1820 it was necessary to pass a remedial law authorizing the Secretary of War to disqualify veterans whom he did not consider in need. He relied on sworn statements by veterans, not too different from the declarations of eligibility described in Chapter 4, which have been considered a modern innovation. It should be remembered that the main concern in 1820 was the veteran of the Revolutionary War and not the veteran of the War of 1812. There is always a time lag between recognition of veterans' needs and appropriate legislation to meet them.

It was not until 1862 that further legislation related to Revolutionary War veterans was enacted: The intention was to render it impossible for heirs to process claims against the government for unpaid pensions of their forebears. Descendants of Revolutionary soldiers *have* been granted pensions, but only by special acts of Congress.

The last widow of a Revolutionary soldier died in 1906, one year after the last veteran of the War of 1812 had passed away. She was receiving a pension at the time of her death, representing the exercise by the nation of more than a century of social responsibility for one war.

"Booty" (goods and merchandise taken by force from other ships at sea) was sold by the Federal government to pay for early pensions. There were also pensions and pension funds for men serving aboard private merchant vessels traveling under arms and allegiance to the United States. They were known as "privateers." A privateer pension fund was established in 1812 and exhausted in 1837 but renewed later with inclusion of privateers' pensions in ordinary pension appropriations.

In an act of February 1871 veterans of the War of 1812 or their survivors were granted pensions only in cases of disability or death during war service. No question of financial need was raised.

An act to grant pension, clearly defining pensions for both officers and enlisted men for service-connected disability or death, was passed by Congress in 1862. The Civil War was an immediate cause for attention to pensions at that time; ten years later a comprehensive law was passed "to revise, consolidate and amend the laws relating to pensions"; it raised officers' pensions to a maximum of $31.50 a month.

In 1861 President Abraham Lincoln had called for 500,000 volunteers to "suppress the insurrection," and Congress stipulated that they be entitled to the benefits of regular service. This act did not make subsequent volunteers eligible; another law in 1879, known as the Arrears Act, applied to this latter group. Civil War veterans and their families continued to be the subjects of significant legislation for the next half-century. Pensions were authorized only for Civil War veterans on the Union side.

President Grover Cleveland vetoed the Dependent Pension Bill in 1887. This bill would have granted pensions to needy dependents of Civil War veterans. President Cleveland declared that, with pensions, employment preferences, and care in soldiers' homes such veterans had "received such compensation for military service as has never been received by soldiers before since mankind first went to war." [1] President Benjamin Harrison, Cleveland's successor, voiced approval of this type of legislation.

Women who had served as nurses for six months or more during the Civil War were authorized to receive pensions in 1900. Men received pensions for having served ninety days or more. In 1920 an act increasing pension payments to survivors of the war with Mexico, the War of 1812, and the Civil War was passed. The last pension law affecting Civil War veterans was passed in 1930.

Pensions to veterans have been reduced only twice in American history: in 1820 after a national depression and in 1933 for the same reason.

The Spanish-American War (1898), the Philippine Insurrection (1899) and the Boxer Rebellion (1900) helped to swell the ranks of pensioners. Veterans Regulations 1 and 3 established pension rates for these veterans and defined five grades of disability: 10, 25, 50, 75 and 100 percent.

The main goal of legislation up to this point was to provide pensions. A pension is authorized and paid to a veteran only for injuries that do not result from his own misconduct. Awards of pensions for temporary disabilities are reevaluated from time to time to establish continuing eligibility. Pensions may then be discontinued, continued at the same rates, or continued at higher or lower rates.

Various national groups are interested in the welfare of veterans. In 1917 the National Conference of Charities and Correction devoted an important part of its agenda to discussion of provisions for disabled soldiers and sailors. The Committee on Labor of the Council of National Defense drafted a bill on the same subject, which was enacted on October 6, 1917. This particular bill was the most significant step up to that time toward expanding services for veterans. Its basic provisions were pensions for disabled veterans or for their families in case of their deaths; allotments for wives and allowances for dependents; voluntary insurance; medical attention for veterans, including artificial limbs; vocational rehabilitation for the permanently disabled.

The matter of allotments to servicemen's wives, former wives, or separated wives without children was taken out of their hands and set at $15 per month. Illegitimate children were also considered if a court had ordered support. In cases in which allotments were made involving more persons than wives the government contributed from $5 to

$50 a month, depending on the number of dependents and the relationships. As one might expect of any regulation to be applied to vast numbers of men, complications arose, including requirements for proof of marriage and paternity, deaths prior to marriage, and unwillingness of veterans and their dependents to cooperate with existing regulations, who felt such requirements were an imposition. A number of amendments, as well as new laws, were passed to correct deficiencies in the program.

Forced vocational rehabilitation of veterans has not been successful. Acceptance of such training was originally made compulsory for men seeking pensions, but the provision was never enforced. The Vocational Rehabilitation Act of June 27, 1918, became a model for retraining veterans. But disabled veterans were being discharged at the rate of more than 23,000 a month in 1919, and the program was impossible to administer. One bottleneck was the centralization of decisions on veteran eligibility in Washington, D.C. Individuals, soldiers' organizations, and the press were extremely critical of this "bureaucratic blundering." In February 1920 a series of articles charging gross mismanagement and inexcusable delays began to appear in the *New York Evening Post*. The articles were written by a reporter who had done research on rehabilitation of disabled soldiers, and they were instrumental in initiating an official investigation by the House Committee on Education. Rehabilitation services for veterans stopped June 30, 1928, as a result of an amendment to the World War Veterans' Act of 1926 permitting dissolution of the program within twenty-four months.

In 1924 a medical council within the Veterans' Bureau was formed to improve the care of veterans. Through the efforts of this council research was encouraged, after a survey conducted by the American College of Surgeons fifty Veterans' Bureau hospitals were accredited, affiliations with schools of medicine were established, and gerontology (the study of the aging process) was studied scientifically for the first time on a national scale.

Inherited Functions of the Veterans Administration

When it was created in 1930 the Veterans Administration inherited a number of existing programs that had never been successfully coordinated in the past.[2]

Compensation for World War I Veterans

On May 19, 1924, an act was passed, over the veto of President Calvin Coolidge, allowing for "adjusted compensation" for World War I veterans. It was to consist of an allowance of $1.25 for each day of overseas service and $1 for each day of service in the United States, the total less the $60 separation pay received at time of discharge. If the remaining amount was greater than $50, the veteran was to receive a "non-participating adjusted service certificate" payable twenty years from the date of issue. Management of this program was subsequently assigned to the V.A. The delayed-payment clause was the issue leading to organization of the Bonus Expeditionary Force of 1932–1935, which is discussed later in this chapter.

Military and Naval Pension Systems

The V.A. processed pension claims as well as making the necessary payments. At that time claims were divided into three groups: those from wars before the Spanish-American War, from the Spanish-American War itself, and from wars after the Spanish-American War. Veterans had the right to appeal pension determinations, and appeals were processed in Washington, D.C.

Medical Care and Hospitalization

Although basically established for the care and treatment of veterans, V.A. hospitals were sometimes also used for active-duty personnel, reservists, and certain government employees.

Payments to State Homes

The National Home for Disabled Volunteer Soldiers had formerly made payments to states that maintained homes for disabled veterans. The V.A. took over this responsibility, as well as that for inspection of such homes to ensure that they met minimum standards for care and treatment of veterans.

Guardianship of Veterans and Dependents

Guardianship of veterans and their dependents is sometimes deemed necessary. The V.A. acts in an advisory capacity to the courts in establishing guardians for veterans rated incompetent or insane and for minor children of deceased veterans.

The Bonus Expeditionary Force

An indigenous social movement sprang up in protest against what veterans believed was injustice in the system of pensions granted them. The Bonus Expeditionary Force was organized, and more than 5,000 men assembled in Washington, D.C., during the summer of 1932. They camped at various locations in the area and some did not leave until a resolution of July 8 gave the Veterans Administration the authority to pay their railroad fare plus per diem expenses of 75 cents.[3] Because many were traveling by automobile, further adjustments were made to permit payment of gas and oil expenses.

There were several riots, and the remaining members of the Bonus Expeditionary Force had to be forcibly removed from the nation's capital. A similar situation began to develop in the spring of the following year, and arrangements were made to avoid the unpleasant scenes of 1932. An army camp near the capital was outfitted by the Veterans Administration to accommodate the "conventioneers." Transportation to and from the city was also provided.

The bonus march was opposed by three large veterans' groups, the Disabled American Veterans, the American Legion, and the Veterans of Foreign Wars. These groups did not want to be identified with a movement that they classified as "un-American." The march of 1934 was considered "mild" by much of the American population, and the march of 1935 never passed the planning stage. Although the demands of this group were not entirely satisfied, the marches did serve to call attention to the problems of American veterans. Later veterans benefited more than did participants in the protest marches of 1932–1935.

Insurance

Because of the extra hazards in time of war, a serviceman is considered a poor insurance risk. An act of October 6, 1917, granted insurance provisions to men who had served in World War I. Various administrative costs were to be paid to private companies by the government. The insurance was voluntary and is best described as an annual renewable term insurance, which could be converted to long-term policies within five years after the end of the war. Many people who were not covered by this program also suffered injury and death, and therefore in 1918 provisions for automatic coverage for servicemen who had been totally disabled or killed between April 6, 1917, and February 12, 1918 were made. Although premiums were deducted from servicemen's pay on the basis of signed authorizations, the Director of the Veterans' Bureau said, "For the purposes of writing this war time insurance . . . there can be little doubt that in many cases an application from men enlisted in the service was more nearly a requirement than a privilege." [4]

Approximately 75 percent of the veterans let their policies lapse after discharge, and there was a great publicity campaign to explain the benefits available to men who were not taking advantage of them. Nevertheless many people did lose the benefits of their military insurance because of ignorance, misunderstandings, or indifference. Special provisions in the law permitted waiver of premium payments to hospitalized veterans.

The Bureau of War Risk Insurance, which had previously been the main instrument through which veterans' problems were channeled, was abolished in 1921, with creation of the Veterans' Bureau. A committee of consultants had recommended a hospital-construction program, and the new bureau took over responsibility for it. Previously medical care had been offered only to those veterans who had at least 10 percent disability. After 1921 any injury or disease entitled a veteran to treatment. As the problem of getting medical services to veterans was gradually brought under control, the letting of contracts to private hospitals for medical services was discontinued. Exceptions were made when removal would endanger the veteran. Females who had served as nurses were also entitled to these services.

Employment of Veterans

Because many returned veterans (and other citizens) were unemployed and in desperate financial straits, the Roosevelt administration assisted veterans to obtain assignments in the Civilian Conservation Corps (C.C.C.), Federal Emergency Relief Administration (F.E.R.A.) camps, or Works Progress Administration (W.P.A.) projects. Seventeen years after the start of World War I these veterans would have been in their thirties and forties, in itself a basis for discontent. These men suffered not only physical problems reflecting their general health but also emotional problems related to separation from their families, unemployment, and threats to their adequacy and masculinity. At the time more than half the patients in the V.A. hospitals were diagnosed as suffering from "neuropsychiatric disease."

Effects of World War II on the Veterans Administration

The Selective Service Act of 1940 imposed upon every male in the United States between the ages of twenty-one and thirty-six the obligation to register at his local draft board. These "inductees" were entitled to most of the benefits that the V.A. had to offer, resulting in an increase in its rolls of approximately 1 million people. The employees of the V.A. at the outbreak of World War II numbered 45,000. It was operating ninety-one hospitals and administering disability compensation and pensions to more than .5 million veterans, 80 percent of whom had served in World War I.

It was during this time that the V.A. became the recognized leader in coordinating mental and physical health. In World War I servicemen had been accepted and assigned with little or no thought to their emotional stability. Many would have been rejected as unfit for service at a later date. In World War II the V.A. not only acted as consultant in many cases but also offered its services to induction stations as well.

A number of problems plagued the V.A. during the early years of World War II. It requested no deferments for employees in general, and physicians were truly scarce. Facilities were inadequate to meet demands, and building materials and labor were not easily obtainable. It had been the practice to review the service record of the veteran in processing his claim, but for injuries suffered in battle records were often not available. The V.A. had been rather lenient in such cases, often accepting sworn affidavits as evidence.

One of the major laws passed by Congress during the few days remaining in 1941 after formal declaration of war was to codify the V.A.'s policy on service-connected disabilities.

The G.I. Bill of Rights

The single law with perhaps the greatest impact on veterans and their families to date was the Servicemen's Readjustment Act of 1944, commonly known as the "G.I. Bill." The nation had experienced problems with returning veterans in the past and wanted to avoid repetition in the future. It was recognized that the reassimilation of this vast number of people would involve a number of difficulties. President Franklin D. Roosevelt appointed a committee to study the possibility of education for the returning veteran. The committee's recommendations applied to related problems as well. In addition to education and training for veterans, they recommended various kinds of loans, vocational counseling, and unemployment benefits (whose recipients were known as the "52-20 club" because the benefits were to be $20 for a maximum of fifty-two weeks); all these programs were originally to be administered by the V.A., but the U.S. Employment Service (U.S.E.S.) assumed the responsibility for locating jobs, screening applicants, and handling payments of unemployment benefits to veterans. More than 11 million veterans returned after World War II, creating a considerable burden for the Veterans Administration. Construction of thirty-one hospitals was only a partial answer to the medical problem. Several surplus army and navy hospitals were transferred to the V.A. Other problems also began to receive attention with the appointment of a new administrator in the postwar years.

Eventually the vast numbers of returning veterans were absorbed into the labor market or into institutions of higher learning. Many were offered opportunities that would not have been available otherwise. The financial assistance given veterans of World War II encouraged and enabled many to begin families that would otherwise not have been economically feasible and thus postponed.

Reorganization of the Veterans Administration

General Omar Bradley, Administrator of Veterans Affairs in 1945, began reorganization of the V.A., setting up thirteen branch offices throughout the nation to administer all V.A. programs on a district basis. A deputy administrator was assigned to each district, which permitted individual decisions to be made in much less time and with much less red tape. During this reorganization the number of V.A. employees increased to more than 96,000.

All did not go smoothly with Bradley, his reorganization, and the administration of benefits to more than 17 million men, however. The national commander of the American Legion protested the appointment of a career military man (Bradley) instead of a businessman and did much to obstruct the efforts of the V.A. At the annual convention of the American Legion Bradley gave one of the frankest speeches in history, describing the lack of cooperation and faith that he had encountered in trying to administer the program. A particularly controversial issue was the eligibility of a veteran receiving on-the-job training to receive full subsistence and a salary, whereas a veteran in college was denied a subsistence allowance. This inequity brought about much criticism of the entire program from what Bradley called a "small minority," but in fact the number of veterans who were college students far exceeded those receiving on-the-job training.

In 1948 the thirteen branch offices serving local areas were replaced by district offices covering regional areas, for the postwar problem had been dealt with effectively, and they no longer seemed necessary. In the same year the number of V.A. employees decreased by approximately 21,000.

An additional problem for the V.A. was the "police action" in Korea, which involved 7 million members of the American armed forces—more than had served in World War I. The problem mainly arose from the technical definition of Korean war service as peacetime service, which meant that Korean veterans were not eligible for training, hospitalization, burial, and other usual wartime benefits. The rejection of a Korean combat veteran by a V.A. hospital on these grounds in May 1951 brought about passage of a law extending normal benefits to veterans of the Korean Conflict.

Veterans' hospitals, especially in the South, had followed local custom in matters of segregation of whites and nonwhites. Segregation in the armed forces was outlawed in 1948 without major opposition. Integration within the V.A. hospitals was then accomplished both without incident and without much notice on the part of patients, employees and the communities. It came to be expected and unquestioned.

The phrase "the best medical care possible" was linked with the V.A. Eventually V.A. hospitals were equipped to deal with any disease, ranging from tuberculosis to various kinds of mental illness. Research and the close ties with medical schools further guaranteed the best in medical care and treatment.

The geriatric program of the V.A. was of a pioneer nature for little attention had previously been accorded aged veterans. For a variety of reasons, it was decided to work out a plan for returning them to their communities. One aspect of this plan was a foster-care program, which places veterans in private homes at substantially less cost than hospitalization would entail. V.A. staff members maintain contact with veterans and ensure that their interests are being looked after properly.

Another innovation within the V.A. hospital system was the concept of the "seven-day hospital." All V.A. personnel are subject to civil-service regulations and work a forty-hour week, but their duty days are staggered so that fuller coverage of services is possible every day. This scheme was initiated at the Coral Gables, Florida, V.A. hospital, and the turnover of patients was increased 15 percent. Getting a veteran back on his job sooner resulted in savings to him, his family, his employer, and the community at large, for he was reassimilated into the economy as a wage earner and taxpayer.

During the four-year term of V.A. administrator John S. Gleason, beginning in February 1961, the first Negro field director, regional office manager, and director of insurance were appointed. During the same time 23 percent of V.A. employees were Negro, and the administration hired or promoted 11,000 Negroes. An equal-opportunity policy was adopted in all V.A. facilities.

The V.A. is also responsible for American veterans who live in other parts of the world, especially Puerto Rico and the Philippines. Veterans also live in areas not under the jurisdiction of the United States: Europe, Asia, and South America. Some 30,000 Americans receive veterans' benefits in other parts of the world. For some time an office has existed in Rome, Italy, to handle such business.

The Veterans' Readjustment Benefits Acts of 1966 was, in fact, a new GI bill. It granted certain benefits to anyone who had served on active duty since January 31, 1955, and was later broadened to include men who had served in the Vietnam campaign. Provisions were made for almost all service personnel, whether actual combatants or not. They also include females and provide for their education after discharge from military service.

Housing

A veteran suffering the loss or loss of use of both lower extremities may receive a grant to pay part of the cost of building, buying, or remodeling a home to meet his requirements. This grant cannot exceed 50 percent of the cost of the home up to a maximum of $10,000.

Jobs

The U.S. Civil Service Commission grants a ten-point preference to any veteran disabled in service and a five-point preference to any veteran who has not sustained a service-connected disability in filling positions under its control. Some states use the same five- and ten-point scale in their respective systems.

Veterans are given priority in referral to appropriate training programs or job openings listed with state employment offices. First consideration is given to disabled veterans.

When a veteran has left other than a temporary job to enter the armed forces and is still able to perform his former duties upon his discharge, he has a right to reemployment, in both the private and government sectors. He is also entitled to all benefits accrued in his absence relative to the job, excluding wages.

Orphans' Education Assistance

Up to thirty-six months of college training are available to orphans of veterans and to the children of surviving veterans who are totally and permanently disabled. They receive $130 a month for full-time enrollment and less on a sliding scale to the point at which no payment is received for less than half-time schooling.

Special restorative schooling or training is available to persons qualified for orphans' education assistance who are unable to pursue their education because of physical or mental disabilities. Speech and voice correction, lip reading, reading and writing Braille, and other types of occupational therapy are supported at rates up to $130 a month.

Pensions

Veterans without dependents whose incomes are less than $600 a year can receive pensions of $104 a month, even though they have no service-connected disabilities. As their incomes rise, pensions are adjusted and discontinued if their earnings reach $1,800. There are special pension regulations for Spanish-American War veterans.

Current Services

A variety of other services is currently available through the V.A.[5] In comparing present services with those originally considered, it is clear how much the program has expanded. To receive these benefits, a veteran must have been honorably discharged. The numerous technicalities and exceptions will not be treated here.

Automobiles

A maximum allowance of $1,600 is available upon request toward the purchase of an automobile, or other conveyance, for a veteran who has lost one or both hands or feet or has sustained permanent loss of their use in connection with his military service.

Aid for the Blind

Electronic and mechanical aids and guide dogs and similar aids, plus certain maintenance allowances, are available upon application to the Veterans Administration for a veteran who is blind in both eyes, whether the blindness is service-connected or not.

Burial

A headstone or grave marker may be provided without cost for any veteran. An American flag used to drape the casket of a veteran may be given to his family or friends after use. Eligible veterans may be buried without cost to survivors at any national cemetery that has available space. A payment, not to exceed $250, may be made to an undertaker toward a veteran's burial expenses.

Compensation for Service-Connected Disabilities

Monthly payments ranging from $21 to $301 may be granted, depending on the degree of disability. These figures apply to 10 percent and 100 percent disabilities respectively. Veterans whose disabilities are rated at 50 percent or more are entitled to additional allowances for dependents.

Death Payments

Compensation payments to survivors of veterans, ranging from $70 a month for a widow with no dependent children to $121 for a widow and one child and $29 for each additional child, are made. A widow and four children would thus receive $207 a month. Receipt of these payments does not prevent an eligible widow or child from receiving social-security death benefits. There are income limitations for surviving widows and children, however. For example, if a widow with one child earns more than $3,000 a year, she is not entitled to receive a pension.

Education

Many veterans took advantage of the G.I. bill after both World War II and the Korean Conflict. The G.I. bill for veterans of World War II expired on July 25, 1956, and for veterans of Korea on January 31, 1965. It is now available to any veteran who has served on active duty for more than 180 days, excluding only those who have previously taken advantage of the benefits. Educational assistance is given for a period of one month in training for each month of active duty, not to exceed thirty-six months. Training must begin within eight years of discharge. These regulations are currently undergoing revisions to increase educational benefits for veterans.

Educational and Vocational Counseling

Either or both educational and vocational counseling are available to veterans through the Veterans Administration upon request.

Hospitalization

An eligible veteran may, upon application, be admitted to a veterans' hospital for any of a number of services.[6] In the event that a particular service is not available in a hospital to which a veteran has been admitted, he can be transferred to a facility that does offer it. Many V.A. hospitals are connected with the medical schools of nearby universities for teaching and training purposes, which increases interest in "uncommon" medical problems. The patients benefit from the skills and knowledge available through the medical schools.

To be eligible for the complete care offered by the V.A. hospital, a veteran must have been honorably discharged from active duty; he is admitted under a priority arrangement involving other factors as well. Top priority goes to a veteran requiring medical attention for a service-connected disability, disease, or injury. A veteran who has been discharged or retired for a service-connected disability and is receiving (or is eligible to receive) compensation and who requires treatment for a nonservice-connected ailment is given the next highest priority. Lower priorities are assigned to other veterans for whom hospitalization is deemed necessary and who swear that they cannot bear the cost of hospitalization elsewhere.

Life Insurance

Eight different kinds of G.I. life insurance have been supervised by the V.A. Many technicalities apply in the administration of life insurance in general. There are even more connected with life-insurance programs because of considerations like wartime disabilities or diseases that would otherwise render veterans uninsurable.

Loans

Many projects entitle an eligible veteran to a V.A.-guaranteed or -insured loan: for example, construction of a home, purchase of a farm and necessary equipment, or undertaking or expanding a legitimate business venture.

Veterans also have an advantage in down-payment requirements for loans insured by the Federal Housing Authority (F.H.A.); they have to put less money down before moving in than do nonveterans. But they must borrow more money on the principle thus increasing interest payments.

The Farmers Home Administration of the U.S. Department of Agriculture gives preference to eligible veterans with farming experience who apply for credit and management advice and farm loans.

Outpatient Care

Domicilary care is available to veterans outside nursing homes and hospitals. They receive full care, including medical treatment, without preempting beds that may be needed for more severe medical problems. Outpatient medical treatment is available to veterans with service-connected disabilities. All disabilities of veterans of the Indian wars and the Spanish-American War (including the Philippine Insurrection and the Boxer Rebellion) are considered to be service-connected. Treatment by private physicians is authorized when travel to V.A. facilities proves impractical.

Outpatient dental treatment is available to certain veterans at V.A. facilities, and it is also possible to receive authorization for treatment by approved dentists in veterans' home communities. This "hometown" plan is preferable when the cost of travel to a V.A. facility exceeds the standard cost of dental treatment locally.

Artificial limbs, braces, trusses, eyeglasses, hearing aids, and cosmetic hands may be fitted and supplied to eligible veterans. Training in the use of such items, as well as replacement, is also authorized under certain conditions.

Free medical or physical examinations are available to veterans to determine the presence of a claimed service-connected condition, for government life-insurance purposes, and for application for hospital or domiciliary care.

Naturalization Preference

It is possible for veterans since World War I to receive naturalization in less than five years, provided that they had been lawfully admitted to the United States before serving in the armed forces.

Retraining

An unemployed or underemployed veteran can seek retraining through the joint efforts of the U.S. Departments of Labor and Health, Education and Welfare under the Manpower Development and Training Act. The eligible person can be trained for jobs within the labor market either in schools or on the job and under certain conditions can receive a training allowance. A trainee can supplement his allowance by outside employment up to twenty hours a week.

Social Security

The U.S. government began matching the contributions of military personnel to social-security funds in 1957. As a result, servicemen on active duty since that time are covered by social security.

Ancillary Services

In addition to the extensive medical and surgical services available at veterans' hospitals, a number of supportive services are available. They include chaplain, dietetic, nursing, laboratory, mental-hygiene, pharmaceutical, psychiatric, psychological, radiosotope, radiological, social-work, hemodialysis, and nursing-home services. The ancillary services are usually under the direction and supervision of the chief of staff of a V.A. hospital, who is a medical doctor. The highest nonmedical officer in the organizational structure is the assistant director. The assistant director has direct supervision of building management, engineering, personnel, fiscal matters, and supply.

The Future

The V.A. today finds itself in the midst of rapid changes, some of which reflect national trends cutting across several major social-welfare organizations. One of the most exciting of these trends is the definition of the type of person to receive service from these organizations, of his "problems," and of the kind of "service" that he needs. Whereas before, V.A. personnel defined their clients as "ill," "mentally ill," "disabled" and "casualties," the current trend is to define clients as any people in crisis. The main kind of service needed is education or reeducation so that the patient or client can *learn* to deal with his particular problems and perhaps go on to teach others how to deal with theirs.

This definition implies many changes in organization in the V.A. and similar organizations. This new way of viewing individuals is less demeaning to the clients, who are treated as "students" with positive rather than negative expectations.

Several V.A. offices have already instituted organizational changes as a result of this new philosophy. There has been an increase in "self-help" hospital wards, leaderless group-therapy sessions, and increased reliance on "grass roots" leaders and workers, clients are becoming both recipients and givers of care.

Because of the increased use of nonprofessional personnel in social-welfare institutions, the shortage of professionals, and the increasing numbers of people needing help, the V.A. finds itself part of another trend sweeping through social-welfare institutions: expanding use of preprofessional and semiprofessional workers. Many social workers believe that the new professional should be less concentrated on direct service and more involved in social action, teaching, training, leading teams, consultation, supervision, and program coordination.

Because the general public, as well as state and national legislators, does not begrudge appropriations to the V.A., further extensions of its coverage can be expected. The new idea of eligibility is as revolutionary as hospital integration, as unconventional as the "seven-day hospital" concept, and as important as the "best medical care possible" principle. Already a trend is apparent. Recent legislation, such as the Omnibus Act, or Sharing Bill, allows for the treatment of nonveterans at V.A. facilities where services ranging from treatment of relatively minor problems to complex technical ones are contracted to other agencies.

In certain areas, the V.A. is beginning to gear itself to seek out clients actively. This approach is well under way with blind veterans in appropriate rehabilitation programs offered by the V.A. It seems appropriate to predict that, as this trend grows, the V.A. will also shift its focus from clinical emphasis (treating casualties) to emphasis on public health (preventing casualties).

The vast system operating for veterans will revert to something like the old public-health hospitals. These hospitals can make their advanced techniques, modern equipment, and trained personnel available to all citizens in need, regardless of race, creed, national origin, or military status. Within a very short time there will be 27 million veterans being served by V.A. If each of these veterans had one spouse and one child, a considerable proportion of the population would be involved either directly or indirectly with the V.A. anyway. Especially as automation of V.A. procedures, which is still undergoing research, develops to a high level, it may prove more economical to provide medical assistance for all citizens than to feed the various qualifications into the computer. This situation is similar to the one that the V.A. experienced immediately after World War II in attempting to process the millions of claims thrust upon an inadequate system. It was less costly to authorize claims than to process them through a complex system requiring time, personnel, equipment, and various supplies. If the cost of minor surgery amounts to $100 and processing a claim costs $200, providing fast and efficient service is far more economical.

V.A. hospitals have in the past been opened to active-duty personnel, reservists, and certain government employees. Other exceptions to eligibility regulations can also be made.

The V.A. is not an entity isolated from the larger society. First, veterans must function in society and not just in V.A. hospitals. Recognition that care is not enough is generating complex interrelations with other service agencies. Second, the V.A. is developing many community resources like foster-home programs, contract nursing homes, and half-way houses. Third, the V.A., like so many other agencies, is coming to base its services on need, rather than on eligibility. It is conceivable that the V.A. will be absorbed into a comprehensive Federal service system, along with community mental-health, public-health, public-welfare, prisons, and other agencies that currently overlap and duplicate services.

NOTES

1. *Congressional Record,* 49th Congress, 2nd Session, 18, Part 2, February 11, 1887, p. 1638.
2. Gustavus A. Weber and Laurence F. Schmeckebier, *The Veteran's Administration: Its History, Activities and Organization* (Washington, D.C.: Brookings, 1943, pp. 42–43). Gives a detailed account of the events leading to the formation of the Veterans Administration in 1930.
3. *The Statutes at Large of the United States of America* (Washington, D.C.: Government Printing Office, December 1931–March 1933), Part 1, 47, 654.
4. *U.S. Veterans Bureau, Annual Report, 1922* (Washington, D.C.: Government Printing Office, 1922), p. 456.
5. U.S. House of Representatives Committee, *Federal Benefits for Veterans and Dependents,* Print No. 4, 90th Congress, 1st Session (Washington,

D.C.: Government Printing Office, 1967). Describes all rights and benefits administered through the Veterans Administration.
6. U.S. Veterans Administration Information Service, *Medical Care of Veterans* (Washington, D.C.: Government Printing Office, 1967).

SUGGESTED READINGS

Bedford, James H. *The Veteran and His Future Job*. Los Angeles: Society for Occupational Research, 1946.

An occupational-guidance book for veterans, with a comprehensive analysis of opportunities in twelve major industries.

Miller, Joseph H. *Veterans Challenge the College*. Binghamton, Vt.: Vail-Ballou, 1947.

A description of the study, planning and work involved in expanding educational facilities for more than 1 million returning World War II veterans.

Pratt, George K. *Soldier to Civilian*. New York: McGraw-Hill, 1944.

Gives advice on problems of transition from military to civilian life, with emphasis on family life, marital problems, community attitudes, and occupational adjustment.

Stagg, Harold G. *Billions for Education*. Washington, D.C.: Army Times, 1952.

A comprehensive description of the provisions of the Korea G.I. bill.

Waller, Willard W. *The Veteran Comes Back*. New York: Dryden, 1944.

A history of veterans' affairs and activities from the Revolutionary War to World War II.

Chapter XI

CURRENT PUBLIC-

WELFARE PRACTICES

Existing policies, practices, and philosophies
on various categories of public assistance
and child welfare are described, and a
descriptive breakdown of welfare clientele
and discussion of guaranteed-income plans
are offered.

A wide variety of public-assistance programs exists throughout the nation, each one different in some respects from the programs of other states. As a consequence of these many differences, there is no single state program that can serve as a model for our discussion. All states have taken an interest in the "disadvantaged," as is clear from the number of programs for the blind, the aged, physically and emotionally disabled children, and so on.

Many people (particularly Negroes from the Deep South) have been too ignorant and too frightened of unpleasant repercussions to consider applying for such temporary assistance to which they may have been entitled. In programs using Federal matching funds discriminatory practices are not permitted. Title VI of the Civil Rights Act of 1964 states that "no person in the United States shall, on the ground of race, color, or national origin, be excluded from participation in, be denied the benefits of, or be subjected to discrimination under any program or activity receiving federal financial assistance."

If a state elects not to seek Federal aid, it may establish any eligibility test it desires. All states do receive Federal aid, however, and some consistency thus exists in public assistance offered throughout the country.

In addition to various programs, there are various views on assistance. F. Emerson Andrews discusses the "undeserving" needy and suggests that attitudes about the "qualities" of recipients have substantial effects on the public image of an agency.[1] If social welfare agencies obtained money only from private philanthropic parties, policy would originate from that source. The private donor subsidizing an agency could demand that his image be favorably transferred to the public. The end result would be an evaluation of the "parent" organization, rather than the quality of the service offered. After passing through a "charity" phase the United States has come to the realization that a person should retain his dignity, no matter how "unacceptable" his problem may be. Great strides were made in acceptance of this philosophy when great numbers of "worthy" people became dependent upon public assistance during the Great Depression. Realization of the need for some national program resulted in the Social Security Act of 1935.

This act provided for financial security for vast numbers of workers and their survivors. Several specific programs were established for this purpose, including Old Age Insurance (OAI). This program underwent changes and later became Old Age and Survivors Disability Insurance (OASDI), which allows for payments to eligible disabled workers or to survivors in the event of workers' deaths. The second major program under this act provided for public assistance. In the remainder of this chapter we shall examine this program.

Public Assistance

The original focus of the Social Security Act was on financial assistance, the result of two main factors. First, the Great Depression had plunged much of the work force into enforced idleness. Second, those in need were not chronic indigents but "substantial" and "worthy" people, and temporary financial help was all they asked.

As the employment situation began to be stabilized, the "relief" rolls dropped considerably. Those who remained financially dependent generally also needed help with other problems that were immobilizing them. Many of these people were unable to enter the labor market because of lack of training. They had had insufficient training before the Depression and were still untrained when the Depression ended. The Depression itself was considered temporary, and individuals postponed such long-term goals as training so long that by the time work was available people could afford no further delay in earning and did not then seek training.

Training for specialized work did not receive its greatest impetus until the 1960s. From the time of the Depression until the end of World War II a person's chances of success in business or as a wage earner, even with less than a high-school education, were greater than they are today. The G.I. bill gave large numbers of veterans the opportunity to obtain college educations, and by 1950 a high-school diploma was considered the minimum requirement for entrance into the labor force for most jobs. By 1960 a college degree was necessary to compete for higher-paying jobs. At the same time recognition that practical training, in addition to formal schooling, was needed for many jobs occurred, and emphasis has been on training and retraining programs since that time.

But the untrained people remaining on "relief" rolls after the Depression did not find such programs to assist them. Instead the Social Security Act of 1935 and its subsequent amendments instituted services to help people with other than financial problems. The 1964 amendments extended service to recipients in an effort to reduce dependence. Four areas were singled out for special consideration: strengthening of family life, social and human relation rehabilitation, prevention of dependence, and self-support and self-care. In order for states to qualify for 75 percent Federal participation, each interview or investigation had to be reported in writing for auditing purposes.

The Secretary of Health, Education and Welfare declared that social services would be provided for aged and disabled individuals in need of protection from exploitation in health, housing, and other related problems; aged and disabled individuals requiring help to remain in or return to their own homes or communities; blind and other disabled individuals with potential for total or partial self-support; and families with dependent children, including unmarried parents and their children with specified problems, families disrupted by desertion or impending desertion, families with potentially self-supporting adults, and children in need of protection.

There are various categories within public assistance programs which are listed below.[2]

Aid to Families with Dependent Children

Aid to Families with Dependent Children (AFDC) includes services to assure children opportunities to grow up in their own family settings, enjoy the economic support and services necessary for health and development, receive education to realize their capacities and participate in their neighborhoods and communities.

Aid to the Blind

Aid to the Blind (AB) assists people of any age whose vision is 20/200 or less with correction.

Aid to the Disabled

Aid to the Disabled (AD) is available to people between eighteen and sixty-five years of age who are totally and permanently disabled physically or mentally. The disability may be congenital, developmental, or accidental.

Old-Age Assistance

Old-Age Assistance (OAA) is available to people sixty-five years and older. Liens are often taken on the property of applicants for this assistance, so that states may recover some of the funds granted these people through sale of their property after death.

Medical Assistance (MA)

Medical assistance pays medical expenses for recipients of OAA, AFDC, AB or AD and others in low-income categories.

General Assistance (GA)

This program is designed for employable and unemployable people under sixty-five years of age. Applicants who are physically able are assigned to works projects.

Eligibility

For each of the programs described, a specific list of questions must be answered by the client in order to establish eligibility, in compliance with regulations under which assistance is granted. Manuals of regulations are one of the things that welfare departments throughout the country are known for. Many a disgruntled welfare employee has complained that there are too many regulations and too much paper work in connection with the regulations. Some people, it is reported, spend as much time keeping their manuals up to date as in interviewing clients.

Complaints of excessive paper work involved in establishing and maintaining eligibility have received much attention. Administrators at county, state, and Federal levels have cooperated in streamlining the numerous forms, many of which are duplications of other forms. Filling out forms is one duty that the caseworker is willing to transfer to a volunteer worker, a clerk, or some other responsible person.

A significant attempt to assist the professional caseworker is the widespread use of the subprofessional, often called a "case aide." The case aide can handle many of the clerical aspects of a case load. For example, there is the work necessary to change all existing records when a client changes his address. The notification of various people and offices is imperative if the client is to continue receiving financial assistance and services without interruption.

Programs using case aides are increasing in number, and experience will determine the most effective use of people at all levels of competence, whether in clerical work or in more complex tasks like intake interviewing. The intake interview is often the client's first contact with a public-welfare department. A case aide could be very valuable in helping the client understand the various regulations and in collecting the information that is still required to establish eligibility.

Although there are still many such eligibility requirements, they are becoming less important and will probably eventually dwindle to a very few specific items. The problem of residence, which has received much attention, no longer causes the same concern. At this writing there are questions being raised that eventually may eradicate residence requirements. Establishment of the medical-assistance program was a significant step toward relaxing residence requirements, for declaration by the applicant of his intention to remain in the state is sufficient to obtain such assistance.

Another problem is the financial responsibility of close relatives. Some states have had laws requiring such responsibility for a long time, and most states require exploration of this possible resource but only as a formality. The 1965 amendments to the Social Security Act make support of a relative a voluntary matter rather than a statutory requirement. This change does not affect the basic responsibility of spouse to support spouse and of parents to support minor children and physically or mentally disabled children regardless of age.

Income has been a great problem in determining eligibility.[3] Problems that would not even occur to the applicant may turn out to be of such consequence that he experiences additional stress instead of the relief that he seeks. Such factors as potential value of livestock, inoperative vehicles, stock in defunct or extinct organizations, sporadic support payments, alimony, gifts, garden and farm products, and past sale of property are investigated to establish need. Certain sources of income like $5 Christmas gifts are considered inconsequential; others, like earnings from a boy's paper route, may be exempt. An applicant may elect not to disclose all the facts for fear that they will render him ineligible. He thus places himself in jeopardy of court action for fraud. Reduction in grants is common, and prosecution for fraud and imprisonment is not impossible. Failure by the client to report changes in circumstances—sometimes forgetfully, sometimes not—is also cause for concern. Often the client is unable to reach his caseworker, and his message is not recorded. Turnover among caseworkers often means that overpayments do not come to light until months after they actually occurred. Overpayments to clients were long classified as resulting from either administrative error or fraud. But the cost of processing the former is becoming higher than the recovery of overpayment warrants. Attention will continue to be paid to cases of fraud and errors, however, because they make assistance to others less possible.

Personnel Problems

Although many new regulations are adopted to allow caseworkers more time with clients, other necessities nevertheless impose restrictions on that time. One of them involves reporting procedures. In order for the U.S. Department of Health, Education and Welfare to justify its various grants to states for public welfare, services must be fully reported. The state becomes party to a contract that calls for accounting for money advanced to it. Without such a system the Federal government could not submit to audits of its disbursement of public funds.

Each caseworker is therefore required to submit monthly a detailed statistical report on his case load. The services of case aides could be useful in this area too, thus freeing the caseworker to spend more time with clients. The caseworker is responsible for knowing each of his clients and being able to assist him as problems arise. Any innovations that can free the caseworker to devote more time to such duties will be welcome.

One frequently encountered problem is the caseworker who pays lip service to his responsibilities to clients but devotes more effort to reporting. This attitude in turn contributes to another problem: the tendency to label clients and to lose sight of their individuality. This tendency is especially characteristic of workers who strive to create an impression of knowledgeability; ironically, they are usually less sophisticated than those who merely describe accurately what they observe.

Still further complications arise from the relative status attached to specific jobs within a given welfare agency. Caseworkers in child welfare (not a category of public assistance but included in Title V of the Social Security Act of 1935) and AFDC are viewed as the "elite." Those in OAA, on the other hand, spend much time justifying their positions because their clients are more difficult to treat, as well as an underlying assumption of a more favorable prognosis for the child than for the elderly. There is a notable lack of enthusiasm in working with the elderly which results in vacancies in this area for longer periods than in other categories of public assistance. In some states interagency rivalry is neither friendly nor professional. More often it is a subtle factor taken into account when considering applicants for other positions; heavier weight is given to some kinds of experience than to others.

The same preference is accorded to supervisory experience over casework experience. In the vast number of welfare departments throughout the nation, the holder of a master of social work degree (M.S.W.) is assigned supervisory or administrative responsibilities within a short period of time after he is graduated. He may be assigned to a case load for only a brief period, whereas most casework is handled by those with bachelors' degrees.

Until recently there was no nationally recognized undergraduate program to prepare people for the helping professions. The Council on Social Work Education (CSWE), a composite of all professional social-work organizations, has taken the initiative in setting standards for and offering accreditation to colleges and universities in the United States and Canada that develop undergraduate social-welfare curricula. These programs are known by various names, but all serve to prepare undergraduates either for employment in the helping professions or for admission to professional schools of social work.

Poverty

Poverty has recently become a major issue among the American people, and almost everybody has his own views on why people are poor. Some Americans believe that welfare clients and other poor people are lazy and could raise themselves out of poverty if they wished. Others, including some welfare officials, maintain that most, if not all, of those on public assistance are victims of circumstances totally beyond their control. Both these views are extreme, however. There are other views, including those of most caseworkers themselves. John K. Galbraith describes "case poverty" and "insular poverty." The former characterizes people who are unable to cope with social demands because of physical and emotional shortcomings. Insular poverty afflicts people living in areas that have been "depressed" for some time.[4]

Until very recently, many welfare workers believed that most clients with whom they dealt had personality disorders and emotional illnesses that prevented their rising out of poverty. The solutions adopted were individual counseling by welfare workers and psychotherapy and psychological testing for severe cases when funds were available. It was assumed that solving the emotional problems of individuals on welfare would result in their rushing out to find jobs that were supposedly waiting for them in vast numbers.

Linked with this treatment approach was the idea that the ultimate purpose of public welfare was to remove clients from the rolls and to send them into the labor market as self-sufficient taxpayers. History has shown, however, that welfare departments across the nation have failed to reduce welfare rolls dramatically. In fact the rolls have increased annually. It is now being recognized that public-assistance programs exist only to provide financial aid and medical and other services to those who can prove that they are in need. The goal of getting clients off welfare is still important, but it is secondary to providing aid to those who have no other source of income. Individual counseling and psychotherapy may have failed to eradicate poverty because there are other important causes besides personality difficulties.

Clients on public assistance can be divided into three broad categories. First, there are the "circumstantially poor," who find themselves in need because of events beyond their control that have prevented breadwinners from working and have exhausted savings and other resources. They are the ones most often attacked by those who think that welfare recipients are bums unwilling to work. Often, however, fathers have lost work because of such medical catastrophes as severe heart disease, strokes, or back injuries. Divorced mothers may be unable to work because they have infant children or lack the skills and education necessary to find jobs. Such mothers and children stay on assistance an average of less than two years, which strongly indicates their determination to become self-supporting as soon as their children are old enough to be cared for by others.

The circumstantially poor are usually eager to get off welfare for two main reasons: They dislike the stigma attached to welfare by conservative politicians and those who write letters to editors complaining that recipients enjoy easy lives and do not pay their bills, and they also wish to raise their standard of living above what welfare grants permit. As welfare grants in the United States amount to less than the income defining poverty, these people would rather work and increase their earnings and buying power.

The second group includes those who are on welfare for psychological or emotional reasons. Among them are alcoholics, drug addicts, neurotics, and psychotics. Many such people have been placed on welfare rolls after receiving institutional treatment and then reentering the community. Many are members of families in which even one more member could present a financial strain thus posing an even greater problem for the rest of the family.

Many welfare clients with serious emotional problems have never received psychiatric care in or out of an institution, however. They present to welfare workers emotional problems and ways of behavior that are dysfunctional in society and have remained untreated for years or even lifetimes. Often a welfare worker may represent the only "therapist" that an emotionally ill client ever knows. This problem is very serious, for most caseworkers have insufficient training to provide therapy, nor do they have adequate time to devote to such demanding clients. These clients tend to use welfare workers as substitute parents. They seek not only financial aid but also the opportunity to remain dependent upon others. It is frustrating to a welfare worker to be expected by the emotionally disturbed client to provide for all his financial, medical, and emotional needs.

Finally, there are those from the culture of poverty, about whom we are only beginning to learn. Their orientation is toward the reality of always being poor. They are typically found in ghettos, on Indian reservations, in racial minority groups in urban areas, and in the rural South. The essential feature of the culture of poverty is that its inhabitants have learned to think, feel, and act in accordance with the deprived conditions under which they live. They find it extremely difficult to postpone immediate gratification and to plan for the future. They are accustomed to living only in the present. They also distrust the middle class and occasionally blame it for their own difficulties. This distrust is not difficult to explain. Many of the landlords, furniture dealers, and other merchants with whom they deal live outside the ghettos, usually in comfortable suburbs, and their contacts with their customers are impersonal. Some of them exploit the poor by selling inferior goods or charging excessive interest rates on long-term installment contracts.

Government services for ghetto dwellers are most often represented by policemen, health inspectors, and welfare workers, all of whom come mainly when there is trouble or to ask questions. Their middle-class perspectives are often not compatible with those of poor people. Therefore the poor have come to dislike representatives of the dominant culture, which is viewed as threatening or exploitive.

Furthermore, poor people generally own no property beyond a few personal possessions. It is not surprising that millions of dollars worth of property were destroyed during the urban riots of the 1960s, for little or none of that property belonged to ghetto dwellers.

It also follows that, although the middle-class American is a great founder and joiner of organizations, the person from the culture of poverty is not. He believes that organizations belong to the dominant culture and that he can derive little pleasure from and exert no power in them. Often, he feels unwelcome even though official policy would not bar him as a member. Discrimination does not take place at the "unofficial" level, however.

The person from the culture of poverty attaches little or no value to formal education. He is seldom familiar with anyone who has gained much from education, and he sees little evidence that he can gain financially or socially himself. Parents generally have received less than high-school education and therefore do not serve as models for children seeking education.

People from the culture of poverty provide the second and third generation of welfare clients. Their whole way of life is one of "just getting by," as opposed to the "getting ahead" typical of the middle class. In addition to its physical and financial aspects, such a way of life soon fixes modes of feeling, thinking, and acting in new generations, who learn to plan only for the present and to take a fatalistic and hopeless view of the future.[5]

The history of public assistance since its inception during the Depression of the 1930s contains many examples of misunderstanding of those receiving aid. Until recently, social workers defined welfare clients as people with mental and emotional problems. The public tends to side with conservative politicians in viewing the welfare client as lazy and content to enjoy existing on small welfare grants. The client had on one hand to manage on an unrealistic budget for his needs, and on the other to maintain his dignity in the face of the public assumption that he was incompetent or indolent.

The triple classification system just presented represents a beginning toward understanding the welfare client as an individual.

Legal Services

Approximately seven people out of every thousand seeking the services of attorneys cannot pay for them. One of the most frightening situations in which a person can find himself is that of having to cope with our legal machinery. As our society becomes more complex, even the most sophisticated person finds it difficult to follow directions precisely, to remember names, and to recall social-security and other numbers. Yet applicants for public assistance are expected to do just that. Legal processes are often set in motion against a person before he has had time to organize and mobilize his resources. The problem may be economic, domestic, or involving property, any one of which may necessitate his appearance in court. If he does not have the money for professional legal representation, he may not be able to obtain justice.

In addition to misunderstanding and disagreement, there is deliberate exploitation of the poor, which brings even greater feelings of helplessness and hopelessness. When a poor person is faced with unethical and unlawful practices by members of the middle class, he has a difficult time exercising his legal rights. In all probability he will fare worse without a lawyer; his misunderstandings, outbursts of temper, and inability to communicate may result in dire consequences indeed.

A recipient of public assistance often has contact with the county attorney, the attorney general, or their representatives. For example, if a father deserts his family a legal effort is often required by the wife before the authorities can deal with him. The proceeding is complicated, and it is not surprising that some people purposely avoid it. In many communities free or very inexpensive legal services are available through the Legal Aid Society and the Legal Defenders Association, and certain programs under O.E.O. in cooperation with local bar associations, depending upon the circumstances of the client.

Establishment of Special Case Loads

As welfare departments grow in size they often recognize problems with special characteristics. For instance, it may come to light that a large number of women on AFDC have husbands in prison, state mental hospitals, or otherwise detained. It is expedient to establish special case loads consisting of these clients. If one caseworker is responsible for all cases involving a member of the family in prison, time and effort are saved, especially in avoiding duplication of service, consultation, and collaborative efforts. As the number of people eligible for vocational rehabilitation grows, a caseworker can "specialize" in this type of case and become quite efficient in offering services.

Training Programs for Welfare Clients

At present poverty programs are geared to aiding the poor indirectly rather than directly. That is, various rehabilitative, educational, and employment programs aim to "help people help themselves" out of poverty. Of necessity, the indirect programs are oriented toward the future rather than toward the present, and one of the realities of poverty is that the poor are in need right now. For example, a multitude of training services for able-bodied people who are providing for their families only through unemployment checks or welfare grants is currently available. But there are no guarantees of jobs after training and no provisions for adequate income during the training period. There are several educational and job-training programs for young people who drop out of high school, but there are few financial supports to help teenagers from poor families remain in high school.

Community Action neighborhood centers, whose objectives are to mobilize available resources for a coordinated attack on poverty, despite all their creative activities, have no direct way of channeling funds into poor homes. They have found ways to communicate well with the poor, and their staffs have made gains with slum landlords and city hall on behalf of the poor. Public assistance programs are able to do little more than help the client deal with a crisis situation. Yet too many poor people have remained poor in the very neighborhoods that are being bombarded with services to alleviate their poverty.

Criticism of the War on Poverty programs is not intended to show that they are unnecessary or ineffective. Rather it is aimed at encouraging immediate and adequate financi٬٬ aid to the poor as a first condition of service. When a wound is severe, bleeding must be stopped before treatment for possible infection is administered.

A plea for adequate income maintenance thus becomes appropriate. Children can stay in school and do better work if their physical needs are adequately met. Adults can perform better in training programs and devote more attention to improving slum neighborhoods if they have the means for subsistence.

One avenue to more and better employment for the poor could involve private industry and business. In fact, the precedent and structure already exist through modern weapons development and production. The Federal government subsidizes private industry through multimillion-dollar contracts for military rocket, missile, and aircraft production, thus creating jobs for thousands of workers. In areas where few other employment opportunities exist, establishment of defense industries has provided an economic boon to individuals and whole communities.

The practice could be expanded to nonmilitary production as well. Water-resource development, smog control, and natural-resource conservation are only three major areas that require development in our nation at the present time. And jobs could more easily be designed to include the marginally skilled worker than is possible in technologically sophisticated nuclear-armament plants.

Welfare Practices and Children

Under Title V of the Social Security Act, Congress is authorized to provide funds to states for such services to children as maternal and child health care, crippled children's care, and child welfare. In 1967 Arizona was the only state that did not apply for and receive such funds.[6] The following breakdown gives a brief sketch of the responsibilities of these services.

Maternal and Child Health Services

One important service to children is provision of practical assistance to mothers and expectant mothers. There are clinics that make available to expectant mothers the services of doctors, nurses, and social workers. Public-health nurses make visits before and after children are born. There are "well baby" clinics that offer medical and nursing consultation, as well as treatment. Dental diagnosis and treatment and immunization against communicable diseases are also available.

Crippled Children's Services

Crippled children's services, of which few people are aware, locate, diagnose, and refer or treat children with medical problems. In almost all participating states, each child is entitled to one free referral and examination. In 1964 the total number of children who received care under the crippled children's program was approximately 423,000, not a high proportion of the children in the United States, all of whom are eligible at least once for such services.

In each state there are clinics to which children are brought for specialized treatment. In states whose populations are widely scattered clinics travel from place to place, but they are staffed by the same interdisciplinary teams that are found in the permanent facilities.

Child-Welfare Services

Child-welfare services include essentially all areas of nonmedical child care, ranging from adoption of infants to day care for older children of working mothers. Adoptions have traditionally been more often the province of private than of public agencies, but foster care has been handled by the public agencies, largely because of the vast expense involved.

Public adoption agencies often receive the older child, who is more difficult to place for adoption, one with a physical handicap perhaps or of a racial minority group.

The goals of child welfare are

1. To eliminate, through casework services, the neglect, abuse, or exploitation of children by their parents.
2. To provide shelter to abandoned, homeless, or dependent children.

3. To shelter for their own safety abused or neglected children.
4. To assist working mothers in providing adequate day care for their children.
5. To intervene with whatever urgency is necessary to protect children whose welfare is endangered.
6. To evaluate objectively, to diagnose, and to assist in the treatment of problems that disrupt families and to strengthen family life.

Other Services for Children

As employment of women in industry increases, it is not uncommon to find female heads of households. Women from the lower classes have traditionally worked outside their homes, whether or not they had children. Until World War II the typical middle-class male considered outside employment for his wife an affront to his dignity as breadwinner. Today working wives are commonly accepted in the middle class. There is controversy over working mothers, but the rate at which they have been employed in industry has been increasing.

As more young mothers have taken work outside their homes, the demand for child-care arrangements has been rising. The 1967 amendments to the Social Security Act specified that AFDC mothers with no preschool children must either begin job training or be already employed. Exceptions are allowed for physical disability, mental illness, or age.

The number of mothers entering training or employment will continue to grow in the future, and this increase will create a still greater need for child-care arrangements. They will probably take the form of centers that can handle numbers of children or private individuals, possibly other welfare recipients, who will take one or two children into their homes.

The cost of day care for children is a major problem; it will have to be kept at a minimum if many young mothers are to afford it. More important than cost is the quality of the child's experience away from his family. As he is going to spend more than one-third of his waking hours under someone else's supervision, many of his learning, play, and socialization needs, as well as his physical needs, will have to be met outside his family.

Whatever specific solutions are reached, there will be a large-scale expansion of day-care resources to meet the growing needs during the next several years. Some organizations already offer such services to their employees. There are already many day-care centers, licensed through state departments of public welfare, that provide supervision for large numbers of children. Neighborhood houses, settlement houses, and other community-sponsored programs will also continue to expand their programs, facilities, and staffs to help meet this growing need.

Guaranteed Annual Income

So far we have described various services designed to serve people with social and financial needs that they cannot handle alone. Many critics believe that such agencies are too bureaucratic to deal effectively with all the problems that they were created to attack. Neither public assistance nor pension programs provide enough income to meet the subsistence needs of the individuals they serve.

The true need of the individual is not the basis for computing benefits under any known pension, welfare, or insurance program. Instead, "eligibility" factors, which differ from one social-welfare agency to another, are the prime consideration in awarding grants or benefits, which are considerably below the standard poverty level of $4,000 a year for a four-member family.[7]

To be raised just to the level of poverty though not above it, a four-member family would have to be assisted to the point that its total income, including grants, reached $333 a month. None of the programs discussed so far can assist a family to that extent.

Regulations in the existing programs are many, varied, and complex and thus not understood by many of those responsible for their interpretation. It is possible for an individual to receive a veteran's pension, an agricultural subsidy or unemployment compensation, a public-assistance grant, and social-security benefits all at the same time. The receipt of each additional payment complicates his eligibility for both earlier and later assistance.

Even with safeguards on amounts and eligibility, the United States gives away many millions of dollars each year. Most of this money goes to subsidize agriculture, industrial development, education, and the defense and aerospace industries. The proposed guaranteed minimum-annual-income programs to be discussed here would represent only a fraction of the appropriations for any of these subsidies.

Any guaranteed minimum-annual-income scheme would have to provide for the basic needs of people with inadequate financial resources on the *basis of need,* rather than of arbitrary figures set by legislators "off the scene."

During the past decade economists and people in the helping professions have questioned the effectiveness of present income-redistribution programs in the United States. The social-insurance and social-assistance programs have not been able to meet the basic economic needs of the 20 percent of the American population that lives below the poverty line. In response to the present basic disparity in needs and resources, several different guaranteed-minimum-income proposals have been put forward. We shall describe some of the elements of these proposals after a discussion of one notable historical example, the Townsend Plan.

The Townsend Plan

On September 30, 1933, the Long Beach, California, *Press-Telegram* published a letter to the editor from Francis Everett Townsend, M.D., in which he suggested that, as industrialization had created pools of untrained and unemployed manpower, people be automatically retired at sixty with pensions of $200 a month, to release more jobs. To maintain eligibility the recipients of these pensions would have to spend the money in the United States within thirty days, thereby returning money back into the depressed economy, which would alleviate costs of many social-welfare institutions involved in the care of the aged.[8]

Although there had been proposals for raising pensions, increasing jobs for younger workers, and providing care for the elderly, the Townsend Plan, put forth in the depths of the Depression, benefited from the respectability of its originator in the mind of the public. Local Townsend clubs sprang up across the nation, claiming a total of 2.5 million members at one time.

Members of Townsend clubs were eligible voters, and they were encouraged to cast their ballots for appropriate programs. Although the Townsend Plan eventually lost its momentum, it was one of the moving forces behind the Social Security Act of 1935, especially the old-age provisions. Various political candidates were forced to adopt old-age pensions as planks in their platforms.

The Townsend slogan was "Age for leisure, youth for work." Many people joined the movement, and great results were achieved. Congressman John S. McGroarty of California introduced the Townsend Old Age Revolving Pension Plan in January 1935.[9] The majority in

Congress, and ultimately in the nation, opposed the Townsend Plan as too costly, unworkable, and unrealistic. Its aims may have been altruistic, but it was defeated by representatives of the people on practical grounds.[10]

Current Plans

The several guaranteed minimum-annual-income proposals that have recently been put forward differ essentially only in their methods of implementation but not in their philosophies. Many such plans would guarantee to all citizens, regardless of their positions in the labor force, sufficient income to maintain a standard of living at or above the poverty level. Under one plan, the Federal government could fix such a level, based on family composition, and those whose incomes fell below it could receive cash warrants raising them to it. Another plan, called the "negative income tax" is based on the existing Federal income-tax structure. Nontaxable citizens could claim portions of their unused exemptions in cash under this system. Guaranteed-employment plans would ensure employable people minimum amounts of work.

There are other plans, programs, schemes, and systems, and still others will no doubt be advanced in the future. They will include "generic" plans, in which all contributions and paid benefits are from one source, and "investment" plans, under which everyone will "deposit" his various benefit checks and draw payment vouchers in return from the cooperative pool that would invest money saved through its increased purchasing power.

Need for Immediate Income

Of the various plans mentioned none has a provision for making money immediately available to those in need. The one agency that does so is public assistance, which is itself a guaranteed-income system. People turn to public assistance when they do not have adequate incomes, often as the result of unexpected layoffs, injuries, illnesses, and personal tragedies.

As a result of the speed with which public-assistance programs can help clients, consideration should be given to another factor: that public assistance is usually the only source of income while other claims for benefits are pending. Some social-security claims take as long as two years to be processed and paid. Although a lump-sum payment of benefits due since the date of eligibility is eventually forthcoming, if no other means is available to the claimant, public assistance will probably be called upon to assist in the interim. Unemployment-compensation benefits are also often delayed beyond the prescribed ten-days-to-two week period from the date of filing.

In order to meet immediate financial needs a guaranteed minimum-annual-wage plan would have to make financial "first aid" similar to that of the public-assistance programs available. There are already sufficient refinements in public welfare-department policies to permit financial emergencies to be met on the date of application. That is, money *can* be disbursed the same day a person makes application when need justifies it.

The various forms of guaranteed income, whether they provide for financial "first aid" or not, are being widely discussed. National business and legislative leaders are endorsing such proposals in popular magazines.[11] Both legislators and their constituents have been exposed to information about the guaranteed-income idea.

Arguments Against Guaranteed Annual Income

There are three main arguments against the guaranteed annual income, which can be labeled the "giveaway," "socialistic," and "cost" arguments. The "giveaway" argument is that the program would destroy the incentive to work, that if people could make more money by "loafing" than by working they would not work. Helen Harris Perlman [12] observes that the public does not consider all men who earn more than $10,000 annually tax dodgers yet there are many income tax chiselers from this economically self-dependent group. Not only do people generalize more about those living in poverty but condemn them as well. Although there is no evidence either to support or to refute this argument, work is a value in our society, at least before retirement. Status and prestige are derived mainly from work, and most people will likely continue to seek them.

The second main argument against minimum-income plans is that they are "socialistic" and "un-American." These schemes *are* socialistic, just as farm subsidies, Medicare, and grants to airlines are. Such plans should be assessed for their contributions to improving human life within American society rather than for their labels. It appears that the real basis for the "socialist" argument is a moralistic attitude that the poor do not deserve better than they have.

The "disadvantaged" person often does not have access to jobs at the upper end of the salary scale because he lacks training and education. He is also more subject to illness, arrest, and dependence on social welfare. It is obvious then that his overall contribution to society is likely to be less than that of a healthy, comfortably employed person.

A third argument against guaranteed-income plans is the cost involved. Any plan that would adequately compensate the large numbers of people falling within the current definition of poverty would cost billions of dollars. Few taxpayers, even those sympathetic to the poor, would welcome tax increases as a solution to the problem, especially on a long-term basis. There would be greater support for such programs if it could be guaranteed that the problem of poverty in the United States would be resolved within a five-year period. People are less prone to participate in social action when they cannot envision results and be present at the conclusion.

The Future

Many kinds of income plans have been proposed and will continue to receive attention, for concern for the poor is not new. At the turn of the century Edward T. Devine suggested that provision be made to assist people with "deficient income" temporarily, in order to restore them to normal self-support.[13]

The Townsend Plan, put forward in the midst of the Great Depression, focused much attention on guaranteed income and was instrumental in achieving national legislation in that area. As income needs continue to be a problem, greater attention will be accorded to it. Only through social action geared to the solution of problems within a society will relief be found. The guaranteed minimum wage may be the answer for one of the United States' most serious internal problems.

The legal profession, through law schools and "internships," will offer more adequate legal services to the indigent. A U.S. Supreme Court decision in 1951 (*Griffin* v. *Illinois*) established an indigent person's right to a free record of his trial at the time he appealed his case. That decision also prescribed other protection of his rights, including appointment of counsel to serve throughout the arrest, trial, and appeal procedure.

Increasing the purchasing power of all citizens will release more money into the national economy, as was demonstrated by Franklin D. Roosevelt's administration when it increased Federal spending and thus reduced by almost two-thirds the number of people in poverty.[14]

Programs geared to a similar end, reducing poverty, will continue to be adopted in the future.

Public awareness of unemployment, poverty, and public-assistance problems will continue to increase. A better-informed public will permit relaxation of measures against the "disadvantaged." To deny adequate assistance to a family because of an additional birth causes suffering to the new child and is not an effective deterrent to the mother's having still more children.

Federal funds will continue to be necessary to help alleviate poverty, both directly and indirectly. In addition to direct grants to the poor, more work-training and other incentive programs will be established. Grants will be made available to those in the service professions to equip them to deal more effectively with poverty problems. One such program involving both poor people and professionals is Operation Head Start, sponsored by the Office of Economic Opportunity (OEO). It demonstrates what can be accomplished through emphasis on alleviating some of the components of poverty. Operation Head Start takes a multifaceted approach to coping with the total needs of the child: health, family relationships, emotional and social development, and intellectual enrichment. By involving the parents and other volunteers in a wide range of tasks the child is given a greater opportunity to observe basic functions of society in a more meaningful way. Professional skills in food preparation, counseling, nursing, library science and teaching further develop constructive skills and attitudes for the children. This program was instituted for the first time in the summer of 1965, and current plans call for its continuation. Subsequent evaluations will reveal the specific limitations of children in poverty and suggest new programs for the future.

NOTES

1. F. Emerson Andrews, *Philanthropic Giving* (New York: Russell Sage Foundation, 1950), pp. 27–32. Andrews analyzes the major areas of philanthropy and the common questions of potential donors. He also discusses the change from traditional charity to philanthropy in all its forms.
2. U.S. Department of Health, Education and Welfare, *Characteristics of State Public Assistance Plans under the Social Security Act*, Public Assistance Report No. 50 (Washington, D.C.: Government Printing Office, 1964). A detailed description of the public-assistance programs

in the fifty states and in the District of Columbia, Guam, Puerto Rico, and the Virgin Islands.

3. George Hoshino, "Simplification of the Means Test and Its Consequences," *The Social Service Review*, 41, No. 3 (September 1967), pp. 16–22. This article clarifies the importance of making determination of eligibility a less confusing and time-consuming process.

4. John K. Galbraith, *The Affluent Society* (Boston: Houghton Mifflin, 1958), pp. 252–253. Galbraith interprets poverty in terms of different theoretical concepts, popular and statistical illusions, social balance, inflation, and the economics of production.

5. Robert R. Bell, *Marriage and Family Interaction* (Homewood, Ill.: Dorsey, 1967), pp. 48–52. This basic text for courtship-and-marriage courses that offers an interesting comparison of different class values.

6. U.S. Department of Health, Education and Welfare, *op. cit.*, p. 21.

7. Michael Harrington, *The Other America: Poverty in the United States* (New York: Macmillan, 1963), p. 182. Portrays the paradoxical culture of poverty in the United States, with special attention to slums, Negroes, the aged, and a classification of poor people.

8. Abraham Holtzman, *The Townsend Movement* (New York: Bookman, 1963), pp. 35–37. Provides a descriptive analysis of one of the first and most popular plans for the elderly.

9. H.R. 3977 (Washington, D.C.: Government Printing Office, 1935).

10. U.S. Senate Committee on Finance, *Hearings*, S. 1130, 74th Congress, 1st Session (Washington, D.C.: Government Printing Office, 1935).

11. T. George Harris, "Do We Owe People a Living?," *Look* (April 30, 1968) pp. 25–27. Now: "A Tax Plan That Pays People," *U.S. News & World Report* (February 14, 1966), p. 63.

12. Helen Harris Perlman, "Are We Creating Dependency?" *Minnesota Welfare*, 9 (October 1963), pp. 11–19.

13. Edward T. Devine, *The Principles of Relief* (New York: Macmillan, 1907), pp. 3–9. This book is an early history of relief and charity, citing typical problems of the nineteenth century.

14. Dwight Macdonald, *Our Invisible Poor* (New York: Hillman Foundation, 1963), p. 12. This pamphlet discusses poverty in the United States, covering numbers, race, programs, and philosophy.

SUGGESTED READINGS

Fink, Arthur E., C. Wilson Anderson, and Merril B. Conover. *The Field of Social Work*. New York: Holt, Rinehart and Winston, 1968.

A critical analysis of the various amendments to the Social Security Act and discussions of other national programs.

Tenbroek, Jacobus, ed. *The Law of the Poor*. San Francisco: Chandler, 1966.

A thorough examination of laws applicable to poor people, with comparisons of results for the affluent and the indigent.

Theobald, Robert. "The Guaranteed Income," *Vital Speeches,* 32 (July 1, 1966), 573–6.

Some of the more recent thinking on guaranteed annual income.

Thursz, Daniel. "Social Aspects of Poverty, Public Welfare," *The Journal of the American Public Welfare Association,* 25, No. 3 (July 1967).

A frank discussion of myths about the poor and a challenge of certain fictions regarding poverty.

Part Three

CONTEMPORARY

SOCIAL FORCES

Chapter *XII*

INDIGENOUS SOCIAL

MOVEMENTS

*Indigenous social movements are defined and
analyzed, showing how attention is brought to
bear upon problems that have been
known but ignored.*

Sociologists differ in their opinions about social movements. William B. Cameron has written an entire book to define them.[1] Ralph H. Turner and Lewis M. Killian [2] while offering a comprehensive analysis of social movements, did not include the term indigenous in their discussion. We define a social movement as an organized body of people working toward change. Because of the necessity of including the indigenous factor, we shall broaden this definition to include a description of the people involved in specific kinds of movements, the processes by which change is to be brought about, and methods for achieving legitimation.

An Organized Body of People . . .

This portion of the definition must be interpreted to include the concept of *indigenous* movements. The employees of the Veterans Administration are an organized body, but an organization generated *from among* its clients would be an *indigenous* organization. This

237

would parallel "grass roots," up-from-the-people types of goal-directed organizations that form without the benefit of a "parent" organization.

. . . Working Toward Change

Some common processes of organizations in general are election of officers, appointment of committees, fund raising, recruiting, and debate. Variations of these elements are also common in social movements, but standard approaches and methods have often failed to bring about desired results, and consequently their repertoire has expanded to include more effective processes like demonstrations, protests, marches, and other actions to "rub raw the sores of discontent." [3]

Legitimation

The final point needed to broaden a definition of a social movement to include an indigenous social movement would be that of legitimation. Historically such movements have begun as protests against established institutions. The causes they espoused have often been labeled "radical," and therefore many protests against unfair practices, discrimination, and prejudice have not been "respectable." In fact, acceptance of the protestors' ideals by society at large has usually signaled the end of the movement, which has its birth in controversy and its death in acceptance.

Phases of a Social Movement

The definition of a social movement thus becomes "an organization of laymen who recognize common problems and seek power vigorously and forcefully in order to further their cause." With this definition in mind, we can analyze the two basic phases of such a social movement: recognition-mustering and organization-action.

In the first phase awareness of common problems grows among a particular group of people. This step is quite elementary but necessarily precedes any other. For example, a group of mothers of young children might become concerned at the lack of a school guard at a busy intersection. Some of them might share their concern with mothers of other children attending the same school. Discovery that apprehension was widespread might lead to enlisting support to seek a solution.

When sufficient strength had been mustered, the mothers would be ready to move into the next phase, organization-action. Presumably a spokesman for the group would have emerged, either voluntarily or through election. In the second part of phase two the mothers might request a crossing guard through the principal of the school, the board of education, or elected county or state officials. The potential danger might be demonstrated by mothers accompanying their children to school and carrying placards and warning signs for motorists. As soon as action favorable to its cause had been taken, the movement could be dissolved.

This example is admittedly simple and without incident, but it illustrates the general principles involved. A more complex example is that of a minority group that is being moved out of its familiar neighborhood. Attempts to relocate such groups have been relatively common during the past two decades, mostly as the result of urban-renewal programs.

During hearings in 1965, 1966, and 1967 members of the U.S. Commission on Civil Rights learned a great deal about the feelings of slum dwellers, those usually displaced by various public and private building programs.[4] The commission's report clearly describes the advantages sought outside the slums: better schools, job possibilities, housing.

The freedom to move from the ghetto is limited by the lack of funds for down payments on houses or apartments, deposits on utilities, cleaning fees, and similar incidental moving costs. When a move is sought these costs are taken into account, but when the move is involuntary they pose additional hardships on already overburdened budgets.

Mass evictions are usually ordered in the name of "progress," whether under Federally funded urban-renewal projects or by private enterprise. The intention is usually to demolish existing buildings to make way for new construction, but usually there are lengthy delays that make it seem as if progress is at a standstill. The former housing sites may be replaced by expressways, parking lots, shopping centers, or industrial complexes. Whatever new construction is intended, the inhabitants are not usually the property owners and have very little voice in the matter. In the face of expanding population and competition for already overcrowded housing, displacement of many residents is a problem in any city.

Employees may be forced to leave the area of their employment. Children who must transfer to other schools may be left back in grade regardless of their ability. A public-assistance recipient in one county or state may experience new eligibility problems if his move (perhaps less than two miles) places him in another county or state; a probationer or parolee also experiences problems in moving to another county or state.

These difficulties are in addition to the psychological impact of being uprooted. The person about to be evicted feels helpless to cope with the many problems that a move imposes upon him. He is faced with a grim future and rightly wonders whether or not his feelings have ever been considered. He is aware of much that is going on around him. He may see buildings already standing vacant but no activity to demolish them and build something else. He soon concludes that certain "decision makers" do not have the benefit of sound plans, informed advisers, or knowledge of "the pulse" of the neighborhood.

As residents become aware of plans to move them out to make way for something else, they begin to recognize the problem as one affecting the community, the first step in phase one. As questions are raised, a common cause materializes, and others are soon recruited. At this point, one of the first of many complications may arise. The momentum so far generated can easily carry over into the second phase, especially if the people are fairly homogeneous. It is unlikely that all the people to be affected by eviction will react in the same way. Some may welcome the event as a long-awaited end to the "undesirable" neighborhood, and they may see no value in fighting for reconsideration of the plan. Others may be so pessimistic that participation in any form of protest seems futile and is therefore unthinkable.

An assessment of the characteristics of people involved in the common problem must be made, in order to complete the mustering portion of phase one. If enough people are willing to involve themselves, phase two can be initiated.

In order to gain a hearing for its cause, a group must organize its "power"—its strength in numbers. Single individuals cannot be as effective as can a large group working toward a common goal. This power can best be wielded by leaders enjoying the trust of all the membership.

The indigenous leader is usually called upon to serve and is less often a self-appointed crusader. Members of minority groups who have risen above their humble beginnings are not usually regarded as logical leaders at such times. By virtue of their "success" these people are often distrusted as much as is the typical middle-class white from outside the area. Consequently, a capable resident familiar with area problems often rises to the challenge and assumes leadership. If no such person exists, no organized activity will be forthcoming. One aspect of an organization is its charter, constitution, or bylaws, the basic rules and regulations under which the organization is to function. The purpose, philosophy, and objectives of the group are usually spelled out in these documents. For purposes of gaining additional power certain coalitions may be formed, perhaps between two neighborhood groups protesting related problems: rats and high rents, for example. Coalitions are as important to social movements as they are to political parties, for the same reason: the increase in organized power.

The second portion of phase two begins after problems of organization have been solved; the types of action that such a group may take are virtually unlimited. The nonviolent, law-abiding approach is unquestionably the least expensive, in lives as well as in money. We hope that violence has served its purpose and that lives and property will no longer have to be needlessly sacrificed in order to register protest. Pressure from sufficiently powerful groups can accomplish the same missions without violence. Some "legitimate" avenues for action, including protests, demonstrations, meetings, and pamphleteering, will be discussed here. Martin Luther King, Jr., the late leading advocate of nonviolence, called such avenues "direct action." [5]

Protests may take other forms but basically must offer objections to existing conditions. A protest may be voiced by a representative, written to an elected official, published in a newspaper, or made public through marches, boycotts, or mass demonstrations of pickets.

Demonstrations include marches to enlist sympathy and to show strength. The wearing of black arm bands by supporters of Senator Eugene McCarthy following his defeat in September 1968 is an example of a demonstration on the part of his supporters.[6] The point of a demonstration is to bring the demonstrators' feelings on a particular issue to the attention of society.

Meetings are useful for fact finding, exchange of information, and organization. The assembly of people with common problems can be used effectively by leaders as a forum in which to answer members' questions. Committee reports can be presented, and officers can be elected, activities planned and progress evaluated.

Written or printed material can be distributed widely. If, for instance, a certain government official has the power to delay action on the eviction of large numbers of people, handbills telling how to get in touch with this man might be distributed. Signs, placards, and banners often bring a message to the attention of passersby. Letters to individuals and newspapers are effective means of attracting attention. A 100-word telegram signed by ten citizens would probably have less impact than a ten-word telegram with 100 signatures, for reasons of sheer numbers and awareness of the dynamics inherent in group action.

After taking advantage of the various avenues of direct action, a social movement may be either successful or unsuccessful in obtaining its goals and public acceptance of them (legitimation). Following is a discussion of factors to be included in evaluation of indigenous social movements.

The age, sexual and geographical distribution of the members is important. If the age range includes enough eligible voters of both sexes, it is possible for such a group to exert political influence. The distribution of the members can affect political decisions and may be most effective if it is sufficiently wide to offer strong support or opposition on municipal, state, and Federal levels.

The number and characteristics of leaders are also important. Study of them would be tantamount to examination of the structural and organizational effectiveness of the movement. It is necessary to find out whether or not boards, committees, and others are capable of carrying out the mandates of the group.

A third factor is how much change results from the group's activities as reflected in local, state, or national legislation. The issues on which a group protests and acts usually require revision of existing rules, regulations, ordinances, or statutes. Favorable legislation is one sign of success.

Many social movements are "blackballed" or ignored by society at large first, in reaction to any protest against the status quo. How far society eventually accepts the protestors' principles is an index of their success or failure. Open housing, for example, is more widely accepted now than in 1950.

A factor of considerable importance in evaluating the success or failure of an indigenous social movement is the degree to which concessions are made on either side to achieve the desired ends. If, in the final analysis, the general attitude of society has undergone redefinition, the tenets of the movement will be considered less radical. These beliefs, by virtue of their acceptance, will no longer be outside the mainstream of opinion but will be considered an integral part of the culture; in fact opposition to them will be regarded as "radical." In an attempt to persuade society of the value of some of its objectives, an indigenous social movement may compromise its position on other objectives; this course can undermine the importance of the movement as a whole unless such compromises are recognized as realignments of policy rather than as retreats from a position. An example of realignment is coalition with another group dedicated to a sufficient number of the same principles espoused by the other to make it possible for cooperative efforts. An example of retreat is a civil-rights group's failure to insist upon housing for a particular minority group.

The final test of the success or failure of social movement, however, is its current image and what organized opposition it has aroused. If the movement is generally considered rational, fair, active, and "worthy," it has already succeeded to a degree. If, on the other hand, it continues to arouse widespread ridicule, suspicion, and doubt of its "genuine" intent, and to be regarded as a group of troublemakers, it has failed.

As an indigenous social movement is successful in making its protests heard and having its problems remedied, other forces will arise to protest the new status quo. Another social movement may arise, and its opposition will include many of those who have just struggled to establish the new status quo. John A. Clausen points out that social movements originate in challenges to social functioning posed by conflicts between values and practices.[7] In these terms, the group that struggles for acceptance of certain principles today may defend the functioning of society tomorrow.

With this general foundation we can examine an actual, and rather successful, indigenous movement, the Woodlawn Organization (TWO).

The Woodlawn Organization

In 1960 three Protestant ministers and a Catholic priest with parishes in a Negro ghetto in Chicago enlisted the aid of Saul Alinsky, a professional community organizer. Alinsky was, and still is, a controversial figure who specializes in "appealing to the self-interest of local residents" and in persuading people that they can solve their problems through community organization.[8] He was then head of the Industrial Areas Foundation (IAF), which had been successful in developing indigenous leadership potential in about fifty communities before 1960. A community often has people with leadership qualities, and IAF helps to develop them. After training the necessary local leadership to assume responsibility for the community organization, IAF withdraws.

Woodlawn, an area adjacent to the University of Chicago, had a population of approximately 100,000 people, mostly Negroes, who were seriously exploited by landlords, merchants, and police. Children attended overcrowded schools in shifts, and various forms of vice were rampant.

After an assessment of the problems as residents saw them, IAF organizers arranged parades, protest marches, demonstrations, boycotts, and other citizen-participation efforts to publicize area problems. As a result, The Woodlawn Organization (TWO) was formed; eventually it hired one salaried administrator. The various activities of TWO forced merchants to cut down on excessive interest charges, short-changing, and improper use of scales for weighing merchandise. Landlords in the area were pressured into repairing buildings and bringing them up to legal minimum-health standards. An urban-renewal proposal by The University of Chicago was effectively blocked. TWO was successful in influencing decisions affecting its members' lives to a much greater degree than before. City Hall, formerly regarded in Woodlawn as an ominous place, was visited many times by area residents, who developed skills in voicing their opinions, suggestions, and complaints.

Conditions in Woodlawn when Alinsky was invited there were so deplorable that the residents believed that they could get no worse. They were frightened and had never experienced success, either jointly or individually, in combating poor conditions, which makes their success all the more remarkable. They needed and received help in the first phase; they also accepted guidance and advice in the second phase until they were capable of administering TWO entirely on their own. Once they had passed through these phases successfully, they had no difficulty continuing on their own momentum.

TWO encompasses approximately ninety groups, representing a total membership of 30,000.[9] These people, led by barbers, mailmen, bartenders, and other residents of the area, were able to muster the power to make their voices heard. They no longer believed that they had to be silent victims of more powerful individuals; through TWO they could influence their own lives.

Neither the experiences of TWO nor those of other indigenous social movements indicate cause for complacency. Regardless of solutions to any number of difficulties unsolved problems still remain in every community. When the existing structure is inadequate to meet its members' needs the situation calls for recognition and mustering followed by organization and action.

NOTES

1. William B. Cameron, *Modern Social Movements* (New York: Random House, 1966), p. 7. Entire publication analyzes the characteristics, memberships, structures, and importance of such movements.
2. Ralph H. Turner and Lewis M. Killian, *Collective Behavior* (Englewood Cliffs, N.J.: Prentice-Hall, 1957), pp. 307–479. This book offers an interdisciplinary survey of collective behavior, through excerpts from diverse sources.
3. Charles E. Silberman, *Crisis in Black and White* (New York: Vintage, 1964), pp. 137–144. This book is a study of the explosive race problem in the United States and the increasing necessity of a solution.
4. U.S. Commission on Civil Rights, *A Time to Listen . . . A Time to Act* (Washington, D.C., Government Printing Office, 1967).
5. Martin L. King, Jr., *Why We Can't Wait* (New York: New American Library, 1964), p. 42. This analysis of the struggle for civil rights also contains Dr. King's famous letter written from the Birmingham, Alabama, jail.
6. "The Government in Exile," *Time*, September 6, 1968, pp. 25–27.
7. John A. Clausen, "Mental Disorders," in Robert K. Merton and Robert A. Nisbet, eds., *Contemporary Social Problems* (New York: Harcourt, 1966), pp. 26–83. This collection furnishes an overview of social disorganization and various forms of deviant behavior.
8. Silberman, *op. cit.*, pp. 321–324.
9. *Ibid.*, p. 319.

SUGGESTED READINGS

Overstreet, Bonaro W. *Understanding Fear.* New York: Collier, 1962.
    Offers an especially interesting thesis about the elements holding small groups together in the chapter "Becoming Members One of Another."

Riesman, David, Nathan Glazer, and Reuel Denney, *The Lonely Crowd.* Garden City, N.Y.: Anchor, 1953.

Discusses pressures for conformity, desires for autonomy, and individual capabilities for more than society demands.

Rose, Arnold M., *The Power Structure.* New York: Oxford, 1967.

Attempts a reconciliation of power theories, through political analysis.

Chapter *XIII*

MILITANT GROUPS AND

CIVIL DISOBEDIENCE

This chapter, in recognition that social change
does not always proceed in an orderly and
"acceptable" manner, describes various
alternative efforts and philosophies.

On July 26, 1967, as a result of widespread discontent, turmoil, and
riots, President Lyndon B. Johnson issued Executive Order 11365,
creating the National Advisory Commission on Civil Disorders, whose
chairman was Governor Otto Kerner of Illinois. Mayor John V. Lind-
say of New York City was appointed vice-chairman on the eleven-
member commission. The need for the establishment of this fact-finding
group stemmed from the costly and extensive riots that took place
throughout the country that year.

The Kerner Report

The commission investigated twenty-four disorders that had taken
place in twenty-three American cities that year. Its report and recommendations were published in *The Report of the National Advisory
Commission on Civil Disorders*, a 1,400-page document containing
250,000 words. We shall draw freely on this report. It addresses itself
to three basic questions: What happened? Why did it happen? What
can be done to prevent it from happening again?

TABLE 2

*Action of Federal Government on State Requests for
Federal Troops*

Date	Incident	State	Action
1838	Buckshot War, violence over political contest	Pennsylvania	Refused
1842	Dorr Rebellion, attempt to seize governorship	Rhode Island	Refused
1856	San Francisco Vigilante Committee, usurping authority of the state	California	Refused
1873	New Orleans racial problems, political unrest	Louisiana	Granted after rioters' failure to heed proclamation
1876	Violence between Ku Klux Klan and Negro militia	South Carolina	Granted
1877	Railroad-strike riots over wage cuts	California, Indiana, Michigan, Ohio, Wisconsin	Granted Federal arms to Ohio, refused troops to all states
1892	Coeur d'Alene mining disturbances	Idaho	Granted for a seven-year period
1894	Coxey's Army, unemployment discontent	Montana	Granted without formal proclamation
1903	Mining-strike disturbance	Colorado	Refused
1907	Mining disturbance	Nevada	Granted but later declared unwarranted by President Roosevelt's investigating committee
1914	Coal strike	Colorado	Granted after failure of negotiation

Date	Incident	State	Action
1919	Race riots	Nebraska, Washington, D.C.	Granted without proclamation
1919	Steel strike	Indiana	Granted without proclamation
1921	Coal-mine warfare	West Virginia	Refused initially; second request granted
1932	Bonus Army, veterans' march on Washington, D.C.	Washington, D.C.	Granted without proclamation
1943	Detroit race riots	Michigan	Granted
1967	Detroit race riots	Michigan	Granted

In attempting to answer these three questions, the commission reviewed the history of domestic violence in the United States, focusing on state requests for Federal assistance during disorders and whether or not it was granted. Table 2 is a chronological summary of such requests during civil disorders and the Federal responses.

The incidents in Table 2 include only those civil disorders in which states requested Federal assistance. There is no mention in the Kerner report of disorders dealt with entirely by the various states themselves, a much longer list. The purpose of the table is to suggest the history of internal violence in the United States and the frequent involvement of the Federal government.

Although the Kerner commission was formed as a result of incidents during 1967, it recognized that violence has played a significant part throughout American history. Of greater concern than the events leading up to the violence of the 1960s were the psychological attitudes of the people resorting to it.

Extralegal group action, as Arthur Schlesinger, Jr., points out,[1] has long been a significant part of the democratic process, though many people refuse to recognize it. Too many American citizens view the nation unrealistically, as peaceful, just, and equally beneficent to all. If that were true, there would have been no unrest and no violence. Most recent disorders have focused on problems connected with race, which led to one basic conclusion of the Kerner commission: that "Our nation is moving toward two societies, one black, one white—separate and unequal." The commission further recognized that race prejudice has shaped the history of the United States. The ambivalence of many people is clear: As long as "race problems" exist elsewhere they are indignant about the treatment of minority groups, but when problems arise in their own communities they become defensive. Wisdom and tolerance exhibited in criticism of another community often disappear in assessing one's own.

These general conclusions were reached after an examination of the second basic question, Why did it happen? White racism, declared the commission, was essentially responsible for the explosive mixture in the cities. The "ingredients" of this mixture were

1. Pervasive discrimination and segregation in employment, education, and housing, which have resulted in continuing exclusion of most Negroes from the benefits of economic progress.
2. Black in-migration and the white exodus, which have produced massive and growing concentrations of impoverished Negroes in major cities and contributed to the growing crisis of deteriorating facilities and services and unmet human needs.
3. The black ghettos, where segregation and poverty converge to destroy opportunity for the young and to enforce failure, result in crime, drug addiction, dependence on welfare, bitterness, and resentment against society in general and white society in particular.

The Kerner report analyzes these ingredients and associated factors, including frustrated hopes and unfulfilled expectations, a climate favoring violence, feelings of powerlessness and the conviction that there is no alternative to violence, replacement among younger Negroes of subservience with racial pride and self-esteem, and belief in the existence of a "double standard" of justice for Negroes and whites.

These conditions surfaced in urban ghetto areas and "sparked" the riots of 1967. Negro slum dwellers have a disproportionate share in unemployment, crime, education, and sanitation problems. Unemployment in these areas is often as much as 8.8 times greater, the crime rate as much as 35 times greater, and infant mortality 58 percent greater than in middle-class white neighborhoods.[2] Protests over these conditions and pleas for help in solving the problems have generally not brought sufficient improvement. It should be stressed that the riots did *not* result from concerted efforts by subversive organizations but were separate incidents based on the same kinds of discontent in various cities.

Negro Protest Movements

Nonviolence

The most noteworthy attempt at organizing a Negro protest movement was that of the late Reverend Martin Luther King, Jr., President of the Southern Christian Leadership Conference (S.C.L.C.). He deplored violence and steadfastly adhered to a philosophy of nonviolence, but he believed in civil disobedience to unjust laws. His position was set forth in a letter replying to objections to his demonstrations expressed by fellow clergymen, which he wrote while detained in the Birmingham, Alabama, jail.[3] His statement is the most pertinent summation of the concept of civil disobedience in this country, based on the distinction between just and unjust laws. An unjust law is one that degrades the human personality, is enacted by a majority group to compel only a minority group to obey, or is binding upon a minority group that has been denied any part in writing the law. Such a law, according to King's philosophy, must be disobeyed, lovingly and in full knowledge and acceptance of the consequences which themselves may need reexamination for equitableness. Such disobedience demonstrates to the public the inequity in the law that should be corrected. This philosophy does not advocate violence or defiance of a just law simply because it displeases a person or group. This differs from the behavior of the insincere and unprincipled agitator who is willing to be destructive for what he purports as a cause but unwilling to seek legitimate avenues for action.

The conservatism of other leading Negro groups reflects this nonviolent philosophy. The National Association for the Advancement of Colored People (N.A.A.C.P.) and the Urban League have been promoting equality for Negroes within the framework of the Constitution for many years. They have avoided extreme policies, especially violence. Other groups that have been formed around the basic issue of race, a major problem in American society, are militant and have helped to promote the concept of two societies, one black and one white. Examples include the Black Muslims and the Student Nonviolent Coordinating Committee (S.N.C.C.).

Black Muslims

The reader should be aware of the history of Negro militance and the "black power" concept. "Black power" is a term denoting the recognition that ethnic pride is needed to gain respect through visible political and economic strength.

Early in the 1960s a former drug addict and ex-convict who had taken the name Malcolm X became an active Negro leader. He had grown up believing that his father had been murdered by white men and became a spokesman and advocate for the Black Muslims. In a speech at the Boston University School of Theology he expressed some of the aims, objectives, and rules of this controversial group, claiming that the Black Muslims were striving for peaceful relations with all races but would retaliate swiftly and violently if molested. He also demanded a Federal land grant and financial aid to establish a separate state encompassing approximately half the territory east of the Mississippi River. Following a split with the Black Muslims and the formation of the Organization for Afro-American Unity, his career came to an end when he was assassinated in Manhattan on February 21, 1965 while speaking to a large group of his followers. His reputation among blacks (a term he insisted upon) was that he did not cower before "Charlie" (the white man). Instead, he was known as a black man not afraid to tell any or all members of the white Establishment "where to go." He was highly praised for his refusal to back down in the face of white or black hostility.

Noble Drew Ali (Timothy Drew), an earlier Negro leader, had promoted the belief that Christianity was for whites and Islam for Asiatics, his term for Negroes, and had further argued that religious faith should not cross racial lines. Drew was responsible for the establishment of Moorish Science temples in six large cities in the eastern United States, patterned after the Islamic religion. Some Moorish American temples still survive, but many of their members were early converts to the Black Muslim movement.

An equally strong influence on the Black Muslims was Marcus Garvey, a Jamaican who had arrived in the United States in 1916 but had never obtained citizenship in this country. He began speaking from a soapbox on street corners and eventually gained control of a newspaper, *The Negro World*, that claimed a circulation of 200,000. He was able to reach the masses of frustrated and disillusioned black migrants from southern states with his plans to take American Negroes back to an unspecified promised land in Africa, a scheme that was also supported by the Ku Klux Klan. The government became alarmed, and the U.S. Department of Justice cited Garvey's newspaper for "radicalism and sedition." England and France, who were interested in preventing Liberia from becoming a nation of free Negroes which they viewed as politically dangerous, brought pressure to bear on Liberia's president, who denounced the "incendiary policy" of the Garvey movement.

Garvey met with opposition among Negroes as well, particularly from the more successful elements of the middle class. They labeled him "bombastic and impractical." Most of his critics recognized that his philosophy was as racist as was white supremacy and would promote inequities, rather than eliminating them. Although Garvey had considerable influence on the thinking of American Negroes, he had little practical success.

Then a door-to-door peddler named Wallace Fard made his appearance in Detroit. His demeanor, dress, and talk convinced people that he was an Arab, and he eventually came to be known as the Prophet. He rented a hall, called it the Temple of Islam, and dubbed his followers Black Muslims. The movement steadily grew in numbers and power. Along with a high degree of organization it offered rigid discipline and formal ritual. A University of Islam was established, as well as classes to teach young women how to be proper Black Muslim wives and mothers.

During these early days Elijah Poole, a Negro from Georgia, was very active in the movement; he was given the name Elijah Muhammad. After serving as chief minister, he split with Fard and gathered the intense, hostile, and fanatical true believers about him. He often spoke of freeing the Negro from the white devil's yoke. He did not, however, want an unruly mob on his hands. Instead, strict measures were adopted to cover all forms of behavior. Members were told to hold jobs and to live respectably. They were forbidden to smoke, to drink liquor, to gamble, or to indulge in other frivolities. Paramount was the dictum to take pride in their race. A form of tithing, reportedly as high as one-third of their earnings, was imposed upon the members.

The appeal of an organization powerful enough to "get the white man's foot off the Negro's neck, his hand out of his pocket, and his carcass off his back" [4] was substantial; the movement appeared to have the potential of overcoming white supremacy.

The devout Black Muslim was expected to pray five times daily, to attend at least two temple meetings a week and to do missionary work. He was commanded to obey duly constituted authority, whether black or white, until the Black Nation had risen to power. Morality is strictly defined, and visits from strong-arm squads punish infidelity and philandering.

The newspaper *Muhammad Speaks* claims a circulation of over 200,000. It offers advice in all matters, including courtship, marriage, and sex. Sexual intercourse between blacks and whites is given as a cause of death and disease.

One Black Muslim goal is to attract 5 million members. Such strength could readily make itself felt politically without violence, though it might be a bitter pill for some whites to swallow. The Black Muslims, regardless of their strength, however, represent less of a potential political threat because of their separatist philosophy. It is impossible to predict the future of this group, but some concessions by the Black Muslims will have to be made before they can influence the American public to the degree necessary to attain their general ends.

Black Power

Another militant attempt to bring about racial change is aimed at "black power," a term that is defined differently according to the interests of each group using it. The Student Non-Violent Coordinating Committee (S.N.C.C.) has drafted a statement of its position, although published excerpts from this statement do not contain the actual term.[5] The position paper includes a number of points, among them:

1. Negroes have never been free from interference by white men and consequently have not been able to organize themselves.
2. Negroes feel intimidated by white men.
3. Negroes need to express themselves.
4. Negroes should form their own political parties and institutions and write their own history books.
5. S.N.C.C. should have no whites on its staff and should accept no white financing.
6. The time for reassessment of white and black social roles has arrived.
7. Whites should no longer assign subservient roles to Negroes.

8. Black people should define white people's roles (so that they might better understand each other).

Martin Luther King, Jr., addressed a crowd composed of members of forty-five local civil-rights groups in Chicago in July 1966, calling the philosophy of black power an evil, a deterrent to Negro progress. Floyd B. McKissick of the Congress of Racial Equality (CORE) also spoke, insisting that black power was neither an expression of hatred nor a call to violence. Both men believed that Negroes could find an effective economic or political voice through unity, rather than through violence.

On October 17, 1966, a large advertisement in *The New York Times* carried a joint statement by seven Negro leaders repudiating black power. These leaders and their affiliations were: Amos T. Holt, executive secretary of the Conference of Grand Masters, Prince Hall Masons of America; Mrs. Dorothy Height, President of the National Council of Negro Women; A. Philip Randolph, President of the Brotherhood of Sleeping Car Porters; Bayard Rustin, Director, A. Philip Randolph Institute; Roy Wilkins, NAACP executive director; Whitney M. Young, Jr., National Urban League executive director; and Hobson R. Reynolds, grand exalted ruler of the Improved Benevolent and Protective Order of Elks of the World. The position of the groups they represented was based on the following principles:

1. Obtaining racial justice through the democratic process.
2. Repudiation of violence and riots.
3. Commitment to integration.
4. Recognition of the need for both whites and blacks to work toward integration.

Dr. King's name was not included among the signers, although he declared his agreement with the principles in the statement.

Controversy over the definition and philosophy of black power have received more attention as Negroes have continued to struggle for their rights. The nonviolent approach has appealed more to the middle-class Negro, who is more patient with the slow pace of progress. Younger, lower-class Negroes are more impatient to obtain and exercise some control over their own destinies. They are weary of nonviolent direct action that is met only with tear gas, guns, and clubs. Such feelings were voiced poignantly in May 1967 in an article that described black power as an attempt to bring about equality *and* opportunity by influencing opposing forces.[6] The article reported an interview with Dr. Nathan Hare, a Negro activist, who speculated in rather descriptive terms that Negroes had too long been "singing instead of swinging," "praying instead of preying," and "playing instead of flaying." His most revealing remark was that the black power movement was an anti-antiblack movement. He meant that there was antagonism toward those who specifically were against the black movement per se rather than a generalized opposition to any white person.

The Negroes' struggle against the injustice of society's antiblack attitude has led to efforts to create racial pride in individual Negroes and to advance Negro rights collectively as other than "second-class citizens." Many factors suggested that a long and bitter struggle still lay ahead; not least among these factors were other movements dedicated to precisely contrary ends.

Opposition

George Lincoln Rockwell, the late leader of the American Nazi Party, has called upon race prejudice, discrimination, and hatred as tools of destruction. As many men of initiative and resourcefulness have done in the past, Rockwell had set himself a specific goal: to become President of the United States. Preaching "white survival," he promoted his own brand of eugenics, involving sterilization for some, subsidies for certain first marriages, and bonuses for childbirth of "good stock." He had a unique plan to end the segregation problem: to offer a grant of $10,000 to any Negro family of five or more members who would move to an industrial area in Africa. His plan for Jews was not so simple. He planned to investigate, try, and execute all Jews who have been involved in "Marxist or Zionist plotting" and to cancel all debts owed to Jews by non-Jews.

Citizenship was to be granted only after the eighteenth birthday, at which time a person would undergo a series of "meaningful" tests and pledge to lay down his life for country and race. Many other social ills would receive attention. There would be free schooling to the limit of each person's capacity and free medical attention for all citizens.

Various groups of people passionately opposed the American Nazi Party, and as a result, it was difficult for Rockwell and his associates to carry on many of their functions without violence. One organization, the American Anti-Nazi Mass Retaliation Party, has been created for the express purpose of "exterminating instead of being exterminated." This group, no larger than the group it opposes, has stated publicly that in a meeting of the two parties not one of the Nazis would leave the area alive. This same kind of resistance has greeted many other militant groups. Violence, however, simply breeds more violence and necessitates restoring order before an attack on the original problem can be made.

Civil Disobedience and Disorders

Men of vision and action have helped to shape the character of civil disobedience, from the early days of Christianity, through the passive resistance of Mohandas K. Gandhi, and more recently in the nonviolent philosophy of Martin Luther King Jr. Ironically, Christ, Gandhi, and King were all victims of the violence that they opposed. In their disobedience they were willing to accept any consequences that followed, and they were sincere not only in their attempts to call attention to inequities but also in mobilization of resources to combat these inequities. The consequences, sometimes out of proportion to the offense, brought much attention to the inequities being protested.

We believe that the militant group does a disservice to its cause when it uses violence instead of more peaceful means. Long-standing discriminatory practices are difficult to change at best, but the opposition aroused by violence can lead to a complete breakdown or postponement of efforts to alleviate them. Violent militants are usually outnumbered by people willing to resolve their differences more rationally. A description of "typical" rioters of 1967 shows that those using violence are proportionately few even among so-called "militants." In its "Profile of a Rioter," the Kerner commission described a typical (and hypothetical) rioter as an unemployed Negro male between fifteen and twenty-four years old, a life-long resident of the city in which the riot occurred. He had attended high school, was working in a menial job, was extremely hostile toward whites, and was better informed politically than were Negroes who were not involved in the riots. The commission concluded that this Negro had been put off with unkept promises and empty gestures for many years.

The rioting that occurred in 1967 resulted from long-standing degradation, insult, helplessness, and futility. Previous programs had not brought results, and many Negroes were convinced that nothing short of violence would bring attention to the situation. Each effort by

Negroes to solve their problems was met with only half-hearted interest in the larger society, and the main source of action was white fear of Negroes.

When a protest group ignores the principle of nonviolence and openly defies the law, it goes beyond the Constitutional guarantee of petition and free assembly, but, when legal protests fall on deaf ears, no alternative to violence seems possible. The Negro has been the victim of ridicule, degradation, derision, and misunderstanding for a long time. He has been able to "wear two hats," so to speak, often pretending to be happy-go-lucky and content with his meager lot. White Americans have placed Negroes in a category from which they are still striving to escape, having long been denied both the opportunity and the means of protest. Grown men have been addressed as "boy," cursed, kicked, lynched, treated as "things." [7]

But Negroes today are becoming more aware of their rights and are finding ways to fight the denial of those rights. It is to be hoped that violence has served its purpose and that more peaceful means can be effective in the future.

Various temporary changes have resulted from recognition of prejudice and discrimination. Prejudice is a matter of attitudes, less tangible and therefore harder to combat than is discrimination. Discrimination is overt and can be more readily identified and attacked through legal and other corrective measures. Changes have occurred throughout history, but after an initial surge of interest attention is usually diverted, and progress slows to a halt. Either direct action or the threat of such action has been necessary to revive interest in the past.

In 1941 President Franklin D. Roosevelt created the Federal Fair Employment Practices Commission (F.E.P.C.) in order to forestall a threatened mass Negro convergence on Washington, D.C. The Federal government thus went farther than had many individual states to prevent discrimination in hiring. It was the F.E.P.C. that set the precedent for treating fair-employment practices as a civil right, although the agency itself was discontinued at the end of World War II. Unfortunately, this beginning did not completely solve the problem; the Kerner commission reported in 1968 that Negro workers were still concentrated in the lowest range of occupations. In addition, the Negro unemployment rate was higher than that of whites. Even in similar employment Negro workers with the same education as white workers are often paid less. Such disparities discourage many Negroes from actively seeking and preparing themselves for advancement.

If the reason for the disparity were lower-quality education and training in segregated schools, the problem could be approached by upgrading education for Negroes. Whatever the reason effective steps should be taken the instant that such discrimination is discovered; much of what is wrong today arises from superficial attention, if any, to such symptoms of injustice in earlier years.

Change will probably never be initiated without precipitating events. Perhaps as the memory of the 1967 riots fades, the nation will once again relax its efforts to stem the rising tide of bitterness. The nonpartisan Kerner report not only is an indictment of the American social system but also suggests that attention to such problems as employment, education, housing, and citizen participation could help to avert a repeat of the tragedies of 1967. It is vital that the Kerner commission's recommendations be heeded, in order not to repeat the cycle that Negroes have experienced since they were brought to this country as slaves. Sociologists have observed that the group most likely to rebel against further oppression is the one that sees hope for improvement of its condition and then is blocked from achieving it. Frustration is intensified when the Federal government fails to follow through on highly publicized programs to encourage such improvement. It is not enough to discover the problem anew every several years. At some point it must be effectively attacked. The next commission appointed to study such problems as rioting should include Negro leaders who understand what is happening and who will know the most effective measures to combat the problem.

To sum up, militancy, civil disobedience, and disorders will continue in the United States. Although there may be more reports and suggestions for halting violence, no equitable solution will be reached until informed citizen participation reaches a new height, with the involvement of indigenous leaders and other members of society. We believe that peaceful, nonviolent demonstrations, sit-ins, and boycotts will continue to be effective in bringing social inequities to the attention of the nation. It is to be hoped that greater interest and awareness on the part of society can help minority groups to achieve equal opportunity in those spheres essential to the survival of a democratic society.

NOTES

1. Arthur Schlesinger, Jr., "The Dark Heart of American History," *Saturday Review*, October 19, 1968, pp. 20–23, 81.
2. "Prescription for Racial Peace," *Time*, March 8, 1968, pp. 26–27.
3. Martin Luther King, Jr., *Why We Can't Wait* (New York: New American Library, 1964), pp. 76–95.
4. Essien Voom, *Black Nationalism* (Chicago: University of Chicago Press, 1962), pp. 201–231. This book is a study of the Nation of Islam by a participant observer.
5. *The New York Times*, August 4, 1966, p. 14.
6. "Black Power—Its Goals and Methods," *U.S. News & World Report*, May 22, 1967, pp. 64–68.
7. King, *op. cit.*, p. 81.

SUGGESTED READINGS

Cook, Samuel DuBois. "The Tragic Myth of Black Power," *New South*, 21, No. 3 (Summer 1966), pp. 19–26.

A comprehensive analysis of what the author calls "four fallacies of black power."

Grier, William H., and Price M. Cobbs. *Black Rage*. New York: Basic Books, 1968.

Explanation by two Negro psychiatrists of white racism as a cause of black wrath.

Murphy, Raymond, and Howard Elinson, eds. *Problems and Prospects of the Negro Movement*. Belmont, Calif.: Wadsworth, 1966.

A selection of writings on the civil-rights movement.

Chapter *XIV*

OTHER FORMS OF

CITIZEN PARTICIPATION

Some avenues by which citizens can become
actively involved in social issues without
going outside the law are explained.

Opportunities for participation in social action are virtually unlimited today. There is, perhaps due to the increased effectiveness of mass communication and an expressed desire on the part of people to become involved in social action, an avenue of participation for everybody. Many people want to become involved in social action. We more often hear about the militant episodes than about others, but it is possible to contribute effectively without risking notoriety, martyrdom, or arrest.

A recent *Time* article discussed the question "What Can I Do?" and explained the motivations for social action.[1] The article pointed out that the majority of both Negroes and whites are not involved in the civil-rights movement. Yet the progress of this cause with relatively few people is evidence that citizen participation can and does bring results.

The ways that a person can involve himself in social action can be divided into two categories: those involving direct interaction and those that involve private accomplishment by individuals.

The first group includes volunteer work, political activities, youth groups, fund-raising for nonprofit organizations, the Welcome Wagon,

Parent-Teacher associations, foster parents, veterans' organizations, employment associations, religious programs, and service and fraternal clubs.

The second category includes letters to the editors, "two-way radio," letters to congressmen, telephone solicitation, financial contributions, "after-hours" tasks, and financing advertisements.

Hospital Volunteer Work

Space does not permit examination of all possibilities for volunteer work, and we shall mention only a few here.

The volunteer is in a unique situation—he can quit any time he wants. Nevertheless many people do devote much of their time to such work. The Veterans Administration Volunteer Service (V.A.V.S.) is the oldest hospital volunteer service in existence and needs volunteer service directors to coordinate various hospital activities. The average number of regularly scheduled volunteers for each of the thirty-six hospitals in the V.A. system, with approximately 500 beds each, was 248 for the 1967 fiscal year.[2] This work includes eleven different services, like escorting patients to worship services, transporting and delivering prescriptions on the hospital grounds, recreational supervision and instruction, and clerical work.

The Red Cross recruits and assigns most V.A. auxiliaries, including youth volunteers. The youth volunteers, mostly teenage girls, wear blue-and-white striped uniforms. Adult Red Cross volunteers, formerly known as "gray ladies," perform some of the more responsible administrative and supervisory tasks. These include the keeping of records, necessary correspondence and representation at meetings, conferences and policy-making boards.

Candy Stripers

The Candy Striper program is staffed by teenage girls who work in other hospitals throughout the country. Their tasks involve reception work, answering telephones, serving refreshments, and other nonmedical functions with patients, similar to those of youth volunteers in V.A. hospitals. The Candy Striper wears red and white stripes.

Pink Ladies

The adult counterparts of the Candy Stripers usually perform tasks such as official correspondence and public relations work that require mature administrative and supervisory qualifications, similar to those of the Red Cross volunteers.

The traditional well-to-do middle-aged female volunteer is being replaced with a more representative sample of the population, including young and old, rich and poor, male and female. Approximately one-third of hospital volunteers are male. There is a volunteer job for virtually everybody, and it is rarely that anyone's services are rejected. Volunteer work is increasing. Much of what has been accomplished in this country has been the result of volunteer efforts. As needs continue to develop it will likewise be evident that very few programs are funded to operate without volunteers. Volunteers have provided the main thrusts in such areas as probation, charity, female suffrage, treatment of alcoholics and drug users, prison reform, civil rights, and civic improvement, as well as others too numerous to mention.

The Council on Volunteer Services, formerly known as the Council on Hospital Auxiliaries, of the American Hospital Association (A.H.A.) coordinates most of the country's private voluntary health services.

Welfare Volunteer Work

Within each welfare organization there are possibilities for lay participation. For convenience, we shall present individual endeavors and then group projects.

Big Brother or Sister

An adult may "adopt" a lonely or confused child and offer him companionship in a relaxed, nonjudgmental atmosphere. As the child develops confidence and trust, he often seeks advice and support from his Big Brother or Big Sister.

Housing Aide

The Kerner report of 1967 described a case in which a recipient's rent allowance was not enough for him to obtain decent housing.[3] A volunteer can work with both clients and real-estate brokers to locate housing and can offer advice about costs of renting, clarify departmental policies, and refer clients with health and transportation problems.

Friendly Visitor

Many people on public assistance never receive personal attention. A confused and discouraged child in foster care may be helped by a visit to *him* unconnected with adult business. An elderly person who can seldom leave his home can be considerably cheered by a show of interest in him. Clergymen make a practice of calling on the sick to express sympathy. This type of visiting obviously need not be restricted to either welfare departments or religious organizations.

Tutor

The "disadvantaged" person may have a great capacity for learning but not necessarily the opportunity. An individual who knows foreign languages can be helpful in tutoring adults whose language difficulties hamper them in obtaining jobs and advancement. Reading, grooming, and mathematics are other important subjects for many clients. Professional training is not necessary to tutor such subjects on a volunteer basis.

Needlework Circle

Women with needlework skills have been working together in groups for many years. Welfare departments often receive items that can be repaired, altered, or used to make other items like quilts. After the women have finished their work the items are then given, or sold at token prices, to welfare clients.

Book Club

Interested groups can canvass neighborhoods for surplus reading material for all ages, ranging from coloring books to great works of literature for donation to hospitals, prisons, neighborhood centers or other social-welfare agency clients.

Craft Club

Skilled craftsmen can show people on limited budgets many ways to produce useful goods at little cost. Equipment for cabinet making, appliance repair, upholstering, and other essentials of household management is often available at public schools outside school hours.

Organizational and Institutional Work

During all months of the year help is needed by organizations in typing, filing, and other clerical tasks. Such work can be done at odd hours on irregular schedules. Institutions like hospitals, prisons, and settlement houses also have such tasks for willing volunteers.

Political Activities

Political candidates, and their respective parties, operate with limited funds and rely heavily on volunteer work. Jobs are available at all levels, so that many individual talents can be used within the organization. Unlike some organizations that use volunteers, political groups assign work that would otherwise have to be done by full-time salaried staff members due to the pressure of time imposed by the voting deadline.

Youth Groups

Many youth organizations rely on adults for supervision and administration. Young people cannot drive, sign contracts, buy insurance, or move about unaccompanied, and mature guidance is thus necessary. Boy and Girl Scouts offer many adults opportunities to develop their own capacities as well as to help mold the personalities of boys and girls.

Fund Raising

Nonprofit organizations either participate in united fund drives or conduct individual drives. In either case, volunteers do much of the door-to-door soliciting, collecting, and related tasks. The Red Cross, the Salvation Army, the Heart Fund, the Boy Scouts of America, the Cancer Society, the Easter Seal Society, the Girl Scouts of America, the National Hemophilia Foundation, the National Multiple Sclerosis Society, the United Fund, the National Association for Retarded Children, the U.N. Children's Fund (UNICEF), and the Young Men's and Women's Christian and Hebrew Associations are organizations that appreciate volunteer help and have learned how best to employ the talents offered.

The Welcome Wagon

As Americans become more mobile, job relocation also becomes more common. For whatever reason a family moves into a new neighborhood, many unfamiliar things cause inconvenience. The Welcome Wagon—an organization of community residents—attempts to familiarize new arrivals with schools, churches, and other public and private resources. Different business establishments offer prospective customers "get-acquainted" reductions. The feeling of having friends in a strange city has made many recipients of this service anxious to offer it to others in similar circumstances.

The Parent-Teacher Association

The Parent-Teacher Association, or the "P.T.A." as it is known throughout the nation, founded in 1924, is open to any person interested in the welfare of children, whether a parent or not. Its roots reach back to 1897, when interest in cooperation between parents and schools developed.[4] It was originally known as the National Congress of Mothers, but in 1908 the organization changed its name to the National Congress of Mothers and Parent-Teacher Association and in 1924 to the National Congress of Parents and Teachers. Through this organization a person can participate in various activities related to health, art, child welfare, illiteracy, juvenile protection, and about thirty others.[5]

Foster Parents

Although traditionally viewed as a public-welfare resource, the idea of temporary homes for "disadvantaged" people is expanding beyond the needs of neglected and dependent children. Hospitals are relying on foster homes to make more bed space available. In communities with juvenile-detention facilities people are volunteering their homes and services so that children do not have to be locked up. Boulder County, Colorado, juvenile court has been involved in such a project, which is beginning to show the positive effects of such foster-home care.[6]

Veterans' Organizations

The American Legion, given authorization to organize by an act of Congress in September 1919, has a vital interest in four programs: rehabilitation of disabled veterans, child-welfare legislation, promoting national security, and "Americanism." An auxiliary of more than 1 million women is also quite active.[7]

The Veterans of Foreign Wars (V.F.W.) was formed in 1914 from the combined membership of three existing veterans' organizations. Its objectives are similar to those of the American Legion: national security, rehabilitation of veterans, assistance to widows and orphans of veterans, and "Americanism." One particular service is the V.F.W. national home at Eaton Rapids, Michigan, which offers children of veterans a wholesome environment during the formative years through high school and possibly college. A ladies' auxiliary of more than 325,000 members is active.

There are other veterans' organizations like the Disabled American Veterans (D.A.V.) and the American Veterans of World War II and Korea (AMVETS) whose principles are similar to those of the American Legion and the V.F.W. A person can be a member of any of these organizations, regardless of his unit, ship, station, or rank. Other groups do limit membership to those connected with particular assignments, military units, or problems.

Employment Associations

In practically every field, vocational, professional, or otherwise, there seems to be an organization of special professional interest. The American Medical Association, for example, has many such special-interest groups within its main body. Other examples are state- , Federal- , and municipal-employee associations.

Associations through which employers exchange ideas and share suggested solutions to mutual problems are also important. They exist in virtually every field of interest from air-traffic control to zoology and are often open to anyone interested in the subject, regardless of the primary source of his income.

Religious Programs

All formal religious organizations, Roman Catholic, Protestant, Jewish or Buddhist, have service programs for their members, ranging from child care and development to gerontology—literally from the cradle to the grave and beyond. Many churches also make their physical facilities available to other legitimate groups, whether sponsored by church members or not. Most church buildings are idle most of the time and can become activity centers, regardless of faith.

Service Clubs

Many organizations operate on a national (and sometimes international) basis to promote good citizenship, welfare, and community betterment. Five such organizations will be described briefly here.

Kiwanis International

Kiwanis International was founded in 1915 for business and professional men and is involved in social welfare, vocational guidance, and community betterment. It sponsors two youth organizations, Key Club International for high-school boys and Circle K International for college youths.

Rotary International

First organized in 1904 as a means of exchanging ideas among business and professional men, Rotary International is interested in the promotion of business ethics, community service, and promotion of world peace and fellowship. It is international in scope and has permanent offices in four different countries. A youth organization similar to Key Club International is named Interact and is sponsored by Rotarians.

Junior League

Women volunteers in the Junior League do community work in health, education, and welfare. Each member is expected to complete a course in the principles of volunteer services. The Association of the Junior Leagues of America (A.J.L.A.) was first organized in 1921 and is nonpartisan and nonsectarian.

League of Women Voters of the United States

The League of Women Voters of the United States, a nonpartisan organization dedicated to the promotion of political responsibility and "getting out the vote," was established in 1920, when American women were given the right to vote. Many programs have been initiated at local, state, and national levels to encourage participation by all members. They include attacks on public-health, public-school, child-welfare and tax problems.

Lions Club

The Lions Club, a community-service club founded in 1917 and now grown to more than 600,000 members, is nonsectarian and nonpartisan. Its activities include interest in agriculture legislation, "Americanism," social welfare, and, most notably, sight conservation and work with the blind. Many children from indigent families have been provided with eyeglasses through local Lions clubs.

Fraternal Organizations

Benevolent and Protective Order of Elks

Since 1868 the service objectives of the Benevolent and Protective Order of the Elks (B.P.O.E.) have been charity, justice, brotherly love, welfare, and "Americanism." It has made significant contributions to hospitalized veterans and to the Boy Scouts and donations to social welfare agencies have been as much as $5 million in one year.

Knights of Columbus

The Knights of Columbus (K.C.), a society for Roman Catholic men, has existed since 1882. Its objectives include financial aid to members, health assistance, promotion of education, and welfare, and religious and patriotic endeavors. It operates Columbian Squires, a recreational program for boys between the ages of fourteen and eighteen. Considerable money has also been contributed toward scholarships, educational trust funds, and essay contests on American history.

Ancient Arabic Order of Nobles of the Mystic Shrine

The Ancient Arabic Order of Nobles of the Mystic Shrine draws its membership from thirty-second degree Masons, and dedicates itself mainly to helping crippled children. There are seventeen Shriners' orthopedic hospitals for children, regardless of race, creed, color, national origin, or Masonic affiliation.

Private Social Action

Several other avenues are open to people who wish to express their opinions and influence social action.

Letters to the Editors

The editorial policies of most newspapers and magazines encourage readers to write letters on subjects about which they are concerned. Letters are reviewed for appropriateness, and many are published in each edition. People complain, praise, insult, challenge, and take every possible view on myriad subjects. Some editors, notably of weekly news magazines, publish letters from their readers that express opposing views. Subjects that are of continuing interest are religion, politics, and sex. Just how much these letters influence social action is questionable, but they remain a common form of citizen communication.

The Letters to the Editor section of *The New York Times* has been of special social significance in that the worldwide circulation of the paper permits it to serve as a public forum for exchange of ideas and current social issues. Government officials and other prominent leaders consider these letters from the public and use this service as a method of response to the public pulse.

"Two-Way Radio"

Rather recently radio announcers have begun to make air time available to listeners by broadcasting telephone conversations. Any member of the audience who can dial the radio station's telephone number can speak from the privacy of his own home. Sufficient research is not available currently to assess the impact of this form of communication on social issues. Emotionally disturbed individuals not infrequently take this opportunity to voice unpopular and sometimes incoherent views.

Letters and Telegrams to Congressmen

The democratic process consists of the people voicing their will through elected representatives. One way that representatives learn the wishes of their constituents is through letters and telegrams. Probably not enough citizens choose to express themselves in this way, but it is nevertheless available. The congressman is committed to the principle of representing and working for his constituents. His staff makes serious attempts to give attention to all correspondence, and it is probable that some response to requests, complaints, recommendations, and other valid communications will be forthcoming.

Telegrams were heavily used during the 1968 Democratic National Convention in Chicago. It was possible to wire any candidate at a nominal cost, and an avalanche of telegrams from all over the nation descended on Chicago during and after the selection of the Democratic candidate.

Telephone Solicitation

Many organizations (political, social, fraternal, and service) must get in touch with large numbers of people by telephone, to solicit funds, call committee meetings, encourage attendance, and so on. Much telephoning can be done at home, including initial volunteering for such work.

Financial Contributions

Organizations often must solicit funds to pay skilled people to perform professional tasks. For instance, most of the funds collected during the March of Dimes campaigns go to research. Medical research is expensive, involving equipment, facilities, and scientific personnel. Any citizen can contribute financial support, regardless of his own talents or skills.

After-Hours Tasks

Various nonprofit organizations use volunteer services both during regular working hours and afterward. Mowing lawns, shoveling snow, general building maintenance, and other tasks involving physical strength and skills may be necessary. In addition, there are after-hours clerical, reception, and office duties that must be performed. For instance, programs must be mimeographed for various events, which can be done at odd hours.

Personally Financed Advertisements

An effective way to participate in social action is through publication of the printed word. Individuals often endorse political candidates in this manner by purchasing space in local newspapers. Each newspaper has established policies for the types of material that it will accept for publication, usually refusing vulgar, obscene, or libelous advertisements. The "underground" newspapers make exceptions to the latter bans, and people may advertise less respectable opinions there.

Other Individual Action

There is hardly any level of activity that cannot be related to social action. Specialized reading may develop expertise on a subject of general interest. There are countless more specialized organizations than those mentioned here, giving scope to almost any individual interest. There are organizations to clothe animals, clubs for displaying antique automobiles, poetry groups, peace and freedom leagues, water-well associations, defenders of wildlife, temperance unions, voluntary-sterilization programs, garden clubs, and untold other societies, federations, groups, clubs and associations.[8] Some of these groups are action-oriented, some are larger than others, but all involve voluntary participation.

Citizens can and do participate in social action. Some people are more adept at speaking and interacting with people than are others. But those who are not adept should not feel that they cannot act at all. Apparently most people do want to voice their opinions and become involved in some way. They will achieve the most satisfaction if they involve themselves in activities for which they are best suited. Not only will they benefit themselves, but their chosen causes will very likely also be advanced.

NOTES

1. Time Essay, *Time*, May 17, 1968, pp. 17–18.
2. Veterans Administration, *Establishment of a Veterans Hospital Community Council* (Washington, D.C.: Government Printing Office, 1968).
3. U.S. Commission on Civil Rights, *A Time To Listen . . . A Time To Act* (Washington, D.C.: Government Printing Office, 1967).
4. Martha S. Mason, ed., *Parents and Teachers* (Boston: Ginn, 1928), pp. 114–116.
5. National Congress of Parents and Teachers, *The Parent Teacher Organization* (Chicago: 1944), pp. 19–25.
6. Boulder County Juvenile Court, *A Home Away from Home: Community Volunteers Empty the Jail* (New York: Government Printing Office, August 1968—Boulder, Colorado).
7. Raymond Moley, Jr., *The American Legion Story* (New York: Deuell, Sloan, 1966).

8. *The World Almanac Book of Facts* (New York: Newspaper Enterprise Association, 1968), pp. 639–654.

SUGGESTED READINGS

Anyone interested in participating in social action should get in touch with the agencies or organizations listed in this chapter for literature pertaining to his particular interests. Referrals to the appropriate service can be made by officials listed under the city, county, state or United States government in the telephone directories of most cities in the country.

Chapter XV

IT LOOKS LIKE RAIN . . .

*The diverse processes likely to affect the
future of social-welfare institutions
are discussed.*

The forecast of rain means many things to many people. It is based on
past experience and thus represents a summation of facts. We have so
far attempted to treat generally the many problems, practices, and
policies of social-welfare institutions. Considerable literature exists on
the specific subjects covered, and we have attempted only to give an
overview and an idea of the practical application of relevant principles. Several points that would bear further elaboration in a more
specialized text have been purposely omitted. But some significant
events in the formation and continuation of social-welfare institutions
have been reserved for this chapter.

One factor that has long been influential in various institutions and
movements is religion. Charity and care of the physically and emotionally handicapped have been shaped by religion, primarily Christianity.
These beginnings influenced subsequent development of secular institutions, services, and movements in this country. Religious institutions, for example, the Southern Christian Leadership Conference, the
Salvation Army, Catholic Charities, the Jewish Welfare Board, also
continue active.

Several movements already discussed have had religious overtones:
the humane, temperance, and feminist movements, for example. Some
of the enthusiasm for "brotherhood" found in the Ku Klux Klan also

had religious roots. These four social movements reached heights of popularity when the nation was undergoing a religious reawakening or revival, closely tied in with the Protestant Ethic and middle-class morality. It was not only important to justify these causes on religious grounds; equally vehement attacks on them were also supported by "the Scriptures." Therefore, it is difficult to evaluate an organization on just its own assessment since some unacceptable and illogical aspects of its organization are rationalized with the intent of creating and maintaining a favorable image to its members and the public.

Although religion plays, and will certainly continue to play, an important role in the society of the future, it may be difficult today to understand the fervor of the faithful in the mid-1850s and later. But an appreciation of history as a process contributes to better understanding of the thinking of participants in social action of another era. If we were to hypothesize a typical family of 1920, its problems would be different from those of the Greene family; even those that were the same would probably exist in different degrees. The difficulty in such an undertaking would be to reproduce an atmosphere that accurately reflected the significance of events impinging on the lives of the family. A multiproblem family like the Greenes would not have found the same services available to it in 1920? The most important difference would be the family's attitude toward asking for and receiving "charity." There would have been no Veterans Administration to assist the father, a veteran of World War I. An alcoholic mother might not only have found no help available; she might also have found it extremely difficult to obtain a drink! In 1920 there was no income insurance that could have benefited a grandmother living with our hypothetical family. Tuberculosis was one of the most disabling and frequently fatal diseases in the nation, and little could have been done for a child who contracted it at an early age. The mother of an illegitimate child would have found little if any outside help available. Her liaison with and pregnancy by a Negro would have been disastrous in most areas of the United States. Today such an event is less disturbing, as miscegenation increases nationally. At that time in history the mentally defective older boy would have found no community resources other than the traditional "insane asylum," which had not yet undergone reform in all parts of the country. As institutional change has occurred, programs to help the retarded have also changed. It is now possible for a mentally defective child to obtain funds through Old Age and Survivors Disability Health Insurance

(OASDHI), which were not even under consideration in 1920. The delinquent son would have faced imprisonment for an offense as serious as drug use, for there was little understanding of the special psychological makeup of adolescents and no other available solution beside confinement. Public schools, for example, had not yet progressed to the point at which they concerned themselves with more than attendance regulations and teaching. The boy's early adulthood would probably have been equally dismal. By the time that he was twenty-five the nation would have been in economic collapse. If he had been fortunate enough to obtain employment, he would still have been in danger of losing his job just as he had taken on the additional responsibilities of a wife and children.

It is unrealistic to suppose that the kinds of problems from which the Greene family suffers did not exist in the 1920s. It is also erroneous to assume that such a family could have done nothing to solve its problems. But the community resources available were fewer and less developed.

These three factors—problems, solutions, and resources—would have to be analyzed in view of the time and place in which the family lived. In 1920 a person suffering from a kidney disease for which an artificial filter was necessary probably died, for filters had not yet been developed. Now, through the efforts of such organizations as the Veterans Administration, a hemodialyzer (an artificial kidney) is available. It is still too soon to speculate on heart transplants, but obviously they will be continually refined until the procedure becomes commonplace.

Employment for people of all ages, especially the mature, will also undergo changes. Technological advances are going to continue in such fields as electronics and automation. The wage earner of the future will have to be better educated to perform the more complex tasks required of him—in itself adequate reason to revise the American educational system. An example of attempts to train specifically for the existing labor market is the Job Corps, operated under auspices of the O.E.O. Young men are offered both vocational and academic courses geared to current manpower needs. The status of the Job Corps is uncertain at present, for President Richard M. Nixon would like eventually to disband it. He proposes that private industry, encouraged by tax credits and incentives, involve itself in providing training for jobs that really exist, with less emphasis on those that may be needed in the future. The rise in status (due to recognized need of those with mechanical aptitudes and capabilities) of vocational and technical schools in recent years is another index of the need for trained technicians in many occupations. The public schools will probably more often combine classroom instruction and work experience, as is already done in driver-education programs, in which principles and practical experience are combined.

The U.S. Employment Service will provide impetus for changes in the educational system by computerizing information on both successful and unsuccessful job applicants so that unmet educational and training needs can be isolated and given attention. Methods to assess limitations of job seekers and to detect deficiencies in the school system or individuals will be devised and be implemented as a continuing process. Once the trends in job possibilities are determined, the school system can better prepare its students to fill the vacancies.

Among the most significant changes likely to come about in social-welfare institutions will be those already pending in the juvenile courts, which have outlived their philosophy, effectiveness, and usefulness. Since the Supreme Court of the United States ruled that children have certain rights that have traditionally been ignored, juvenile courts have become adversary courts. One of the rights guaranteed is representation before the court by an attorney, which results in a contest between the child's attorney and the attorney for the court. This system ensures the child that his rights will not be ignored even "in his best interests." For example, an attorney may object to the judge's reading records of the child, his family, associates, and general school adjustment before hearing the facts of the specific case at hand. Juvenile-court judges have not always been impartial observers, rendering judgment only after arguments for both the prosecution and the defense. Instead they have usually involved themselves in administrative, counseling, and social tasks not provided for in legal training. Juvenile courts have had power unequaled by most other courts; to take a child from his parents permanently and to place him for adoption against the wishes of his parents. They also have had the power, and the duty in some states, to commit a child to an institution for the remainder of his minority for an offense that, if committed by an adult, would incur a small maximum penalty. For example, a fifteen-year-old boy could spend six years at a juvenile institution for an act that could have cost him no more than six months in jail and a fine of less than $300 had he been classified as an adult.

Another impetus to change in juvenile courts is their incapacity for dealing adequately with underlying problems, rather than merely with symptoms. Juvenile courts are corrective rather than preventive agencies. A child cannot be taken to a juvenile court until he violates the law or otherwise comes under its jurisdiction. We believe that children who have been "processed" by juvenile courts only once have merely been lucky, and have received no guidance that might help them to avert similar situations in the future.

There is thus growing evidence that juvenile courts have outlived their usefulness. Juvenile courts already can bind children over to trial in district courts if they are fourteen or older. Unmanageable and untreatable delinquents often circumvent the treatment aspect of juvenile courts by their insincere but convincing verbalizing to probation officers who may be inclined to err in "giving the kid a break."

A final flaw in the juvenile-court system is the absence of total family involvement. Some juvenile courts approach children as if they lived in a vacuum, rather than in interaction with their families and communities. Parents have been relieved to hear juvenile courts insisting that children accept full responsibility for their behavior and its consequences. Parents are permitted to evade responsibility for the problems underlying the behavior that has brought their children into court. One obvious answer lies in the future establishment of a family court to deal with the interrelated problems of parents and children. Only through an approach that involves all the participants can any kind of permanent solution be found.

There will be more opportunities for leisure in the future, as well as high-speed transportation and income necessary to take advantage of more activities. The shorter work week and gradual retirement will provide this extra leisure. Younger workers will spend less time on the job, and older workers will have more and more time as they adjust in stages to full-time retirement. Both young and old people will find more ways to use leisure to benefit not only themselves but others as well. Because young adults are experiencing longer delays in entering the labor market, there will be periods of leisure (school recesses and summer vacations) to be considered in training them for employment.

For some time the barren, silent lonely "old folks' home" has been giving way to the nursing home, which attempts to provide activity programs and counseling in addition to medical attention, partly so that the elderly can recover sufficient strength to return to their communities rather than spending the rest of their lives (however brief) away from family and friends. There is also genuine interest in providing something worthwhile for elderly people to do when they return home. This type of community attitude is promising for older Americans, an assurance that somebody cares enough to consider his problems.

Correctional philosophy and practice in the United States have already undergone significant changes and will continue to do so. As suggested in previous chapters, prisons in the future may very well be part of the community, no longer isolated by walls and fences. Not that some inmates will not have to be kept in close custody for the protection of society, although this need is truly an indictment of our ability to focus on helping deviants to alter their behavior. One need is for a sound theory to explain the differences in response to incarceration, preceded by a theory of deviant behavior that accounts for criminality among people with all the advantages, as well as for law-abiding lives of service among people who have very few. More refined knowledge, techniques, and skills are necessary before we see these significant changes in the field of corrections, and the institutions will change before assistance to inmates in working out their problems becomes common.

Several important changes presently affecting correctional philosophy were mentioned in Chapter 9, all of them significant for the time and place in which they occurred. One of the most far-reaching concepts is that of the indeterminate sentence. The opportunity to leave prison in less time than prescribed in his maximum sentence may motivate an inmate to adjust, although there are problems in determining what is an adequate adjustment. If he cannot get along with the other inmates, he may become involved in quarreling, fighting, or attempts to escape, which have always been sufficient grounds for extending a sentence. Yet there is no adequate research to affirm or refute the validity of such a response. We do not know, for example, all the reasons that compel a man to escape. It is not uncommon for boys and girls awaiting release from institutions to run away within hours of the arrival of parents coming to take them home. Adults often imply that they have no pressing reason or rational explanation for having made such attempts. It may be that for some the mere existence of "escape-proof" facilities is a challenge.

Research on corrections should go beyond problems of prisons and inmates to law enforcement itself, especially as applied to juvenile offenses. As an offender's first contact with the law influences his initial attitudes, it is to be hoped that better-trained police officers will deal with offenders in a more professional manner than is common now and will attempt to understand and cope with the resentment, hostility and confusion offenders often exhibit. Inmates often characterize police officers in terms of fairness, understanding, and professional demeanor. Clearly an offender's processing leaves a lasting impression that might be used to his advantage in the treating of his problem by analyzing his actions and seeking remedial help for underlying causes of his behavior.

Future veterans of the armed forces will continue to receive benefits —schooling, as well as what are now considered traditional medical, surgical, dental, and disability benefits. The impact of returning World War II veterans on the American labor market and institutions of higher education was considerable. Not only did the vast numbers of veterans benefit from attending college but they also remained out of a crowded labor market in transition from a wartime to a peacetime economy. This precedent has been reinforced with each subsequent "police action," "situation," "incident," and war in which the United States has used its troops. There is no reason to believe that educational benefits will not continue, for the earning power of a veteran who has obtained formal education increases. His contribution to the Gross National Product is thus greater, which benefits the country.

Veterans Administration hospitals, as they are now constituted, assist in training more medical doctors than does any other single organization in our history. The many facilities and personnel under their control cooperate with medical schools throughout the country. Because of the facilities and services under its administration, the V.A. will begin offering nonveterans assistance on a lower priority than veterans. Eventually the hospitals may be returned either to the Public Health Service or turned over to some other national agency in order to make hospital services available to all citizens. Under current regulations, a person who wishes to enlist in the armed forces but is rejected for a physical disability cannot receive medical attention at a V.A. hospital. If medical attention is viewed as a "right" the entire hospital system will change. Artificial kidneys, because of scarcity (particularly outside the V.A. system) may at present be denied to dying patients because they are not veterans. Yet, when the proper equipment is available, requirement of eligibility based on military service seems pointless and even inhumane.

No immediate solutions to public-welfare problems are apparent. The nation is aware of a cycle of poverty that breeds problems of unemployment, inadequate housing, poor schools, and improper diets. Yet if current resources are concentrated mainly on children, adults must do without attention. Centering attention on adults could result in failure to meet children's needs and thus perpetuate some of the attitudes that help to keep people poor. One program worthy of research and study is that of the Job Corps, in which boys have been removed from basically unproductive environments and given the opportunity to break the poverty cycle. Education, often regarded as a panacea, must go far beyond removing a person from an environment unconducive to successful adjustment in the American culture; it must reach all generations in all vital areas, and it must have both long-term and immediate value. The migrant worker's child should have the same educational opportunities, however difficult it is to provide them, as does the child of the successful executive.

Welfare recipients, cognizant of their rights and responsibilities, will become more active in voicing opinions of the system of which they are a part. Indigenous leadership is already being developed through community-action programs, under the O.E.O. The recipient gains a voice in decisions that have direct effects on his circumstances, the first time in history that he has broken out of the role of supplicant. This independence is similar to that already achieved by women, workers, and Negroes. Clients, too long left out of decisions affecting them, must also be brought into conferences as recognized experts. They have experience in day-to-day survival on welfare grants and could become valuable sources of information for administrators and caseworkers on feelings, attitudes, and conditions among clients.

It is quite likely that a new era has dawned for social movements in the United States. People have been accustomed to change through peaceful, law-abiding efforts, which has given them incentive to participate in causes in which they can believe. Many people will continue to use their talents in such diverse areas as sign painting, bookkeeping, fund raising, administration, and public speaking for such movements. The indigenous leaders developed in these movements will pattern their plans after those of successful organizations similar to their own. Inasmuch as they can benefit from the trial and error procedures of others, their effectiveness can be increased. Although the causes around which social movements form will differ, politics and civil rights will remain two main areas of activity.

The Watts riot in Los Angeles "sparked" a series of civil disorders throughout the country. There was a sudden rise in militancy among the "disadvantaged," mainly Negroes. The Kerner report warned the nation that change is inevitable but that it will be peaceful change only if remedial action is taken immediately. More than investigations and commission reports is necessary. Negroes may well believe that riots and disorders are their most effective weapons, just as workers came to realize that only strikes would move recalcitrant industrialists. Militant organizations may meet denials of their demands with violence. Instead of examining a disaster only after it has occurred, we should focus on averting future disasters. This effort must involve everyone concerned, from the middle-class merchant and politician to the welfare recipient and militant leader. There will be disorders in the United States for some time. True progress will have been made only when disasters, disorders, and riots can be avoided through the combined efforts of people at all levels of society, working toward peaceful solutions of social problems.

The future holds the possibility of social participation by citizens of all ages, incomes, races, and occupations. More agencies, social movements, political parties, and churches will seek volunteers and will learn how to use them more effectively. There are and will continue to be many jobs for people willing to involve themselves in social action. Participation does not have to be regulated, uniform, or in organized groups; there is room for innovation and individual action as well.

One of the goals toward which many Americans will work is a better-informed community. People know, for instance, that there is widespread corruption in public office throughout the nation. They have watched elected officials compromise principles in favor of political expedience.

Many changes that can be expected in the future will be based on the fact that all behavior is learned and that new behavior can be learned to cope with new problems. This principle may have an impact on education at all levels, especially for the helping services. More emphasis will be placed on formal education geared to employment. People with the necessary time and money will be able to continue with liberal-arts education, but they will always be fewer than those who mainly seek practical information on particular subjects. Changes within the various social-welfare institutions are not likely to be swift and revolutionary. More likely they will continue to be gradual.

The processes described in this text have evolved over many years. There will be much research in the area of social-welfare institutions in the future to develop better planning, feasible programs, more equitable practices and applicable theories in helping people solve their problems. It is hoped that the reader of this text has gained a better understanding of these processes and will be able to help put such principles into practice.

Appendix A

ABBREVIATIONS OF
AGENCIES, PROGRAMS
AND ORGANIZATIONS

AA	Alcoholics Anonymous
AAMC	Association of American Medical Colleges
AARP	American Association of Retired Persons
AB	Aid to the Blind
ADA	Average Daily Attendance
AFDC	Aid to Families of Dependent Children
AFL-CIO	American Federation of Labor and Congress of Industrial Organizations
AHA	American Hospital Association
AJLA	Association of the Junior Leagues of America
AMA	American Medical Association
AMVETS	American Veterans of World War II and Korea
AOA	Administration on Aging
AWOL	Absent Without Leave
BPOE	Benevolent and Protective Order of Elks
BSA	Boy Scouts of America
CAP	Community Action Program
CCC	Civilian Conservation Corps
CORE	Congress of Racial Equality

CSWE	Council on Social Work Education
CW	Caseworker
CWA	Civilian Works Administration
DAV	Disabled American Veterans
DOT	Dictionary of Occupational Titles
DPW	Department of Public Welfare
FBI	Federal Bureau of Investigation
FBP	Federal Bureau of Prisons
FECA	Federal Employees Compensation Act
FEPC	Fair Employment Practices Commission
FERA	Federal Emergency Relief Administration
FIND	Friendless, Isolated, Needy, Disabled
FLSA	Fair Labor Standards Act
FSSA	Family Service Society of America
GA	General Assistance
GAI	Guaranteed Annual Income
GI	Government Issue
GNP	Gross National Product
GSA	Girls Scouts of America
HEW	U.S. Department of Health, Education and Welfare
IAF	Industrial Areas Foundation
KC	Knights of Columbus
KKK	Ku Klux Klan
MA	Medical Assistance
MDTA	Manpower Development and Training Act
MSW	Master of Social Work
NAACP	National Association for the Advancement of Colored People
NEA	National Education Association
NLN	National League for Nursing
NOPHN	National Organization for Public Health Nursing
NRTA	National Retired Teachers Association
NYA	National Youth Administration
NYC	Neighborhood Youth Corps
OAA	Old Age Assistance
OAI	Old Age Insurance
OASDHI	Old Age and Survivors Disability Health Insurance
OASDI	Old Age and Survivors Disability Insurance
OEO	Office of Economic Opportunity
PA	Public Assistance
PHS	Public Health Service

PTA	National Congress of Parents and Teachers
PWA	Public Works Administration
SCLC	Southern Christian Leadership Conference
SCORE	Service Corps of Retired Executives
SNCC	Student Nonviolent Coordinating Committee
TWO	The Woodlawn Organization
UF	United Fund
UN	United Nations
UNICEF	U.N. International Children's Emergency Fund
USDA	U.S. Department of Agriculture
USES	United States Employment Service
VA	Veterans Administration
VAVS	Veterans Administration Volunteer Service
VFW	Veterans of Foreign Wars
VISTA	Volunteers in Service to America
WCTU	Women's Christian Temperance Union
WHO	World Health Organization
WPA	Works Progress Administration
YMCA	Young Men's Christian Association
YMHA	Young Men's Hebrew Association
YWCA	Young Women's Christian Association
YWHA	Young Women's Hebrew Association

Appendix B

MILESTONES IN
SOCIAL WELFARE

Date	Event	Significance	Implications	Contemporary Effects
1531	English statute licensing begging	First significant effort to combat poverty	Solution sought for old custom and practice	Dignity of individual considered in programs like public assistance
1547	Mary of Bethlehem Hospital	Nickname "Bedlam" resulted from institutional conditions	Patients eventually unchained and understanding of problem sought	Fewer restraints and modern concept of treatment
1557	London Bridewell Prison	Alternative to other forms of punishment	Prisons became panacea for control of the deviant	Rehabilitation evolved from punitive incarceration
1593	England first offered assistance to veterans	Early acknowledgement of nation's debt to veterans	Compensation for the interruption of military service	Variety of benefits and bureaucratic structure to meet veterans' needs
1601	Elizabethan Poor Law	More effective way to administer poor relief	Basis for charity, relief, and public assistance in United States	Increased client involvement and interest in welfare administration
1619	First Negroes imported to New World	Institution of slavery inherited by United States	Negroes kept in bondage for more than two centuries and freed only through Civil War bloodshed	Prejudice, discrimination, and Negro demands for rights
1622	Act of Settlement (England)	Relieved parishes of responsibility for itinerant indigents	Residence requirement becomes obstacle to eligibility	Less emphasis on place of residence in American public assistance
1703	Ospizio di San Michele (Rome)	Segregation of, and labor for, young male inmates	Program to combat idleness	Productivity viewed as essential to rehabilitation
1760– 1804	Industrial Revolution	Transition of rural societies to industrial bases	High-density living	Potential threat of automation and problems resulting from it
1772	Workhouses for poor (England)	Extraction of service in return for "charity"	Opposition to giving "something for nothing"	Less emphasis on Work projects

Year			
1776	Pension plan for veterans in Colonies	Crude effort to compensate men who had sacrificed for the nation	Greater numbers of veterans needing services after each war	Prior planning since World War II
1776	Boarding of Federal prisoners in local facilities	Lack of Federal facilities	Development of Federal Bureau of Prisons	Most progressive Federal prison system in existence
1790	Opening of Walnut Street prison (Philadelphia)	Innovation of silence and solitary confinement	More humane approach	More prevalent relaxation of harsh discipline
1793	Cotton gin invented	Increased productivity and beginnings of factory system	Created greater manpower needs and concomitant problems	Legislation protecting women and children from labor abuses
1844	Mentally ill prisoners transferred to mental hospitals	Recognition of inadequacy of prison to care for all inmates	Laws for treatment of criminally insane	Prevalence of inmate classification and diagnostic centers
1847	American Medical Association founded	Practitioners combine to improve medical conditions	Concerted attacks on education, training, treatment, and quackery problems	Numerous AMA committees devoted to improving all phases of medicine and health
1852	Massachusetts compulsory school law	Recognition of family inadequacy as sole source of education	Widely emulated to raise educational standards	Concern for both advanced and slow learners
1854	Dorothea Dix made appeal to Congress for aid to the insane	Rising public concern for the mentally ill	Funds and facilities eventually set aside for treating the insane	Mental hospitals in all states
1865	Salvation Army established	Private social service on local basis	Active religious involvement in organized social-service programs	Updated services to meet current needs

Date	Event	Significance	Implications	Contemporary Effects
1866	National Labor Union formed	Early protest of unfair labor practices	Increased recognition of workers' need to unite	Complex labor organization and responsible legislation protecting workers' rights
1866	Society for the Prevention of Cruelty to Animals	Became involved in fighting cruelty to children in 1874	Shifting emphasis from animals to children	Much legislation and organized treatment of both children and animals
1871	American Indians made wards of Federal government	Deprived of autonomy	Ultimate Federal betrayal of treaties and confinement to reservations	Degrading conditions on reservation and only token efforts at improvement
1872	American Public Health Association formed	Medical concern for the entire population	Minimum standards of protection against disease	Diversified services and higher standards
1874	Women's Christian Temperance Union organized	Widespread concern about the evils of alcoholism	Prohibition	Indecision on legalization of control and sale of liquor
1876	Elmira (New York) reformatory	Parole and indeterminate sentence first used in United States	Goal of incarceration becomes reform	New innovations in treatment of offenders encouraged
1882	First American immigration law enacted	States' power to tax immigrants held unconstitutional	Quota system developed (1924) to control immigration	Shift to more just quota system and more relaxed regulations
1886	AFL formed	Various labor groups combined for greater power	Spread of unionization	Unions a significant part of American society
1887	General Allotment (Dawes) Act	Further reduction of Indian tribal holdings	Deterioration of unrepresented Indians' circumstances	Federally-funded programs for Indians
1896	*Plessy v. Ferguson*	Allowed segregation in schools under the "separate but equal" doctrine	Widespread legal segregation, especially in the South	Resistance to and slow implementation of 1954 desegregation decision

Year	Event			
1899	Juvenile court established in Cook County, Illinois	First separate court for children	Emphasis on not treating children as criminals	Continuing legal concern for special problems of youthful offenders
1902	Statutory minimum age of ten years fixed for labor	Governmental entry into this area of social problems	Changing status of children	Child-labor legislation in force
1908	*The Mind That Found Itself* published	Exposure by former mental patient of inhumane hospital practices	Reform of mental hospitals	Mental hygiene a separate field of study
1912	U.S. Public Health Service founded	Centralized authority and responsibility for health standards	Research as important base for expanded services	Services offered through prisons, immigration service, communities, and foundations
1915	Revival of the Ku Klux Klan	Arousal of hatred for "un-Americanism"	Negroes particular targets of atrocities and discrimination	Klan leadership in efforts to resist desegregation and Federal involvement in social issues
1918	Vocational Rehabilitation Act passed	Growing awareness of need for veteran training	Early model for later acts increasing benefits	Applicable to emotional, as well as physical, handicaps
1922	Volstead Act (Prohibition)	Forbade manufacture and sale of alcoholic beverages	Flourishing gangsterism	Organized crime entrenched
1924	Indians granted citizenship	Indians obtain equal rights and privileges	Beginning efforts to improve Indians' conditions	Integration still slow and difficult
1929	Stock-market crash	National economic disaster	Federal intervention in all phases of American economy	Governmental efforts to prever recurrence
1930	Veterans Administration established	Combination of several agencies handling veterans' affairs	Organizational expansion and centralization of services, followed by decentralization	Largest agency of its kind st growing
1930	Federal Bureau of Prisons established	National scope and central administration of system	Internal specialization possible	World's most progressive tem

Early form of citizen protest

Date	Event	Significance	Implications	Contemporary Effects
1932	Bonus Expeditionary Force	Protest demonstration over inequities in postwar veterans' benefits		Strikingly similar to Poor People's March on Washington, D.C., 1968
1934	Wheeler-Howard Act	Transfer of initiative from Bureau of Indian Affairs to tribal councils	Continuing effort to establish Indian rights	Authorized loans, self-government, and tribal ownership of businesses
1935	Social Security Act	Financial assistance for the majority of needy people	Prevention of widespread destitution stimulated by Great Depression	Expanded program of retirement benefits for most workers and their survivors
1938	Federal Juvenile Delinquency Act	Informal court procedures and indeterminate sentences	More responsibility for his own treatment placed on youthful offender	Refinements in diagnosis and classification
1938	Fair Labor Standards Act	The legal end to child labor	Minimum age of sixteen set for work during school hours	Encouragement to pursue education
1940	Selective Service Act	Military obligation for all eligible males	Compulsory service as answer to military manpower problem	Legal and illegal opposition to draft laws
1944	Servicemen's Readjustment Act	"G.I. bill" to provide educational benefits	Changing educational aspirations	Substantial numbers of veterans benefiting from this act
1947	Taft-Hartley Act	Union membership or non-membership not to be basis for employment	Attempt to combat discrimination in employment	Continuing discrimination *within* unions and thus also in employment
1952	McCarran-Walter Act	Set quotas for immigration to United States	Aside from people with special skills, discriminated in favor of north and west Europeans	Higher quotas and shifting emphasis to keep families together and permit naturalization of Orientals
1954	*Brown v. Board of Education*	Supreme Court decision against segregation in schools	Majority acceptance and conflict over minority refusals to comply	Slow progress toward actual integration

Date	Event	Significance	Implications	Contemporary Effects
1955	AFL and CIO merger	Larger union membership	Shift in balance of power between labor and management	Union power to press demands
1957	Civil Rights Act	Reaffirmed rights of all citizens	Stimulated assertion of legal rights by civil-rights groups	Continuing struggle for minority rights becoming more militant
1958	National Defense Education Act	Low-interest loans to college students	Educational opportunities for the "disadvantaged"	"Forgiveness" of repayment provided for added inducement
1962	Migrant Health Act	First legal attention to needs of migrant workers	Growing attention to serious economic and social problems of this group	Agitation for additional programs for these workers
1964	Economic Opportunity Act	"War" on domestic poverty declared by President Johnson	Outline of neglected problems of American society	Involvement of millions of citizens in resulting programs
1967	Riots in American cities	Widespread destruction	Report of investigating commission revealing War on Poverty still unsuccessful	Tension and unrest continuing and spreading
1967	The *Gault* Decision	Juvenile delinquency reexamined	Due process guaranteed to juvenile offenders	Adversary system triumphs over informality
1968	Minimum wage raised to $1.60 an hour	Helped to eliminate substandard labor conditions	Higher living standards	Arouses caution against inflationary surge in economy

Abbott, Grace. *The Child and the State*. Chicago: University of Chicago Press, 1938.

Ackerman, N. W. *The Psychodynamics of Family Life*. New York: Basic Books, 1958.

Ade, George, Ray Long, and Richard Smith. *The Old-Time Saloon*. New York: Smith, 1931.

Ad Hoc Committee on the Triple Revolution, The. *The Triple Revolution*. Santa Barbara, Calif.: 1964.

Alexander, Charles C. *The Ku Klux Klan in the Southwest*. Lexington: University of Kentucky Press, 1965.

Allen, Hollis P. "Federal Aid and the Problem of Control," in William O. Stanley, *et al.*, eds., *Social Foundations of Education*. New York: Dryden, 1956. *The Auxiliary Leader*, (January 1967).

Andrews, F. Emerson. *Philanthropic Giving*. New York: Russell Sage Foundation, 1950.

Arthur, T. D. *Ten Nights in a Bar Room*. Chicago: Donahue, c. 1913.

Ashbury, Herbert. *The Great Illusion*. New York: Doubleday, 1950.

Bancroft, Gertrude. "Multiple Job Holders in December, 1959," *Monthly Labor Review*, 83, No. 10 (October 1960), 97–121.

Barnes, Harry E., and Negley K. Teeters. *New Horizons in Criminology*. New York: Prentice-Hall, 1951.

Barron, Milton L. *Minorities in a Changing World*. New York: Knopf, 1967.

Barry, Ruth, and Beverly Wolf. *Modern Issues in Guidance Personnel Work*. New York: Columbia University Press, 1963.

Beauvoir, Simone de. *The Second Sex*. New York: Knopf, 1953.

Bedford, James H. *The Veteran and His Future Job*. Los Angeles: Society for Occupational Research, 1946.

Beers, Clifford. *A Mind That Found Itself*. Garden City, N.Y.: Doubleday, 1925.

Bell, Robert R. *Marriage and Family Interaction*. Homewood, Ill.: Dorsey, 1967.

Bettelheim, Bruno, and Morris Janowitz. *Social Change and Prejudice*. London: Collier-Macmillan, 1950.

Bisno, Herbert. *The Place of the Undergraduate Curriculum in Social Work Education*. New York: Council on Social Work Education, 1959.

"Black Power—Its Goals and Methods," *U.S. News & World Report*, May 22, 1967, pp. 64–68.

Blauner, Robert. *Alienation and Freedom*. Chicago: University of Chicago Press, 1964.

Bottomore, T. B. *Critics of Society: Radical Thought in North America*. New York: Pantheon, 1968.

Boulder Country Juvenile Court. *A Home Away from Home: Community Volunteers Empty the Jail*. Washington, D.C.: Government Printing Office, 1968.

Brophy, William A., and Sophie D. Aberle, eds. *The Indian—America's Unfinished Business*. Norman: University of Oklahoma Press, 1966.

Burrow, James G. *AMA, Voice of American Medicine*. Baltimore: Johns Hopkins Press, 1963.

California State Department of Education. *The Education of Emotionally Handicapped Children*. Sacramento: March 1961.

Cameron, William B. *Modern Social Movements*. New York: Random House, 1966.

Cavan, Ruth. *The American Family*. New York: Crowell, 1953.

Cherrington, Ernest H., ed. *The Anti-Saloon League Yearbook, 1916*. Westerville, O.: Anti-Saloon League, 1916.

Clausen, John A. "Mental Disorders," in Robert K. Merton and Robert A. Nisbet, eds., *Contemporary Social Problems*. New York: Harcourt, 1966.

Clawson, Marion. *Statistics on Outdoor Recreation*. Washington, D.C.: Government Printing Office, 1958.

Cohen, Nathan E. *Social Work in the American Tradition*. New York: Dryden, 1958.

Coleman, James C. *Abnormal Psychology and Modern Life*. 2d ed. Chicago: Scott, Foresman, 1956.

Congressional Record, 49th Congress, 2nd Session, 18, Part 2, 1638 (Feb. 11, 1887).

Cook, Samuel DuBois. "The Tragic Myth of Black Power," *New South*, 21, pp. 19–26 No. 3 (Summer 1966).

Cremin, Lawrence E. *The Transformation of the Schools*. New York: Knopf, 1961.

Davis, Allison. *Social Class Influences upon Learning*. Cambridge, Mass.: Harvard University Press, 1950.

Della-Dora, Delmo. "The Culturally Disadvantaged: Educational Implications of Certain Social-Cultural Phenomena," in Staten W. Webster, ed., *Understanding the Educational Problems of the Disadvantaged Learner*. San Francisco: Chandler, 1966.

Department of Public Welfare, Utah Division of Staff Development. "The History of Welfare." Unpublished paper, 1964.

Devine, Edward T. *The Principles of Relief*. New York: Macmillan, 1907.

Eddy, Elizabeth M. *Walk the White Line.* New York: Praeger, 1967.

English, O. S., and G. H. J. Pearson. *Emotional Problems of Living.* New York: Norton, 1963.

Esman, Aaron H., ed. *New Frontiers in Child Guidance.* New York: International Universities Press, 1958.

Feldman, Frances L., and Frances Scherz. *Family Social Welfare.* New York: Atherton, 1967.

Fink, Arthur E., C. Wilson Anderson, and Merril B. Conover. *The Field of Social Work.* New York: Holt, Rinehart and Winston, 1968.

Flexner, Eleanor. *Century of Struggle: The Woman's Rights Movement in the United States.* Cambridge, Mass.: Harvard University Press, 1959.

Fourth Annual Southern Conference on Gerontology. *Economic Problems of Retirement.* Gainesville: University of Florida Press, 1954.

Galbraith, John K. *The Affluent Society.* Boston: Houghton Mifflin, 1958.

Gendell, Murray, and Hans L. Zetterberg, eds. *A Sociological Almanac for the United States.* New York: Scribner's, 1964.

Goates, Bruce. "The Referral Process." Unpublished paper, Community Mental Health Center, Salt Lake City, Utah, 1966.

Goldstein, Bernard. *Low Income Youth in Urban Areas: A Critical Review of the Literature.* New York: Holt, Rinehart and Winston, 1967.

Goodman, Paul. *Growing Up Absurd.* New York: Vintage, 1960.

Gordon, Milton M. *Assimilation in American Life.* New York: Oxford, 1964.

"Government in Exile, The," *Time*, September 6, 1968, pp. 25–27.

Grier, William H., and Price M. Cobb. *Black Rage.* New York: Basic Books, 1964.

Grimes, Alan P. *Equality in America.* New York: Oxford, 1964.

Hadden, Samuel B. "A Way Out for Homosexuals," *Harper's* (March 1967), pp. 107–120.

Hapgood, Norman. *Up from City Streets.* New York: Harcourt, 1927.

Harber, Sidney, Aaron Paley, and Arnold S. Black. "Treatment of Problem Drinkers at Winter Veterans Administration Hospital," *Bulletin of the Menninger Clinic*, 1949, vol. 13, pp. 24–30.

Harrington, Janette T. *Who Cares?* New York: Friendship, 1962.

Harrington, M., and P. Jacobs, eds. *Labor in a Free Society.* Los Angeles: University of California Press, 1959.

Harrington, Michael. *The Other America: Poverty in the United States.* New York: Macmillan, 1963.

Harris, T. George, "Do We Owe People a Living?", *Look*, April 30, 1968, pp. 25–27.

Harrison, Shelby M. *Public Employment Offices.* New York: Russell Sage Foundation, 1924.

Hernández v. Texas, 347 U.S. 475, 74 S. Ct. 667, 98 L. Ed. 866 (1954).

Hess, Robert D. "Maternal Teaching Styles and Educational Retardation," in E. Paul Torrence and Robert D. Strom, eds., *Mental Health and Achievement.* New York: Wiley, 1965.

Higham, John. *Strangers in the Land.* New York: Atheneum, 1963.

Hill, Ruben. *Families Under Stress.* New York: Harper, 1949.

Hitchcock, Arthur A. "Milestones in the Development of Personnel Services in Education," in Nelson B. Henry, ed., *Personnel Services in Education.* Chicago: University of Chicago Press, 1959.

Holtzman, Abraham. *The Townsend Movement.* New York: Bookman, 1963.

Horton, Paul B., and Gerald R. Leslie. *The Sociology of Social Problems.* New York: Appleton, 1965.

Hoshino, George. "Simplification of the Means Test and its Consequences," *The Social Service Review,* 41 (September 1967), 16–22.

Howard, John. *The State of Prisons.* New York: Dutton, 1929.

Johnson, Lyndon B. *Message to the Congress of the United States on the Economic Opportunity Act of 1964.* Washington, D.C.: Government Printing Office, March 16, 1964.

Journal of the American Medical Association, 32 (June 10, 1899), 1337.

Journal of the American Medical Association, 34 (June 16, 1900), 1547.

Keve, Paul W. *Prison, Probation and Parole.* Minneapolis: University of Minnesota Press, 1954.

King, Martin L., Jr. *Why We Can't Wait.* New York: New American Library, 1964.

Klein, Philip. *From Philanthropy to Social Welfare.* San Francisco: Jossey-Bass, 1968.

Koller, Marvin R. *Social Gerontology.* New York: Random House, 1968.

Laurence, John. *A History of Capital Punishment.* New York: Citadel, 1960.

Levy, John, and Ruth Monroe, *The Happy Family.* New York: Knopf, 1938.

Linden, Maurice C. "Preparation for the Leisure of Later Maturity," in Wilma Donahue, Woodrow W. Hunter, Dorothy H. Coons, and Helen K. Maurice, eds., *Free Time.* Ann Arbor: University of Michigan Press, 1958.

Lutz, Alma. *Created Equal.* New York: Day, 1940.

McCrea, Roswell C. *The Humane Movement.* New York: Columbia University Press, 1910.

Macdonald, Dwight. *Our Invisible Poor.* New York: Hillman Foundation, 1963.

McWilliams, Carey. *Brothers under the Skin.* 2nd ed. Boston: Little, Brown, 1964.

Marden, Charles F., and Gladys Meyer. *Minorities in American Society.* New York: American Book, 1962.

Mason, Martha S., ed. *Parents and Teachers.* Boston: Ginn, 1928.

Miller, Joseph H. *Veterans Challenge the College.* Binghamton, Vt.: Vail-Ballou, 1947.

Moley, Raymond, Jr. *The American Legion Story.* New York: Deuell, Sloan, 1966.

Moore, G. Alexander, Jr. *Realities of the Urban Classroom.* New York: Praeger, 1967.

Murphy, Raymond, and Howard Elinson, eds. *Problems and Prospects of the Negro Movement.* Belmont, Calif.: Wadsworth, 1966.

Myers, George E. *Principles and Techniques of Vocational Guidance.* New York: McGraw-Hill, 1941.

National Congress of Parents and Teachers. *The Parent Teacher Organization.* Chicago, 1944.

National Education Association and American Medical Association. *School Health Services.* Washington, D.C.: 1964.

The National Elementary Principal, 43, No. 5 (April 1964), p. 5 "Educational Notes."

Neigher, Alan. "The Gault Decision: Due Process and the Juvenile Court," *Federal Probation,* 31, No. 4 (December 1967), 8–18.

Nisbet, Robert A. *The Sociological Tradition.* New York: Basic Books, 1966.

"Now: A Tax Plan That Pays People," *U.S. News & World Report,* February 14, 1966, p. 63.

Oates, Wayne E. *The Christian Pastor.* Philadelphia: Westminster, 1963.

Office of Economic Opportunity, *The First Step on a Long Journey.* Washington, D.C.: Government Printing Office, April 1956.

Overstreet, Bonaro W. *Understanding Fear.* New York: Collier, 1962.

Perlman, Helen Harris. "Are We Creating Dependency?" *Minnesota Welfare* (October 1963), vol. 9, pp. 11–19.

Pete Hernández Case, The, U.S. Supreme Court Reports, Washington, D.C.: Government Printing Office, October Term, 1953.

Philp, Albert Frederic. *Family Failure.* London: Faber and Faber, 1963.

Pittman, David J., and Charles R. Snyder, eds. *Society, Culture and Drinking Patterns.* New York: Wiley, 1962.

Polier, Justine W. *A View from the Bench.* New York: National Council on Crime and Delinquency, 1964.

Potwin, Marjorie A. *Cotton Mill People of the Piedmont.* New York: Columbia University Press, 1927.

Pratt, George K. *Soldier to Civilian.* New York: McGraw-Hill, 1944.

"Prescription for Racial Peace," *Time,* March 8, 1968, pp. 26–27.

President's Commission on Law Enforcement and Administration of Justice. *The Challenge of Crime in a Free Society.* Washington, D.C.: Government Printing Office, 1967.

President's Council on Physical Fitness. *Four Years for Fitness—1961–1965.* Washington, D.C.: Government Printing Office, 1965.

"Prescription for Racial Peace," *Time,* March 8, 1968, pp. 26–27.

Pumphrey, Muriel W. *The Teaching of Values and Ethics in Social Work Education.* New York: Council on Social Work Education, 1959.

Reder, Melvin W. *Labor in a Growing Economy.* New York: Wiley, 1957.

Richmond, Mark S. *Prison Profiles.* Dobbs Ferry, N.Y.: Oceana, 1965.

Riesman, David, Nathan Glazer, and Reuel Denney. *The Lonely Crowd.* Garden City, N.Y.: Doubleday, 1953.

Riessman, Frank. "The Culture of the Underprivileged: A New Look," in Staten W. Webster, ed., *Knowing the Disadvantaged.* San Francisco: Chandler, 1966.

"Risks of Protest, The," *Time,* October 11, 1968, p. 49.

Ritchie, Oscar W., and Marvin R. Koller. *Sociology of Childhood.* New York: Appleton, 1964.

"Roman Catholics," *Time,* September 13, 1968, p. 58.

Rose, Arnold M. *The Power Structure.* New York: Oxford, 1967.

Rosenthal, Robert, and Lenore F. Jacobson. "Teacher Expectations for the Disadvantaged," *Scientific American*, 218, No. 4 (April 1968), pp. 19–23.

Rowe, Clarence. *An Outline of Psychiatry*. Dubuque, I.: Brown, 1965.

Rubel, Arthur J. *Across the Tracks*. Austin: University of Texas Press, 1966.

Rubin, Sol, Henry Weihofen, George Edwards, and Simon Rosenzweig. *The Law of Criminal Correction*. St. Paul: West, 1963.

Salt Lake Tribune (April 2, 1968), p. 13.

Saltzman, Glenn A., and Herman J. Peters. *Pupil Personnel Services: Selected Readings*. Peacock, 1967.

Samora, Julian, ed. *La Raza—Forgotten Americans*. South Bend, Ind.: University of Notre Dame Press, 1966.

Schlesinger, Arthur, Jr. "The Dark Heart of American History," *Saturday Review*, October 19, 1968, pp. 20–23, 81.

Schlesinger, Benjamin. *The Multi-Problem Family*. Toronto: University of Toronto Press, 1963.

Sethna, M. J. *Society and the Criminal*. Bombay: Leaders', 1952.

Shibutani, Tamotsu, and Kian M. Kwan. *Ethnic Stratification*. New York: Macmillan, 1965.

Shilman, Catherine S. *Growing Up Poor*. Washington, D.C.: Government Printing Office, 1968.

Silberman, Charles E. *Crisis in Black and White*. New York: Vintage, 1964.

"Simplification of the Means Test and Its Consequences," *The Social Service Review*, 41, No. 3 (September 1967), pp. 16–22.

Smallenburg, Harry. "Studying the Elementary Guidance Program," *The National Elementary Principal*, 43, No. 5 (April 1964), 15–18.

Smalley, Ruth E. *Theory for Social Work Practice*. New York: Columbia University Press, 1967.

Smith, Edmund A. *Social Welfare—Principles and Concepts*. New York: Association, 1965.

Somers, Herman M., and Anne R. Somers. *Workmen's Compensation*. New York: Wiley, 1954.

Stagg, Harold G. *Billions for Education*. Washington, D.C.: Army Times, 1952.

Statutes at Large of the United States of America, The. 47, Part 1, Washington, D.C.: Government Printing Office, December 1931–March 1933.

Stein, Herman B. "Observations on Determinants of Social Work Education in the United States," in *An Intercultural Exploration: Universals and Differences in Social Work Values, Functions and Practices. Report of the Intercultural Seminar, The East-West Center, Hawaii, February 21–March 4, 1966*. New York: Council on Social Work Education, 1966.

Strom, Robert D. *Teaching in the Slum School*. Columbus, O.: Merrill, 1965.

Tappan, Paul W., ed. *Contemporary Correction*. New York: McGraw-Hill, 1951.

Tenbroek, Jacobus, ed. *The Law of the Poor*. San Francisco: Chandler, 1966.

Theobald, Robert. *Vital Speeches*, 32 (July 1, 1966), 573–6.

Thursz, Daniel. "Social Aspects of Poverty, Public Welfare," *The Journal of the American Public Welfare Association*, 25, No. 3 (July 1967), pp. 29–36.

Time, October 11, 1968, p. 49.

Time, May 17, 1968, pp. 17–18.

Turner, Ralph H., and Lewis M. Killian. *Collective Behavior*. Englewood Cliffs, N.J.: Prentice-Hall, 1957.

U.S. Bureau of Prisons. *Thirty Years with the Federal Prisons*. Washington, D.C.: Government Printing Office, 1960.

U.S. Commission on Civil Rights. *A Time to Listen . . . A Time to Act*. Washington, D.C.: Government Printing Office, 1959.

————. *With Liberty and Justice for All*. Washington, D.C.: Government Printing Office, 1956.

U.S. Department of Health, Education and Welfare. *Characteristics of State Public Assistance Plans under the Social Security Act*, Public Assistance Report No. 50. Washington, D.C.: Government Printing Office, 1964.

U.S. Department of Labor, Manpower Administration. *Highlights of the 1968 Manpower Report of the President*. Washington, D.C.: Government Printing Office, 1968.

U.S. Employment Service, Division of Occupational Analysis. *Dictionary of Occupational Titles*, *Vols. I, II*. Washington, D.C.: Government Printing Office, 1965.

U.S. House of Representatives Committee. *Federal Benefits for Veterans and Dependents*, Print No. 4, 90th Congress, 1st Session. Washington, D.C.: Government Printing Office, 1967.

U.S. News & World Report, February 14, 1966, p. 63.

U.S. News & World Report, May 22, 1967, pp. 64–68.

U.S. Public Health Service. *Bibliography on Religion and Mental Health 1960–1962*, Publication No. 1599. Washington, D.C.: Government Printing Office, 1967.

U.S. Senate Committee on Finance. *Hearings*, S. 1130, 74th Congress, 1st Session. Washington, D.C.: Government Printing Office, 1935.

U.S. Senate Committee on Labor and Public Welfare. *The War on Poverty*, Report 1218, 88th Congress, 2nd Session, Senate Document 86. Washington, D.C.: Government Printing Office, July 23, 1964.

United States Statutes at Large, 1919–1921, 66th Congress, 2nd Session, Vol. 41. Washington, D.C.: Government Printing Office, June 2, 1920.

U.S. Veterans Administration. *Establishment of a Veterans Hospital Community Council*, Interim Report No. 2, Pilot Study No. 1. Washington, D.C.: Government Printing Office, 1968.

U.S. Veterans Administration Information Service. *Medical Care of Veterans*. Washington, D.C.: Government Printing Office, 1967.

University of the State of New York, Bureau of Elementary Curriculum Development. *Educating Migrant Children*. New York: 1968.

Vander Zanden, James W. *American Minority Relations*. New York: Ronald, 1966.

Velie, Lester. *Labor U.S.A*. New York: Harper, 1959.

Voom, Essien. *Black Nationalism*. Chicago: University of Chicago Press, 1962.

Wagley, Charles, and Marvin Harris. *Minorities in the New World*. New York: Columbia University Press, 1964.

Waller, Willard W. *The Veteran Comes Back*. New York: Dryden, 1944.

Weber, Gustavus A., and Laurence F. Schmeckebier. *The Veteran's Administration: Its History, Activities and Organization.* Washington, D.C.: Brookings, 1934.

Wilensky, Harold L., and Charles N. Lebeaux. *Industrial Society and Social Welfare.* New York: Free Press, 1965.

Williams, Robin M., Jr. *Strangers Next Door.* Englewood Cliffs, N.J.: Prentice-Hall, 1964.

World Almanac Book of Facts, The. New York: Newspaper Enterprise Association, 1968.

Wylie, Ida. "The Little Woman," *Harper's* (November, 1945), pp. 402–409.

SUBJECT INDEX